The
OCCULT
and the
SUPERNATURAL

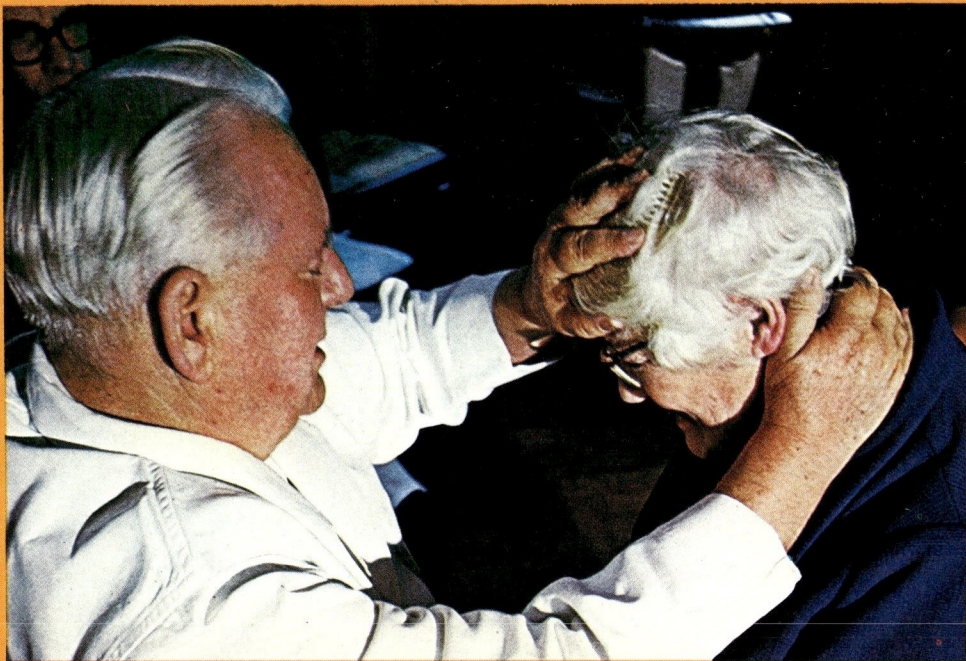

The OCCULT and the SUPERNATURAL

octopus

in association with
Phoebus

Contents

The Supernatural

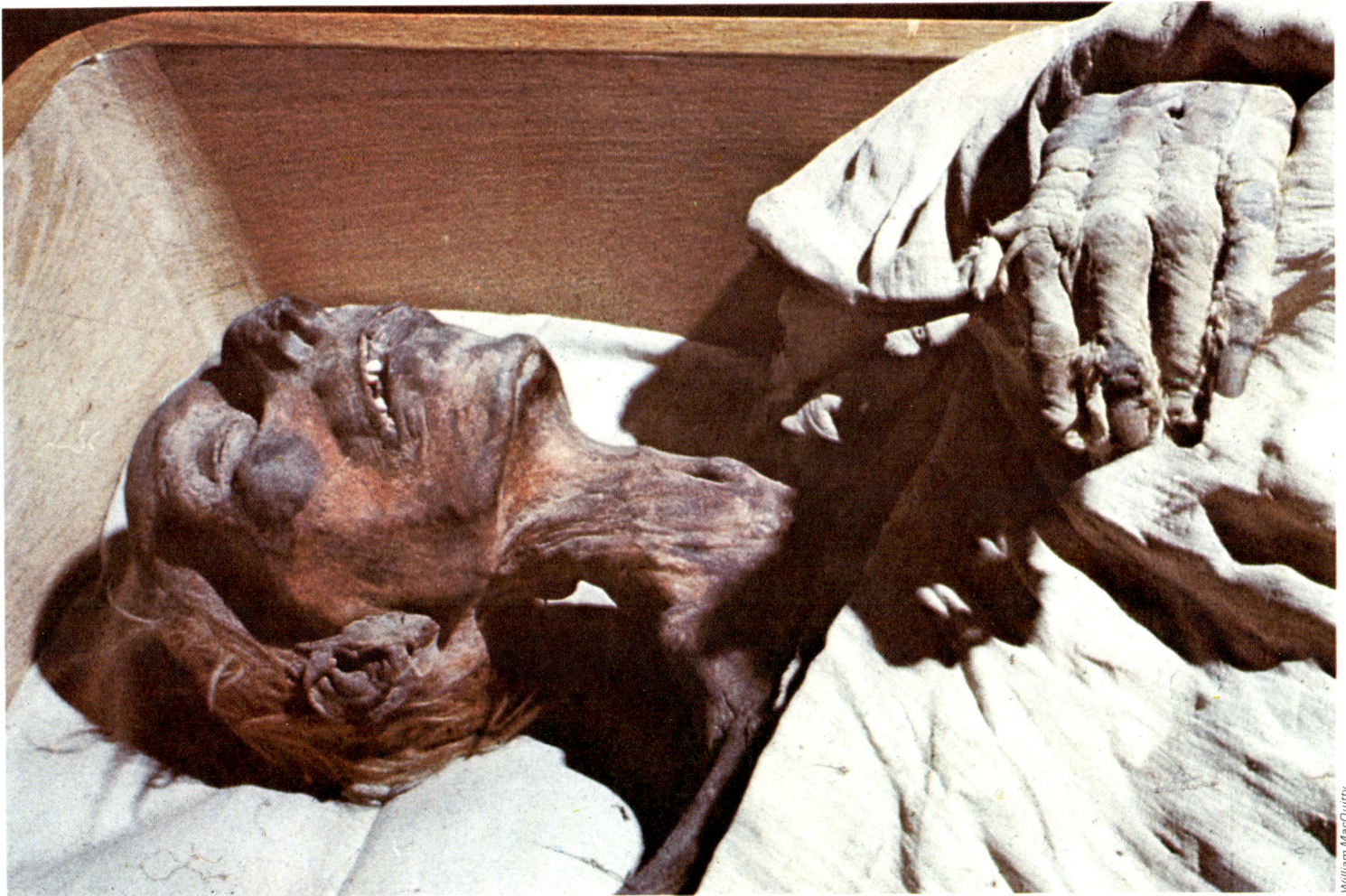

BEAUTY, ENCHANTMENT AND HORROR

The supernatural is the night sky of our minds, the shadow side of our mental 'daylight' of reason and hard fact. Like the night, it contains mystery, beauty, enchantment and horror. It has a powerful attraction and almost every one of us on earth, one way or another, is involved in it.

Above *Mummified corpse of Rameses II, ruler of Egypt, who died in 1225 BC* Opposite *From the ancient world to the present day, dreams have been regarded as ventures into a mysterious otherworld. Sir Edward Taylor emphasized the importance of dreams in causing man to conceive of himself as possessing a soul*

Many people, still, are religious. Many people still believe in astrology, palmistry and a variety of superstitions. It is scarcely possible to live very long without acquiring an interest, however reluctant, in the question of life after death. And each of our minds has its shadow side, where old terrors mingle with old truths.

The supernatural surrounds us still, at many different levels: in churches, synagogues, mosques; in dreams; in the antiseptic corridors of parapsychology laboratories, where experimenters test the strange powers of the mind; in attempts to make contact with the dead; in children's games and nursery rhymes; in experiences induced by LSD and other drugs; in newspaper stories of witchcraft, the black art and the desecration of churches; in reports of poltergeists and exorcisms; in faith healing; in the increasing interest in primitive religions and magic, in oriental religions, yoga and meditation.

The last hundred years have been the most flourishing period in the history of magic and occultism in the West since the 17th century. They have also seen the rise of the modern study of comparative religion, the modern interpretation of mythology, the attempt to test objectively such phenomena as ghosts and telepathy, and the application of modern psychology to beliefs about the supernatural.

11

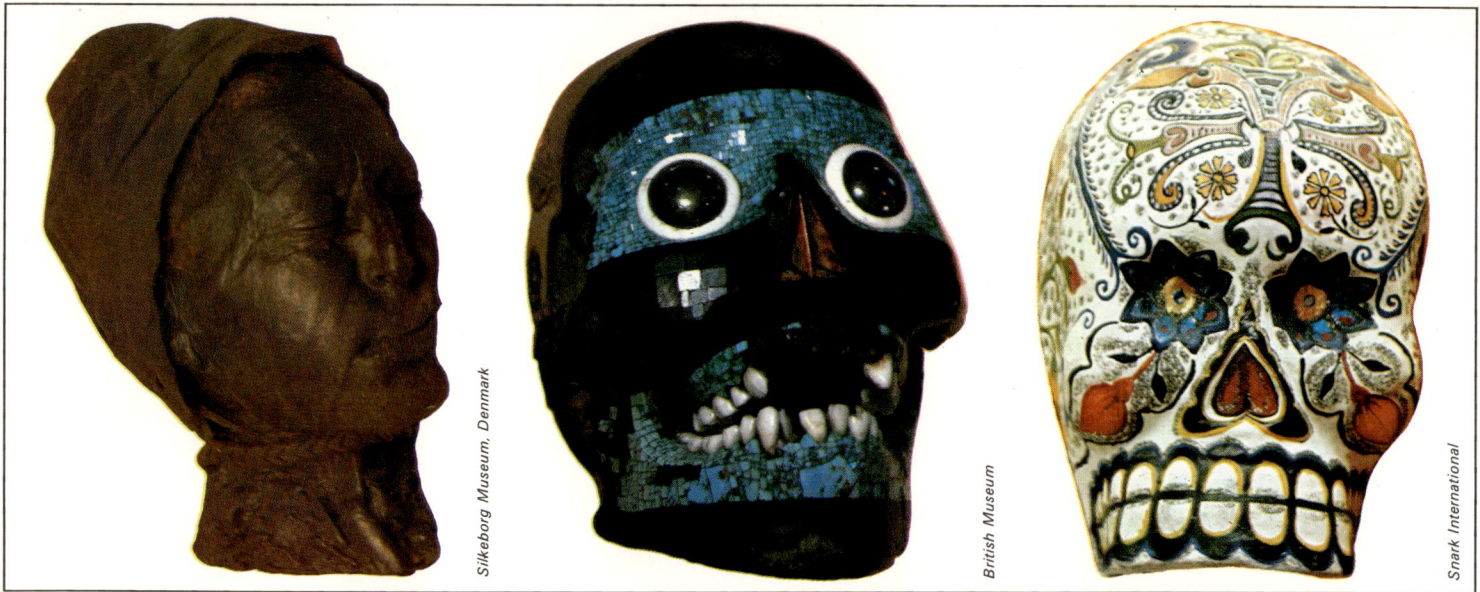

No one escapes death and yet from the beginning men have hoped and believed in a world beyond death. Mummification points to the belief in survival of death which goes back to the beginnings of human history and is suggested by Neanderthal burials more than 50,000 years ago. The rise of Spiritualism in the 19th century centred on the attempt to get in touch with the dead. The question haunts us still – is there life after death? Above left Iron Age ritual murder: the head of the hanged man of Tollund in Jutland. The bodies of sacrificed men were thrown after death into lakes, some of which dried up and became peat bogs, where the bodies were preserved Centre Aztec skull encrusted with turquoise mosaic, believed to represent Tezcatlipoca in his black aspect as lord of misfortune Right Mexican skull made of marzipan. An offering to the dead of Mexico, who are believed to revisit the earth on 31 October each year, and are given food, sweets and cigarettes. Part of an exhibition of popular art in the Muséo Anahuacalli Right 'Behold, a pale horse, and its rider's name was Death, and Hades followed him: and they were given power over a fourth of the earth, to kill with sword and with famine and with pestilence and by wild beasts of the earth.' Death on a Pale Horse, the Fourth Horseman of the Apocalypse, by the mystic, poet and painter, William Blake Opposite One of the most celebrated medium acts of the 19th century was that of the Davenport brothers. The debate over their authenticity was marked by the violent scepticism of the famous escapist Houdini

Across the Threshold

'Supernatural' is a convenient word for a huge area of human speculation about things believed to exist beyond the threshold of our ordinary day-to-day existence, our normal trudging journey from birth to death. John Wesley, the great preacher whose eloquence sent some of his hearers into ecstatic convulsions, believed that he showed his flock 'The Demonstrative Evidence of things unseen, the Supernatural Evidence of things invisible, not perceivable by the Eyes of Flesh, nor by any of our natural senses or faculties.'

The supernatural includes cases in which the normal order of Nature appears to have been momentarily upset: miracles, for instance; or the appearance of an otherworldly being in visible form; or levitation, the ability to rise from the ground and hover above it, unsupported – like the famous St Joseph of Copertino in the 17th century who was always shooting up into the air, to the embarrassment not only of himself but also of his ecclesiastical superiors.

But the supernatural also includes the

operation of forces which are perfectly natural but whose workings are not generally admitted or understood. When men long ago saw lightning, they thought it supernatural and ascribed it to the gods. We know that they were wrong in thinking it non-natural but right in observing its existence.

Similarly, a hundred years ago, those who observed the existence of the strange powers of the human mind which we call extrasensory perception or telepathy or clairvoyance often thought that they had dis-

ST. JAMES HALL,

ON SUNDAY EVENING, FEBRUARY 23d, 1879.

FAREWELL TOUR!

AFTER SIX YEARS ABSENCE IN FOREIGN COUNTRIES,

IRA E. DAVENPORT

Survivor of the World Renowned

DAVENPORT BROTHERS

— AND —

PROF. J. F. DAY

Previous to their departure to Mexico and South America.

In Unique and Startling Wonders!

Mysterious displays, and unaccountable Mysteries, which have been given in the presence of the Crowned Heads and Nobility of Europe, and before large and intelligent assemblages throughout the civilized World.   Their profoundly

MYSTERIOUS POWERS

Have astonished the wisest of all countries, and the most learned have been forced by overwhelming evidence to acknowledge them as inexplicable. *No complicated or glittering apparatus for deception used.*

Witches are associated with demons, night, sensuality and evil. They still horrify and delight the imagination: and they still exist Above Asmodeus was originally the Persian 'fiend of the wounding spear', a storm spirit and personification of rage. Later he developed into a supernatural force of lechery. He is represented as having three heads: those of a bull, a man, and a ram Right St Anthony of Egypt was a 3rd century Christian ascetic who withdrew from the world and was plagued by bizarre and nightmare visions, which included multitudes of demons in frightening animal forms. The Temptation of St Anthony, engraved by Martin Schongauer

covered something supernatural. There is some evidence now that these powers exist and if they do, they are natural powers and people in the past were wrong to think them anything else. But they were right in observing their existence, and it may be that in the future other peculiar phenomena may be found to stem from real and, of course, natural capacities of the human mind.

The Supernatural World

The world of the supernatural includes the great living religions alongside an astonishing variety of peculiar cults and groups, from the Holy Rollers and snake-handling sects of the United States to the new prophetic cults in Africa and the modern cargo cults of the Pacific. It ranges from some of the noblest expressions of the human mind in the lives and writings of mystics and the founders of religions to some of the ignoblest in the Black Mass or the smelling out of witches or the myths of race. It varies in importance from matters like survival after death and the existence of the soul to superstitions which – at least at first sight – are very trivial: from themes like fate, sin, sacrifice to tea-leaf reading, ouija boards and lucky numbers.

The supernatural even has room for humour, usually unintentional, as in this spell found in 1865 in the house of a magician called John Rhodes who had written it for one of his customers.

I adjure and command you, ye strong, mighty and most powerful spirits who are rulers of this day and hour, that ye obey me in this my cause by placing my husband in his former situation under the Trent Brewery Company.

There is music in the world of the supernatural, from primitive drumming and dancing to the splendours of Masses and Requiems. There is art, from the cave paintings and the lumpy, obese 'Venuses' of prehistoric men through the works of a Blake, a Bosch, a Botticelli to the nightmare drawings of Austin Spare and the paintings of modern Surrealists. There is a treasure of symbolism, from the rich religious and magical ideas associated with numbers, letters, architecture, the moon and the sun, to the myths and folk beliefs connected with the horse or the dog or the cat, the wren or the raven, the salmon or the spider.

Shadows in the Mind

It has only recently begun to be recognized that myths, rituals, folklore and magic are not a tangled mass of trivial mumbo-jumbo but a vital part of the human experience and a vital sector of the study of man..

Beyond the interest in the supernatural of which we are conscious, in ourselves or in others, there are all kinds of magical ideas which are deeply embedded in our minds.

One of the oldest and most important components of magic is the principle of mimicry. To injure an enemy, you make a

Musées Royaux des Beaux Arts, Belgium

Jacqueline Mackay

doll of wax or clay or rags, which resembles the enemy as closely as you can manage. If it doesn't look much like him, you can christen it with his name, to make sure you hit the right target. You torture and destroy the doll, you burn it or stick pins through it or wring its neck, in the belief that your enemy will suffer the same agonies in reality. By imitating an event, you hope that you will be able to make it happen.

This notion may seem to be one which we sensible moderns have outgrown but if you keep a watchful eye on yourself, you may discover that you are not free of it. If you are being driven too fast in a car, you may find yourself pressing your foot hard down on an imaginary brake on the floor of the car. On the surface of your mind, you know perfectly well that doing this will not affect the driver, but deeper down in your subconscious is the old magical principle of mimicry.

The Magic of Names
The magical use of names is rooted in many civilized people's minds today, as it was in ancient and primitive societies. In magic, the name of a thing *is* the thing. The name 'cat' is not merely a term of reference for a furry and charming creature with pointed ears, four legs, a tail and disquieting eyes; the name contains in itself the essence of the animal's being, the quality which makes it what it is and not something else. After all, a primitive magician might say, if it was not called 'cat' but 'dog', it would not be itself but something different.

The same principle applies to gods, spirits and human beings. In some primitive societies a man's real name is kept secret because if it becomes known to a hostile magician, he has power over the man and can destroy him. The man himself may not know his own real name, so secret is it, and he goes by another name, a cover name, a name which is not really him.

In the ancient world, to injure someone you hated, you could write down his name and a curse on a bit of lead or pottery and bury it. 'As the lead grows cold, so grow he cold' or 'I put quartan fever on Aristion to the death'.

This again seems a far cry from us but the principle survives among the many modern parents who take trouble over choosing a name for a child because they have at the back of their minds the feeling that the name chosen will affect the child's character. To name a boy Cedric, for instance, seems to many people at the moment to be running a serious risk of stamping a weak and weedy personality on the unfortunate infant. And if we call him James or Henry, won't he grow up to be like some nasty James or Henry that we know? It is a magical idea, deep in the mind, and a widespread one.

People who join occult (or religious) orders very often take new names, to show that they are starting a new life as new people. For instance the occult name of the black magician Aleister Crowley was Perdurabo, 'I will endure'.

The magic of names is also partly responsible for the feeling, still held by many, that someone who tries to get onto first name terms with you too quickly is invading your privacy: the feeling is that by using your own personal name he is trying to grasp the real you too soon.

Fate and the Future
Another set of supernatural notions survives in our attitudes to fate and the future. The powerful impulse not to 'tempt fate' comes up from some dark well in the mind below the level of reason. People constantly refrain from saying – or are horrified if they do say – that they have done well in some test, that the future looks bright, that all will go well; because they are frightened of an unseen power that will punish their presumption.

We sometimes mix this up with modesty but the desire not to seem conceited fails to explain the type of guilty horror that immediately afflicts many of us when fate is tempted. And even modesty implies the same principle at the root: not merely the wish to avoid offending other people but the idea

Above left The Young Sorceress, *a painting by A. Wiertz in which the aspiring sorceress, blindfolded, bestrides a broomstick, surrounded by malevolent figures. It has been suggested that witches originally danced with broomsticks between their legs as a phallic rite. They were said to fly on hobby horses, forked sticks, eggshells, bunches of straw and shovels, long before the broomstick (sometimes smeared with flying ointment from the fat of an unbaptized child) was associated with them* Above *Recent photograph of modern witches performing their rites*

15

of self-effacement in the sense of not attracting the attention of the gods, the fates, the unkind powers that rule men's destinies.

The Burning Galley

Not only do magical ideas survive in our minds but they seem to be needed. Quite a number of ceremonies and rituals have been either revived or invented in the last hundred years. A good example is the spectacular fire-ceremony which involves most of the population of Lerwick, in the Shetlands, in late January each year.

About seven in the evening, in cold and pitch dark, five or six hundred guisers – dancers in grotesque and eerie costumes – light torches and parade through the town, singing and pulling along a replica of a Viking war-galley, with the head of a dragon at its high prow.

The long-ship is hauled in procession to an open space and the marchers surround it, several ranks deep. At a signal they hurl their blazing torches like a rain of shooting-stars into the air and down onto the galley, which catches fire and burns fiercely until the dragon's head bows to the ground and the timbers splinter and char away. Through the rest of the night the guisers go from place to place dancing, and a sizeable percentage of the town's population gets itself genially drunk.

The interesting thing about this ceremony

A Christian hero-myth: St George and the Dragon, *by Uccello*

is that its dramatic central feature is not a survival of an ancient pagan rite but a modern invention. The wearing of sinister costumes, the dancing and drinking, are genuinely old customs but the burning of the galley goes back only to the late 1880s. Down to 1889, the guisers carried blazing tar barrels round the town, a survival of a pagan fire-festival which celebrated the freeing of the sun from the chains of winter. Men made light and heat on earth to revive the sun and to make it give out increasing light and heat in the sky. In 1889 the tar barrels left the Shetland stage and the Viking galley made its first entry.

In his book *Orkney and Shetland*, Eric Linklater says that a man named Haldane Burgess probably had a good deal to do with inventing the galley ritual. He was a blind poet and Christian Socialist who wrote the words of the guisers' song.

> Of yore, our fiery fathers sped upon the Viking Path;
> Of yore, their dreaded dragons braved the ocean in its wrath . . .
> Our galley is the People's Right, the dragon of the free,
> The Right that, rising in its might, 'brings tyrants to their knee;
> The flag that flies above us is the Love of Liberty;
> The waves are rolling on.

For all the bathos of this dotty song and although the ceremony is a modern invention, in the years since 1889 it has grown into a genuine folk institution: it effectively

expresses a big, vague but powerful central idea in the minds of those who take part in it. Perhaps whoever devised it saw the force of adding a ritual patterned on a ship-burial, which involved the liberation of the spirit from the body at death, with songs about the defeat of tyrants, to the relics of a ceremony which saluted the liberation of the sun from the tyrant grip of winter. The ship-burning reminds the Shetlanders of their Viking ancestry and it is a declaration of the Shetland-Norse nationalist and separatist feeling which has grown steadily stronger all through this century.

Magic, Myth and Poetry

Why are magical ideas still rooted in our minds? We have thrown off many of the attitudes of the past, why not these? Because magical thinking is natural to the human mind: which is why rational thinking is generally agreed to be difficult and why there is a strong human sense that rational thinking is not enough.

Behind magic, and at the roots of mythology and religion, is a kind of thinking which is not random and which has its own curious logic, but it is not rationalist logic. It works through analogies, allegories, symbols – which means making connections between things which outwardly and rationally are not connected: the doll and the enemy, the tar barrels and the sun. It looks to man's deep inner wells of inspiration, imagination, insight, instinct as constituting the supreme paths to truth. Magical thinking, in fact, is poetic thinking.

National Gallery/Michael Holford

In this light, it is not surprising that myth and legend have been largely the creation of poets, and that the importance of myths and legends for us is their poetic appeal. The great classical myths, for instance, or the story of Adam and Eve in Eden are *true* stories to us, not because we think they ever happened but because, like poetry, they contain truth about human beings and human life, truth which cannot be fully translated into plain statement. This is the source of our contemporary fascination with the theme of the killing of the divine king, which lies behind some of the myths we have inherited and which has inspired several outstanding, and poetic, modern novels. It is the source of the great

psychologist C. G. Jung's preoccupation with the symbolism of alchemy and mythology. And the myth of the hero continues to absorb men, as it always has.

The Secrets of Superstition

It was suggested earlier that superstitions are trivial things 'at least at first sight'. If you try to explain them, you find yourself in areas which are the reverse of trivial. And they can be explained, or many of them can, because idiotic as they may look, they are not random and senseless but the products of poetic logic.

For example, why is the number 3 supposed to be lucky? If you set out to find the answer, you will come across a host of odd

but minor matters like the fact that in German folklore a werewolf must be stabbed three times in the brows to reveal the real person behind the hair and claws, or the custom in the Spanish royal family of calling a dead king three times by name before burying him. But before long you will come to the Christian Trinity, a doctrine of the highest significance for multitudes of men.

We long to know the future, and search for it in the stars and the hand, in cards and numbers Left The Hanged Man, a card from the Tarot pack, still used in fortune-telling Right Astrological diagram showing the parts of the body which each zodiac sign is supposed to affect

Brompton Studio

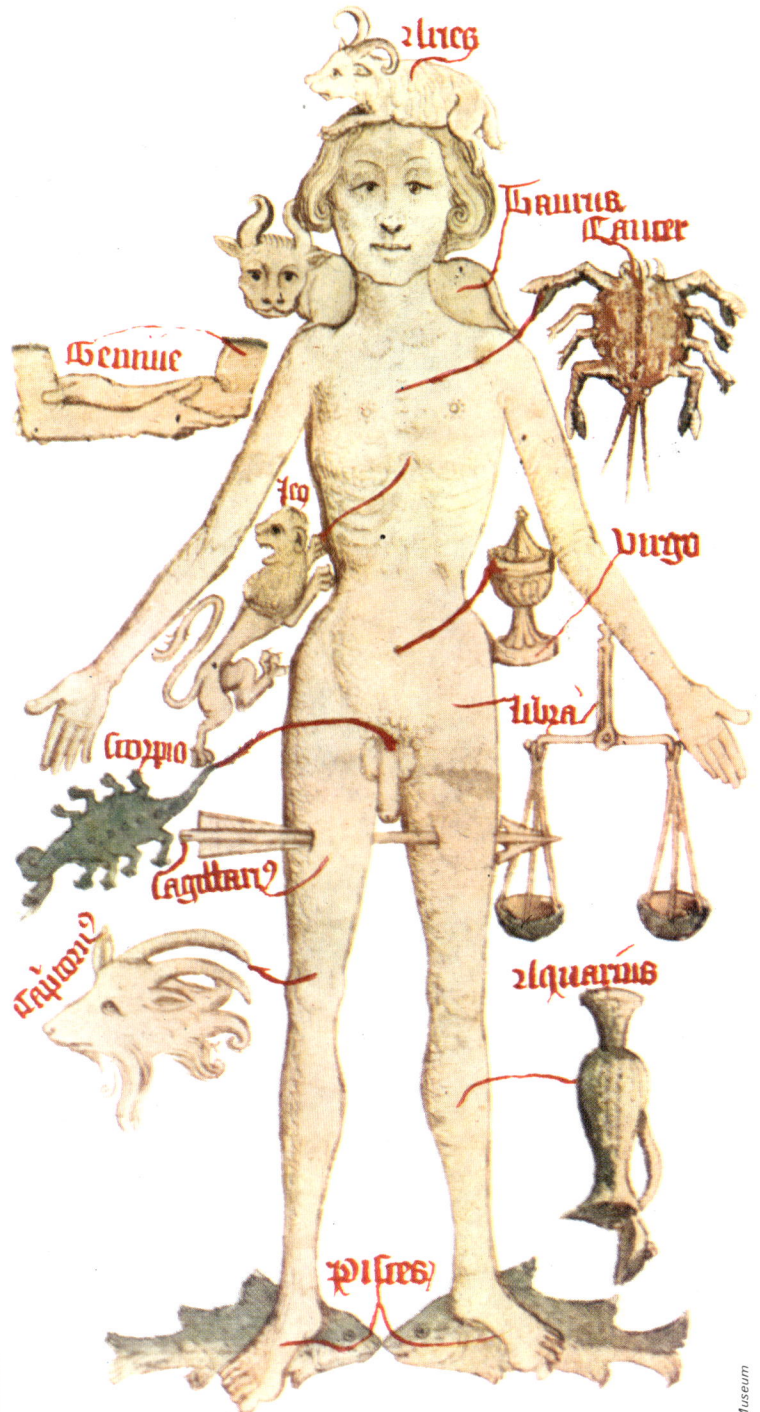

British Museum

17

Mysticism

THE RELIGION OF LOVE

Mysticism is a term that tends to be very loosely used; and so it will be as well to state at the beginning what it is not. In ordinary speech it is often associated with the occult

Above Drugs are sometimes used as aids to *mystical illumination: an 18th century painting shows dervishes meditating while they smoke* ganja, *the dried leaves of the hemp plant, and drink* bhang, *also made from hemp Opposite William Blake's* The Whore of Babylon: *the 'scarlet woman' of the Book of Revelation, riding on a beast with seven heads and standing for the pleasures of this world, on which the mystic turns his back. The magician is more likely to see them as sources of power*

and with paranormal phenomena such as thought-reading, telepathy or levitation.

Etymologically the word mysticism derives from the Greek *mueo*, meaning to 'initiate' into a secret cult – into a 'mystery'. Among Christians, however, the word has come to mean a direct experience of God; and since, in theory at least, Christianity is the religion of love, the 'mystical' experience is spoken of as union with God or as a 'spiritual marriage'.

Theology is concerned with God and man, mystical theology with God alone. Speculative theology leads to knowledge of God – turning its pupils into learned scholars and theologians; mystical theology leads to love of God – turning out intensely affectionate

lovers. This is the traditional Christian point of view: mystical experience is the immediate experience of the love of God, and any experience in which neither God nor love were felt to be present would scarcely be taken seriously as mystical.

But in the course of the last century or so, the word has taken on a wider meaning. There seems to be two reasons for this: the rise of the secular 'science' of psychology; and the dissemination of knowledge of the religions of India and China, in both of which the mystical element is prominent. And yet in neither Buddhism nor in Taoism does love, or indeed God, play a significant part. In what sense, then, are they mystical? At the risk of over-simplifying I would define

The famous story of St Catherine's vision of her betrothal to Christ is typical of the Christian view of the mystical experience as a 'spiritual marriage': The Marriage of St Catherine *painted by Veronese*

'mysticism' as 'a direct apperception of eternal being', whether this eternal being is conceived of in personal terms or simply as a state of consciousness. This may take many forms, but perhaps the characteristic lowest common denominator is the loss of the sense of personality or ego-consciousness in a greater whole.

This kind of experience is usually called 'Nature mysticism'. It is as if one's everyday personality – one's ego – were dissolved and merged into the 'All'; and through this merging into the totality of existence the mystic now feels that he lives with the life of the All and therefore cannot die. This experience is perhaps not so uncommon as is often supposed: it comes unheralded, lasts only for a short time, but brings with it an absolute conviction of its reality. Examples of it turn up in the mystical traditions of Christians and Moslems but on the whole it is not central to them. On the other hand, it seems to constitute the core of the experience which the Zen Buddhists call *satori*, though it is quite different from what the early Buddhists called *nirvana*.

This Nature mysticism which R. W. Bucke, a Canadian doctor who wrote at the turn of the century, called 'cosmic consciousness' and which Freud called the 'oceanic feeling',

can strike anyone at any time; and it can also be induced by yoga techniques and by drugs. It is not necessarily associated with religion of any kind but is liable to infiltrate the mystical tradition of any religion. Its most disturbing characteristic is that through it the mystic feels that he has transcended all the 'opposites' and contradictions of life, including good and evil. Bucke himself had such an experience and (as is the custom of most Nature mystics) he drew from it the most unwarrantable conclusions. According to him, cosmic consciousness 'shows the cosmos not to consist of dead matter governed by unconscious, rigid, and unintending law; it shows it on the contrary as entirely immaterial, entirely spiritual and entirely alive; it shows that death is an absurdity, that everyone and everything has eternal life; it shows that the universe is God and that God is the universe, and that no evil ever did or ever will enter into it; a great deal of this is, of course, from the point of view of self-consciousness, absurd; it is nevertheless undoubtedly true.'

This is typical of the attitude of the Nature mystics. Their experience is usually momentary, but it is overwhelming in its impact: they simply cannot doubt that they have entered into a totally new and different form of consciousness which represents a truth of which they had never dreamt before and which they find it almost impossible to describe. Their attitude is that they have seen the truth and that they therefore know. They are, however, the amateurs at this very hazardous game and unfortunately

they rarely think it necessary to consult the professionals. The professionals are, of course, the religious mystics; and of them the Indians are without doubt the most important. They are important because (unlike believers in Judaism, Christianity and Islam) they are not bound by dogma. Hence they feel no obligation to express their experience in terms of any given religious framework. Thus if love does not form part of their experience, they will not speak of love, the idea of love being only peripheral in their sacred texts.

It is a common error to suppose that 'mysticism is essentially one and the same, whatever may be the religion professed by the individual mystic', for any study of the Hindu and Buddhist mystical texts will very soon convince us that this is not true. There are varieties here which it is simply not possible to overlook: it is not a question of interpretation but of the experience itself. And it would seem that there are three recognizable types of mystical experience, all of which are to be found in the Hindu and Buddhist classics. The first is 'cosmic consciousness'; the second is the realization of eternity and 'deathlessness' within oneself from which the whole universe of change and time and space is excluded; and the third is the experience of the union of the soul with the Absolute or God in a supreme act of love. The first is typical of the *Upanishads*, the sacred mystical texts of the Hindus; the second is typical of early Buddhism; and the third is characteristic of Christianity, Islam and later Hinduism.

The Spiritual Marriage

Christianity is, in theory, the religion of love, and its mysticism therefore naturally expresses itself in terms of love. But Christianity also exalts virginity as one of the greatest virtues, and virginity is not compatible with human love as it expresses itself in wedlock. This is rather awkward for Christians, the more so in that their mystics *experienced* the love of God as a spiritual marriage, the consummation of which bore an uncomfortable resemblance to the sexual act in the physical world. Origen, who had castrated himself for the love of God, was painfully aware of this, but it did not prevent him from writing a commentary on the frankly erotic Song of Solomon.

Love and marriage, of course, are only possible between two *persons*. The God of the pantheists – of cosmic consciousness – must therefore also have his personal side. In the *Upanishads* this is only occasionally recognized. In one of the later *Upanishads*, however, the existence of God as creator and sustainer not only of the physical universe but also of the timeless eternity called Brahman, is admitted.

In the imperishable, infinite city of Brahman
  Two things there are –
Wisdom and unwisdom, hidden, established there:
Perishable is unwisdom, but wisdom is immortal:
Who over wisdom and unwisdom rules, he is another.

This distinction between the personal God and the impersonal Brahman and the relationship between the two becomes even more apparent in the *Bhagavad Gita*, a dialogue between Krishna, who is God incarnate, and his friend Arjuna. It is in the eyes of the Hindus the spoken word of God. The final revelation is, in essence, the Christian revelation too. Not only is man required to love God but God on his side loves man in return: 'And now again listen to this my highest word, the most mysterious of all: I love you well. Therefore will I tell you your salvation. Bear Me in mind, love Me and worship Me, sacrifice, prostrate yourself to Me . . . Give up all things of law, turn to Me, your only refuge, for I will deliver you from all evils; have no care.'

Two Kinds of Unity

In all traditions, even in those which start from the love of God, there is a tendency to mistake the stage of 'isolation' for identity with the Absolute and therefore beyond all relationships of any kind including the consummation of the spiritual marriage. This tendency becomes the official teaching of the non-dualist Vedanta in India. But as the *Gita* makes plain, what is taken to be identity with the godhead turns out to be only the experience of the oneness and eternity of one's own soul.

There is, then, a mysticism of the soul as it is in itself and a mysticism of the love of that soul for God. In the Christian tradition the two are rarely distinguished, for love is God, and God is timeless eternity.

This 'spiritual marriage' type of mystical experience is also recorded in certain forms of Hinduism: the lives of Krishna and the gopis could be allegorized to represent the love between God and the soul

What Christian mystics call the apex of the soul is the top of the mountain; and standing here the soul looks down and contemplates all the transitoriness of the world, realizing its own changelessness. Men, however, are not angels: they do not have wings. Hence it is impossible for the soul to rise higher than the top of the mountain. If it is to go further, then it must receive wings, and this can only come about by the grace of God. As Richard of St Victor writes:

Let a man rise up by himself above himself, and from self-knowledge to the knowledge of God. Let a man first learn from the image of God, let him learn from the likeness of God what he ought to think about God . . . A mind which does not raise itself to consideration of its own nature, how can it fly away on the wings of contemplation to that which is above itself? . . . If the mind has not yet been able to gather itself into a unity, and does not yet know how to enter into itself, when will it be able to ascend by contemplation to those things which are above itself?

It must, however, beware of resting content on the mountain-peak under the delusion that this is the journey's end, for this may lead to complacency and spiritual pride.

21

MAGIC AND MYSTICISM

The Laws of Magic

The science and art of magic is based upon three principles. The first principle declares the existence of a subtle substance called the Astral Light, the medium through which communication with other realms is made.

The Astral Light is beyond the range of our senses but its existence is suggested by mysticism, psychology and the new physics. Its fluidity makes it easily suggestible. Even the most tenuous ideas impress or influence it. By directing the current of his will, ritually motivated, the magician is able to cause changes in the Astral Light.

The Astral Light is an ocean of unconsciousness to which we are all linked. Its existence makes prophecy and clairvoyance possible. It was Eliphas Levi who applied it to magical operations. Levi, who died in 1875, was the first to undertake the task of rehabilitating magic after the discredit into which it had fallen.

The Astral Light or Astral Plane contains or constitutes the Cosmic Memory which is a repository of everything that has ever been thought or done. The Cosmic Memory is thus a vast, impersonal record of impressions which have been received since the beginning of time. Another name for the Astral Light is the Akasha; for this reason the Cosmic Memory is also called the Akashic Records. As these records are in picture form, they are recoverable by a competent skryer or medium. Madame Blavatsky (1831–1891) and Rudolf Steiner (1861–1925) claimed to have read in the Akashic Records data about the lost continents of Atlantis and Lemuria.

The second fundamental principle of magic is the belief in the limitless power of the magician. In theory, there is nothing that he cannot do through the exercise of his will. He can create thunderstorms or turn a man into a camel, as Aleister Crowley is alleged to have turned his pupil, Victor Neuburg (1883–1940) during 1909 in the Algerian desert following a dangerous magical ceremony during which they had evoked Choronzon, the Demon of Chaos.

The third principle of magic is the Law of Correspondence or Doctrine of Signatures; that is, the belief that external characteristics correspond to inner qualities; the external characteristics serve as signs by which it may be possible to discover everything internal and invisible for men.

Man into God

If you magically pronounce, say, a god's name, it engenders a stress in the Astral Light and a lineal figure typifying the nature of the god appears. (Compare the patterns formed by particles of sand with the wavelength of a violin bow drawn across the strings.) And that, of course, is the origin of the form of magic seals, sigils, yantras, mandalas (magic circles). The ancient seers of India saw the lineal representation of the Great Mother as a pattern of interlaced triangles called the Shri Yantra. The 'signature' of a god is thus his lineal figure. The seers reveal these great glyphs or symbols to the worshipper, and the worshipper, by concentrating his mind on the tangible representation of the glyph enters into communion with the deity.

The Law of Correspondences also plays a great part in the history of mysticism which has been defined as the science of ultimates, that is, the science of the union with the Absolute. To that extent, yoga is a mystical activity, for the aim of yoga is the achievement of complete detachment from the world: the yogi who has attained Samadhi (ecstasy) is absorbed by the Great Mother whom all the Lords of the innumerable worlds worship.

The pervading tone of the writings of Eliphas Levi and Aleister Crowley is one of power – desired or achieved power. This is markedly in contrast with the tone of the

Left Padre Pio, the saintly Italian friar who died recently and who, like St Catherine, was believed to have the stigmata, the wounds of Christ on the cross Right Madame Blavatsky, a modern magician who tried to unite the eastern and western occult traditions

Abresch Federico

John Symonds

writings of mystics. Instead of exalting their will, they do their best to extinguish it entirely. At the height of the magician's ghostly operations, he sees the image of the god he is invoking; he harmonizes himself with the nature of this god to the point of identification, and he loses consciousness of his human identification. 'Behold! he is in me, and I am in him.' According to Crowley, this identification of magician and god irrefutably links magic with mysticism. But there are gods and gods, and the Christian mystic would flee from some of the gods Crowley called forth. In any case, Crowley was thinking of Eastern as opposed to Western mysticism; he knew that the Eastern mystic entranced in the bliss of Samadhi cries 'I am Buddha'. But no Christian mystic who has attained the unspeakable experience of 'union with God' would say, 'I am Christ,' but that 'Christ is in me'. Jung remarks that the difference that there is between the two viewpoints is immeasurable.

God into Man

It is not surprising that mystics are critical of magic as a way of escape which man has offered to his soul. According to Evelyn Underhill the experiences of both magicians and mystics are initially similar. Both pass into the plane of consciousness which the Astral Light represents, but whereas the magician stays there, the mystic goes into a higher sphere. Magicians would of course disagree. Crowley talks about a spiritual plane above the Astral Plane. Dion Fortune, foundress of the Society of the Inner Light, thought that magic was as good a way of achieving divine union as any. As a magician she was unable to accept the view that the mystic enters into a higher sphere of suprasensible reality. Whether this is so or not, the approach of these two explorers of hidden realms is clearly different. The magicians have been likened to the cherubs who are filled with perfect knowledge, the mystics to the seraphs who are aflame with perfect love. Love seems to play little or no part in the attitude of the magician who begins by invoking, by devout supplication, the god of the sphere in which he is working, but ends by issuing commands.

The mystic becomes passive, his eye turns inwards; his aim is to transcend or shift his intellectual, emotional and volitional points of view. It is a most difficult thing to do. Years may go by before the Veil of Isis is raised – if it is raised, for few succeed, as few among the thousands that try, succeed at yoga. The mind keeps on interfering. The language of mystics, like the language of yoga texts, becomes somewhat less than precise because of the incommunicable nature of the experience. But to put the matter in a nutshell, the play of opposites, which is the outstanding feature of the prison of sense, is overcome. The distinction between subject and object, good and evil, long and short vanishes, and the eye of the mystic gazes and feasts upon the perfect consummation of the Love of God, which is the ineffable Reality.

LIGHT

In religion, legend and symbolism light is primarily connected with good and with creative powers. Gods and saints are said to radiate light, and 'illumination' is a term frequently used for the revelation or discovery of the divine, not merely as a symbol but as a description of an actual experience, an encounter with light. When the apostles received the gift of the Holy Spirit on the day of Pentecost, 'a sound came from heaven like the rush of the mighty wind, and it filled all the house where they were sitting. And there appeared to them tongues as of fire, distributed and resting on each one of them' (Acts, chapter 2). St Paul was converted on the road to Damascus, when 'a light from heaven flashed about him' and he heard the voice of Jesus (Acts, chapter 9).

The sight of light playing on the surface of a dish stimulated in Jacob Boehme a mystical experience which he called a 'spiritual triumph' and which could only be compared with 'that where life is born in the midst of death'. Ghazali, the great

Moslem mystic, was saved from scepticism by 'a light which God threw into my breast'. In the Indian tradition, among the experiences of the adept who successfully awakens the kundalini is 'a vision of light, which passes from a bright glow to a heaven full of brilliant dots, like stars', eventually followed by a 'suffusion of shining whiteness that is . . . an awareness of the supreme Radiance itself'.

Mircea Eliade says that 'for Indian thought the Light mystically perceived denotes transcendence of this world, of profane and conditioned existence, and the attainment of another existential plane – that of pure being, of the divine, of supreme knowledge and absolute freedom. It is a certain sign of the revelation of ultimate reality – devoid of all attributes. This is why it is experienced as a dazzling white Light . . .'

In the *Mahabharata* the god Vishnu reveals himself in a flash of lightning as bright as the light of a thousand suns, and we are told that 'by penetrating this light mortals skilled in yoga attain final deliverance'. In the *Bhagavad Gita* when the god Krishna shows himself in his true form, he is compared to the radiance of a thousand suns shining at once. 'I see the splendour of an infinite beauty which illuminates the whole universe. It is thee with thy crown and sceptre and circle. How difficult thou art to see! But I see thee; as fire, as the sun, blinding, incomprehensible.'

Light of Battle

That divine beings radiate light is accepted in all the major religious traditions. There is a Buddhist legend that a crowd of gods went to visit Buddha, who was meditating in a cave. The cave was filled with brilliant light, which some said was the radiance of the assembled gods but others said came from the fiery ecstasy of the Buddha himself. In Japan, Amida is 'Lord of Boundless Light', his head is encircled by a halo of light and he is more glorious than the sun at noon. Mohammed's face shone with his own light, and so, according to mythology, did the face of the Scandinavian god Balder.

The face of Jesus shone like the sun and his garments became as white as light when he was transfigured before his disciples on the mountain and the voice of God pronounced, 'This is my beloved Son' (Matthew, chapter 17). In Christian art the Father, the Son, the Virgin Mary and the saints have haloes of radiant light and the Holy Spirit emits fiery rays of light, for example, in El Greco's *Annunciation*.

Not only does sanctity emanate light but in legends and folktales so do beauty and blood-lust. There are Indian folk stories, for instance, of a prince who marries a woman so lovely that she lights up the bridal chamber on the wedding night. In the *Iliad* (book 18), when Achilles went out in berserk fury against the Trojans, the goddess Athene 'shed a golden mist around his head and caused his body to emit a blaze of light.' When the great Irish hero Cu Chulainn was roused in battle, the warrior's light rose from his forehead as long and as thick as a whetstone. We talk of the 'light of battle' being in someone's eye. Similarly, the 'heat of battle' is a familiar figure of speech, and

when Cu Chulainn's dreaded battle frenzy was upon him, the heat he radiated was so intense that he boiled and burst two vats of water.

The radiating light of sacredness is also the light of spiritual vision. Eliade quotes Eskimo shamans who say that you cannot become a shaman without going through an experience called 'illumination' or 'lightning'. After long preparation, the shaman suddenly feels in his head and body a mysterious light, 'an inexplicable searchlight, a luminous fire'. This light enables him to see in the dark, not only literally but in the sense that he becomes clairvoyant. He also has the sensation of rising upwards – 'it is as if the house in which he is suddenly rises; he sees far ahead of him through mountains, exactly as if the earth were one great plain.'

The sensation of rising upwards is one of the distinguishing marks of being in what western occultists call the astral body or 'body of light', which is also an inexplicable searchlight that casts its rays on things not visible to ordinary sight.

The astral plane is said to include but extend beyond the physical plane of our everyday world, and the astral light (the light created by God's command 'Let there be light', according to Eliphas Levi) transmits the rays or waves or vibrations of human will-power, thought, feeling and imagination. In terms of Jungian psychology it is the medium of the archetypes, the basic ideas and symbols of the collective unconscious. In the astral plane thought, fancy and emotion have the same concrete reality as a solid object here on the physical plane, and the astral light is a great reservoir of occult power (like the *mana* of the Polynesians or the *orenda* of the North American Indians). Every human thought makes an imprint on the astral light, it is said, and in it the seer can read the history of the distant past in the Akashic Record or Cosmic Memory, through it the occultist can discern the reality behind the surface appearance of things, with it the magician works as a smith works with metal in his forge, shaping the subtle substance of the astral light with the tools of concentrated imagination and will.

> Each act that we perform, each thought that enters our brain, each emotion as it leaves the heart, registers itself on the astral matter, remaining there for all time as an eternal record so that those who are able to may see and read. On this topic Eliphas Levi has significantly remarked that 'The Book of Consciences which, according to the Christian doctrine, will be opened on the Last Day, is nothing more than the Astral Light in which are preserved the impressions of every Logos, that is every action and every form. There are no solitary acts and there are no secret acts; all that we truly will . . . is written in the Astral Light.'

> Israel Regardie *The Tree of Life*

In ancient Greek religion there is a contrast – though not clearcut as far as is concerned – between the Olympian gods who lived in a 'comprehensible and business-like atmosphere of daylight', and the chthonian powers who lived underground, shrouded

in mystery and approached by night. Behind this is the broad contrast between the worship of sky gods who live in the light of day, and the worship of the Great Mother whose roots are believed to lie deep within the darkness of the earth.

The Divine Spark

The Manicheans, who drew heavily on Zoroastrianism, taught that there were two eternal and uncreated entities, God and Matter, which could also be called Light and Darkness or Truth and Lie. As a result of a complicated succession of mythological events, the powers of darkness were able to seize some of the particles of the divine light, which meant that they had captured part of the essence of God. To keep these ill-gotten spoils in their grasp, they fashioned Adam and Eve, in whom they imprisoned the captive light. Adam and Eve were ignorant of the light within them, until they were redeemed by a heavenly messenger, himself sometimes called 'Jesus the brilliant light'.

The theme of the divine spark, the gleam of heavenly light imprisoned in man and matter, also appears in the Gnostic systems of the eastern Mediterranean and has had a profound influence on mysticism and occultism in the West. It is a way of expressing the belief that in a man's innermost being there is an element of the divine. The discovery and liberation of this inner potential godhead, the true self, is a basic theme of European magic and occultism.

A magician is usually very ready to think of himself as a potential god but for a mystic the problem is to avoid putting man on a level with God while claiming that there is a divine element in human nature. In the 14th century, for instance, Meister Eckhart said that there is a spark of divine light in man but emphasized that his soul is a mere receptacle of God's light. A German Protestant mystic of the 16th century, Hans Denck, said: 'No man can see or know himself, unless he sees and knows, by the Life and Light that is in him, God the eternally true Light and Life . . . He must find God in himself and himself in God.' And again, 'The Kingdom of God is in you (a reference to Luke 17.21) and he who searches for it outside himself will never find it; God, the all-highest, is in the deepest abyss with us, and is waiting for us to return to him.'

In the 17th century the doctrine of the 'inner light', the divine light within each human being, was central to the teaching of George Fox and his first followers were sometimes known as 'Children of Light'. In the 18th century William Law took up the same theme: 'Consider the treasure thou hast within thee: the Saviour of the world, the eternal Word of God lies hid in thee, as a spark of the divine nature . . .'

The Splendid Lights

In the Cabala the process through which the hidden God makes himself known is described in terms shot through with the

The sun as the creator of light and heat has a prominent place in many mythologies. Major Egyptian deities were shown with the disc of the sun as an emblem of power and creativity: Horus with sun disc

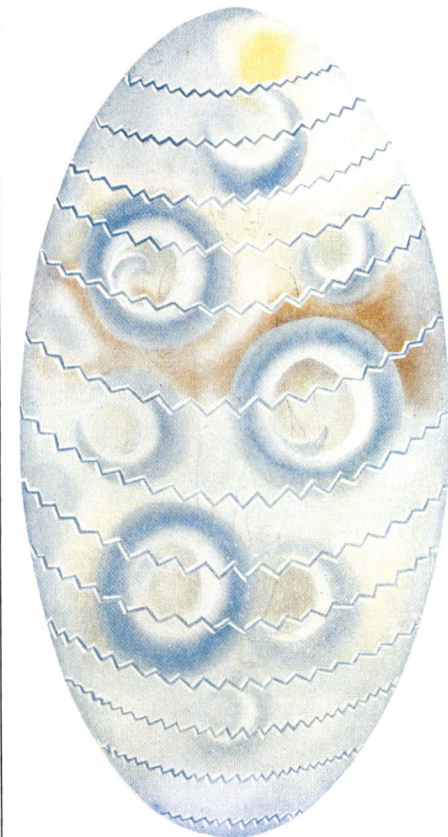

Left *And God said, 'Let there be light': in Genesis God creates light before fashioning his other creations: 12th century manuscript* Above *The sun as the creator of light and life is traditionally linked with gold, the most valuable of metals, and the aim of alchemy was to create the life-giving radiance of the perfect gold: from* Splendor Solis Right *Gods, heroes and holy men have long been believed to radiate light, and* many occultists maintain that human beings, especially in strong emotional states, emit a luminosity called the aura, which can be seen by peculiarly sensitive observers: two illustrations from C. W. Leadbeater's book Man Visible and Invisible; 'Intense anger' (above): the red zigzag lines represent the arrows of uncontrolled rage. 'A sudden rush of devotion' (below): a spiritual experience sweeps over a nun at prayer

imagery of light. It begins with a concentration of divine energy in a 'luminous point'. The sefiroth, which are aspects of God and stages in the process of divine self-revelation, are called 'splendid lights' in the *Zohar*, and God is 'an absolute light but in himself concealed and incomprehensible', who can be comprehended only through the 'luminous emanations' of the sefiroth.

The *Zohar* also contains the doctrine of the divine spark, the element in man which can eventually find reunion with God from whom it came. According to the Lurianic Cabala the infinite light of the godhead retracted itself, to create a vacuum into which God infused his light. But the vessels containing the light shattered and some of the divine sparks fell into chaos.

In the early Church baptism, the initiation into Christianity, was sometimes described as 'illumination' and it was the custom for the candidates at the baptism service to carry torches. Whether this piece of symbolism was borrowed from the mystery religions is disputed but at the climax of the Eleusinian Mysteries there was a sudden blaze of torches.

But nothing, in symbolism or in reality, is a simple, clearcut antithesis. The darkness of love-making, of dreams, of the womb or the depths of the mind, has its own powerful radiance of the sun but also the scorching and destroying flame that withers the desert (which, conversely again, may be a symbol of revelation and the presence of God in the wilderness of asceticism). Ghosts emit a faint and ghastly radiance, the luminescence of putrefaction. The flickering will-o'-the-wisp leads the unwary traveller astray. Satan puts on the guise of an angel of light.

I CHING

Probably the oldest extant book in the world, the I Ching or Book of Change is certainly one of the most extraordinary. This abstruse Chinese classic is known to English readers by several names. I Ching (pronounced Ee Jing) is the official romanized Mandarin spelling, while Yee King, Yik King and so on are spellings representing certain Chinese dialects. Often called the Book of Changes, it is better rendered in the singular form; either would suit the Chinese characters, but its authors were concerned with the principle of everlasting change which governs the exquisitely balanced universal harmony; the transient individual changes that result are of secondary importance. Though this ancient work has long been used primarily for divination, it is revered also as a source of wisdom and as containing in cryptic form the quintessence of an incredibly ancient philosophy.

For well over 2000 years, philosophers have been debating the purpose and meaning of the I Ching. The discrepancies in the various English versions are an indication of the profundity of the Chinese text. Its hoary antiquity, its extreme terseness and the mystical nature of its contents all combine to make it highly enigmatic. Chinese scholars who have devoted whole decades to its study disagree on many points; and the scores of Chinese commentaries, both ancient and modern, are similarly at variance with one another. It is indeed quite possible that the enigmas are intentional, that the I Ching, like many other mystical works, was written in a secret language whose significance was revealed only to initiates.

There have been stern scholars who believed that so lofty a classic was shockingly besmirched by being put to use by soothsayers. For all that, it is certain that it has been used for divination since before the days of Confucius (550–480 BC). Certainly it owes much of its reputation – now swiftly extend- ing to the West – to the surprising accuracy claimed for its predictions. Today in China, Japan, Korea and Vietnam – the four countries where scholars readily under- stand the Chinese script – there are countless people, ranging from pious mystics to street fortune tellers, who peer into a future revealed by means of its curious diagrams. The present Chinese government, in its cam- paign against 'ancient superstitions', is likely to have banned its use but it would not be surprising to learn that Communist generals and administrators still seek its advice in secret. They must know, for example, that in 17th century Japan, Yamaga built up the Samurai into the finest fighting force in Asia by teaching them a type of strategy that accorded with a special interpretation of the I Ching. Though it is not a military book, it teaches how all activities benefit from being made to harmonize with the universal cycles of everlasting but orderly change, involving advance and retreat, progress and retro- gression, each in due season.

System of Diagrams

The I Ching is the product of a religion that antedates both Confucianism and Taoism and goes back to the very beginning of Chinese civilization. According to its teach- ing, the womb of the universe is a limitless, imperceptible void – T'ai Chi, the Absolute. In it all objects have their being and each owes its transient individuality to a partic- ular combination of Yin (negative) and Yang (positive).

A system of diagrams illustrating this con- cept is attributed to Fu Hsi, who is said to have lived 30,000 years ago.

Even assuming that he never existed or that so vast a stretch of time is a fanciful exaggeration, the fact remains that the diagrams are perhaps more ancient than any others in the world. Probably these diagrams had already existed for thousands of years when, if the traditional belief is accepted, King Wen (c 1150 BC) and his son Duke Chou provided each of them with an explanatory text. Modern scholars believe the text to have been much later as Confucius regarded it as belonging to high antiquity. This text, coupled with a commentary written either by Confucius or by some of his immediate disciples, forms the work as it now stands. Since Confucius lived some 2500 years ago, the main text must be somewhere between 2500 and 3100 years old and the commentary, just about 2500.

The main body of the book consists of 64 sections, each headed by a different diagram in the form of a hexagram (figure made up of six broken or unbroken lines). The hexagram is followed by a short explanatory text attri- buted to King Wen. Here is an example: 'Integrity. Sublime success. Righteous per- sistence brings rewards. Those opposed to righteousness meet with harm. It is not favourable to have any goal (or destination) at this time.' Next follows a terse Confucian commentary which amplifies the meaning of the text and usually explains how it came to be derived from the hexagram. Then comes a brief note on the symbolism and its impli- cations: 'This hexagram symbolizes thunder rolling across the whole earth; from it all things receive their integrity. The ancient rulers gave abundant and timely nourish- ment to all!' So much for the hexagram as a whole. Next come notes on each of its separate lines, attributed to Duke Chou: 'Line 1. Moving onward with integrity brings good fortune.' Each note is followed by a Con- fucian commentary on the line text: 'What is willed comes to pass.'

Obviously a book containing so many sections, each composed of terse, disjointed aphorisms, does not make for smooth read- ing. There are readers who, believing that an inner significance relates the parts to one another, read and re-read the book from cover to cover as regularly as devout Christ- ians read the Bible. But mostly it is read a section at a time in connection with the act of divination. The soothsayer (who may be anyone at all) burns incense, prostrates him- self thrice before the silk-wrapped book and, by a complicated manipulation of yarrow stalks (a plant also used for divination in the West) or by tossing three coins six times, receives in answer to the question in his mind one hexagram or, in many cases, two of them, usually with the emphasis directed to one particular line. As there are 64 hexagrams, each capable of giving seven answers (either with reference to one of the six lines or with- out emphasis on any of them), the total number of basic answers is 448. As two hexa- grams are often drawn and more than one line may be stressed, the number of possible answers is much larger. They are considered sufficient to take care of any eventuality, though in one sense all of them are variations on four themes – proceed energetically, proceed with caution, stop, or go back.

High Moral Tone

In another sense this is a gross oversimpli- fication, for almost every word in the text, the commentary, the note on symbolism and the individual line or lines particularly stressed is carefully weighed for its bearing on the question and on the circumstances governing both question and inquirer. Be- cause of the seemingly mechanical means of obtaining an answering hexagram, this method could be dismissed as fortune telling of the most arbitrary sort were it not for at least two special characteristics. First and foremost, the I Ching does not regard the future as fixed, so that ordinary fortune tell- ing is out of the question. The answers tell the inquirer, not what will happen, but how he should act. Secondly, the book's high moral tone makes it quite useless to people who intend to act from selfish motives. The an- swer 'cautious progress' does not mean that the inquirer will act in that way, which is what a fortune teller would be likely to imply, nor does it mean that to progress cautiously would be to the inquirer's immediate material advantage. What it does mean is that, under the circumstances, it would be morally right to do so and therefore it would redound to his ultimate good and perhaps to his immedi- ate advantage, but in the higher sense. Doubters open-minded enough to persist for a while in using the I Ching are, it is said, often astounded by the accuracy of the answers and by their sometimes extraordin- ary appositeness both to the question and to the surrounding circumstances. According to a commonly accepted belief, it does not

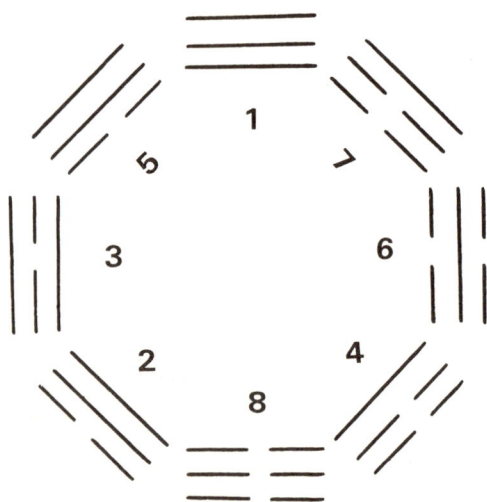

Circular arrangement of the eight trigrams used in charms for warding off evil

take long to discover that the responses are random or even discourteous when the act of divination is performed for fun; whereas they are most likely to be strikingly correct when the 'diviner' acts in all seriousness and when, while putting questions and interpreting the answers, he allows his mind to enter a state similar to that reached in the early stages of Buddhist or yogic meditation. From this one may infer that Jung was perhaps right in supposing that the symbols and words which constitute the oracle convey messages directly to the mind at a level beyond everyday consciousness.

It is apparent that the Book of Change is wholly concerned with the attainment of inner serenity and of harmony with man's surroundings and not at all with material success, except to the extent that, in a universe governed by moral law, material success may well be the ultimate result of righteousness. There are Chinese philosophers and mystics who read it for its spiritual counsel, using it less often (if at all) for divination, and they appear to be untroubled by the disjointed nature of the aphorisms. . Perhaps they really are able to discern a sublime pattern hidden from ordinary readers. Chinese tradition claims that the book reveals the secret workings of the universe; also, that its careful study would lead a man to live a blameless life largely free from frustration, because all his thoughts and actions would be in serene accord with the mystical order of being that governs the activities of the ants and the bees, the smooth progress of the seasons and the majestic movement of the stars.

All Versions Satisfactory

Of the three available translations in English, Legge's was produced about a century ago, under the inevitable handicaps of those days – lack of dictionaries and reference books and of learned teachers fluent enough in English to check what he wrote. It is an extremely literal translation and thereby doubly puzzling. Richard Wilhelm's, rendered into English from his German version, is on the whole excellent; it is marred by a few sentences of which the sense is far from clear, but that is perhaps to be expected in a book designed for use as an oracle. His notes and explanatory chapters are most valuable. Blofeld's rendering is less scholarly and has much less detailed explanatory material; it is a popular version with introductory chapters which were specially written with a view to making the book's use as an oracle as straightforward as possible for everyone.

By a complicated manipulation of yarrow stalks, one of 64 possible hexagrams is obtained; the inquirer then consults the appropriate section of the I Ching for the answer to his question

BOOK OF THE DEAD

It became the custom in ancient Egypt from about the 18th Dynasty (1580–1320 BC) to place in the tombs of the dead papyrus scrolls inscribed with texts. These texts were designed to help the dead to rise to life again and obtain a happy lot in the next world. The name Book of the Dead is a modern one, given by Egyptologists. The ancient Egyptian title was 'Chapters for Coming Forth by Day'. This title described what the texts would do for the dead, according to Egyptian belief. Briefly, it meant 'ability to leave the tomb' and it involved many strange and complex ideas about human nature and destiny. The Book of the Dead was the product of a long development of faith and ritual practice concerning death and the dead in Egypt. Many of the texts can be traced back through two earlier collections of funerary texts, the Pyramid Texts and the Coffin Texts.

The Pyramid Texts have a unique place in human records; for they are not only the earliest records we have of Egyptian thought, but they are also the earliest body of religious writings we have of mankind as a whole. They are called 'Pyramid Texts' because they are inscribed, in hieroglyphic characters, on the interior walls of certain pyramids at Sakkara, the necropolis or burial place of the ancient city of Memphis.

The inscriptions were collected and arranged by the priests of Heliopolis, near Cairo, which was the ancient cult-centre of Atum-Re, the sun god. In composing these texts, the Heliopolitan priests attempted to provide the dead kings, buried in the Pyramids concerned, with the magical means of securing resurrection from death and ascent to the sky, where they might join the sun god on his unending journey through the sky by day and the underworld by night. The sun

Probably the finest existing copy of the Book of the Dead is the papyrus made for Ani, a royal scribe who lived in Thebes in about 1320 BC. In this illustration, of his funeral procession, mourners are shown following the boat-shaped hearse on which his mummified body is lying

god was imagined to make this journey by boat, and in the Egyptian mind eternal bliss was thus conceived as being for ever in the company of Atum-Re as he made his unceasing circuit of the universe.

Guide to the Afterlife

The Heliopolitan priests were not skilful at literary composition, and the Pyramid Texts include rituals for use in embalming and funeral rites, hymns, incantations, magical spells, prayers and myths in no apparent order. It appears that any material deemed to have a religious or magical efficacy was included. Some of it was evidently of a very primitive character: for example, the so-called Cannibal Hymn, which represents the dead king as eating the gods, doubtless reflects a practice of ritual cannibalism that had once, long before, existed in Egypt.

The following translated extracts give some idea of the diction and imagery of the Pyramid Texts. First, an incantation designed to enable the dead king to join the sun god Re:

> He flieth as a bird, and he settleth as a beetle on an empty seat that is in the ship of Re . . . He roweth in the sky in thy ship, O Re, and he cometh to land in thy ship, O Re.

The next illustrates the way in which the dead Pharaoh Unas is ritually identified with Osiris, so that, invoking the principle of imitative magic, he is one with Osiris in his resurrected life:

> Thy (Osiris's) body is the body of Unas. Thy bones are the bones of this Unas. (If) thou walkest, this Unas walks; (if) this Unas walks, thou walkest.

During the period from c 2160 to 1580 BC, the nobility of Egypt adopted the custom of burying their dead in large wooden coffins, on the sides of which were painted texts designed to help the dead to pass safely to a blessed afterlife. The Coffin Texts are particularly characterized by the concern expressed by the deceased that he should have an adequate supply of food and drink,

lest he should be forced to feed on his own excrement. He also asks that he should be assured of a supply of fresh air to breathe and that the integrity of his body should be preserved. Belief in the potency of magic is also abundantly attested.

The scales or balances, which were to be used in the dread judgement that faced the dead, are mentioned. The following passage, which takes the form of an invocation of the sun god, gives some idea of the terror this grim ordeal inspired. The balance is personified as an awful demonic being.

> Thou canst protect me from this god of mysterious form, whose two eyebrows are the two arms of the balance, who casts his lasso over the wicked (to hale them to) his block, who annihilates the souls, in the day when evil is assessed, in the presence of the Master of all! Who is this god, whose two eyebrows are the two arms of the balance? It is Horus who presides at Letopolis. Others say: it is Thoth, it is Nefertem, the son of Sekhmet, this one who raises his arm.

The Pyramid Texts were compiled by the priests of Heliopolis for the exclusive use of the dead pharaohs; no reference is made in them to the fate of other folk. The Coffin Texts reveal that later on nobles and other important persons had begun to take over this ancient royal ritual.

The process of democratization continued into the period from 1580 to 1090 BC, and it finds its complete expression in the Book of the Dead. By this time, any person who could afford the essential minimum of what was once the royal mortuary ritual could hope to enjoy the resurrection to a new life which had once been the privilege of the pharaoh. To enable the dead to achieve this resurrection, and to pass safely through all the grisly perils of the underworld to everlasting happiness, assistance had to be provided as it had been for the pharaohs in the Pyramid Texts and later for the nobles in the Coffin Texts, selections of appropriate texts were provided by scribes, written on sheets of papyrus and deposited in the tomb.

THRONE MYSTICISM

Quotations from Old Testament prophets illustrate the visionary tradition of beholding the glory and majesty of the Lord upon a high and exalted throne. This tradition goes back to early prophets, like Micaiah who declared to King Ahad: 'I saw the Lord sitting on his throne, and all the host of heaven standing beside him on his right hand and on his left' (1 Kings 22.19). It was no doubt indebted to ancient Near Eastern forms and patterns of kingship. During the latter part of the Second Temple period and in the Rabbinic period (the period preceeding, and the centuries which followed, the destruction of the Temple in 70 AD), these records of prophetic visions provided the basis of the visionary, ecstatic early Jewish mysticism.

But the more rationalist and non-mystical thinkers also concerned themselves with these biblical passages, since they raised a basic problem of theology and religious philosophy – that of anthropomorphism. Was there a throne in heaven? Could a purely spiritual God be 'seen'? Were these visions, if taken literally, not gross and crude heresies rather than expressions of mystical spirituality? Many of the great medieval Jewish thinkers discussed these questions and suggested various solutions: the biblical accounts were allegorical figures of speech; or perhaps God created visible forms of glory in order to enable mortal eyes to behold a reflection of the splendour of the invisible Godhead, a symbol of the ineffable, terrifying reality.

The Ascent of the Throne

But in the circles of visionary mystics these philosophical analyses played a minor role. The earlier Jewish mystics cultivated an ecstatic kind of mysticism which taught its initiates ways and techniques of achieving the visionary experience of the divine glory and splendour of light: the throne. In the literature of these mystics, the throne (Hebrew *kisse*) which is the object of the ecstatic vision is more often called 'chariot' (Hebrew *merkabah*), probably under the influence of Ezekiel's great vision with its description of wheels, and wheels within wheels. This is therefore known as Merkabah or throne mysticism, and it can be quite clearly distinguished from later forms of Jewish mysticism, which were largely speculative, and whose practice of meditation and contemplation culminated in the experience of communion, if not union, with God.

The Merkabah mystics seem to have experienced ascensions of the soul, which were not without danger. In rabbinic circles only chosen disciples were permitted to engage in these mystical disciplines, known

as *ma'aseh merkabah* (the work of the chariot). The 'perils of the soul' which the adept encountered during his ascent through the various celestial spheres are described realistically and convincingly enough in the ancient texts. To overcome these dangers and pass the various celestial barriers the adept had to use mystical formulae and 'seals'. Hence Merkabah mysticism also had its magical side: an apparatus of incantations, spells and conjurations.

Within the Merkabah practice proper the magical part was subservient to the essentially mystical goal of the vision of the throne (and possibly of the splendour of the divine majesty on the throne). The outstanding feature of this kind of mysticism is its emphasis on the transcendent, majestic, tremendous and awesomely numinous character of the deity. The experience of loving communion, so common in later mysticism, is absent here. The initiate rises through worlds, spheres and heavens guarded by all kinds of terrifying celestial keepers until, at last, if all goes well and he be found worthy, he stands in awe and trembling before the supreme and blinding vision of the divine splendour.

CABALA

The Cabala, strictly speaking, is a system of Jewish mystical thought which originated in southern ·France and Spain in the 12th and 13th centuries. Yet even for the founders and early masters of this school, Cabala was but one among many terms (true knowledge, inner knowledge, knowledge of the mysteries, hidden wisdom) used to designate their secret lore, and it was only later that Cabala became the term generally used. Later the word was used for Jewish mysticism and occultism in general, and later still Christian Cabalists gave it an even wider meaning.

Cabala or Cabbala or Qubbalah are among the English spellings of a Hebrew word whose more correct transliteration is Kabbalah and whose meaning is 'receiving' or 'that which is received'. By the 2nd and 3rd centuries AD, the word had the technical sense of 'tradition', and especially of tradition handed down by word of mouth, as distinct from the written Scriptures. At this date it still had no 'secret' or mystical connotations but referred to acknowledged legal, ceremonial and religious traditions.

Creation and Splendour

The *Sefer Yetsirah* or 'Book of Creation' which was written at some time between the 3rd and 6th centuries in Palestine or Babylonia, has a theory of the universe which derives the world from 32 elements, which are the first ten numbers and the 22 letters of the Hebrew alphabet. The book is obscure, perhaps deliberately, but its doctrine of ten *sefiroth* (which here means numbers) and its emphasis on letter mysticism clearly influenced the later Cabala. All reality is a reality of the letters, which are the ultimate elements of which the cosmos is constructed. This conception easily links on the one hand with the cabalistic doctrine of the cosmic process as an unfolding of the mystical name of God (that is, of the Hebrew letters constituting his name), and on the other hand with the theory and practice of magic which endeavours to manipulate reality by means of these letters.

From Palestine and Babylonia some of these esoteric and magical texts and traditions spread to the Jews of Spain, Italy and France, and led to the formation of the German 'Hasidism' which flourished in the 12th and 13th centuries. The practical emphasis was on piety, humility and self-effacement, on penitential and ascetic discipline, and on the practice of devotional contemplation – particularly at prayer – in the form of meditation on the Hebrew letters and their numerical values. In due course German Hasidism merged with the new Cabala that developed in the 12th and 13th centuries, at first in Provence, in southern France, and subsequently also in northern Spain.

It is precisely this new system of mystical theosophy (or 'knowledge of God'), and its continuation into the 16th century and beyond, which constitutes the Cabala in the strict sense of the term. Its origins still

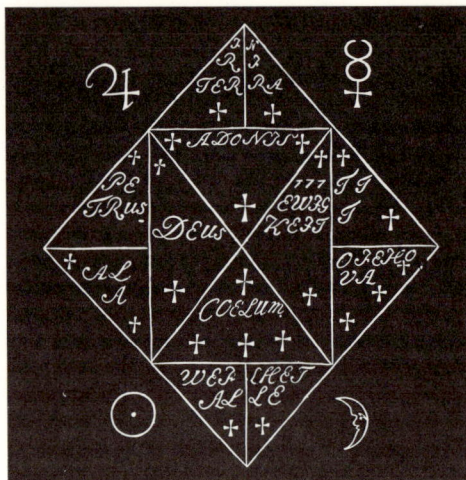

Above In ·magic the cabalistic preoccupation with letters and names of God, as containers of secret knowledge and objects of mystical speculation, turned into the attempt to use them as sources of power. Left Diagram believed to give the magician control of all evil spirits. Right The harmony of God, the universe and man, by Robert Fludd

need further clarification, for it is evident that many different influences coalesced in its emergence: Gnostic and Merkabah traditions, elements deriving from other oriental sources, and philosophical theories of various kinds.

The principal work of the Spanish Cabala, the *Zohar* or 'Book of Splendour' was written in the years after 1280 AD. The *Zohar* draws on many of the cabalistic doctrines and traditions which had evolved by then, but there is no reason to consider it the work of an 'editor' who merely combined ancient sources or texts. The author, Moses de Leon of Guadalajara, wrote the work in a peculiar imitation-Aramaic. The *Zohar* in due course became the classical main text for the Cabalists. Subsequent cabalistic works, whether expounding similar or different doctrines, could not affect the prestige and central position of the *Zohar*. Even the completely new cabalistic system evolved by Isaac Luria in the 16th century pretended to be a profounder interpretation of the mysteries of the *Zohar*.

The backbone of the cabalistic system is its doctrine of the deity, which distinguishes between the inaccessible and unknowable *deus absconditus* (the hidden god) on the one hand, and the self-revealing dynamic God of religious experience on the other. Of the former not even existence can be predicted. He, or rather 'It', is the paradoxical fullness of the great divine Nothing. The Cabalists called it *En Sof*, literally the 'infinite'.

En Sof is so hidden in the abyss of its Nothingness that it is not even mentioned in the Bible, let alone addressed in prayer or accessible in contemplation. Scripture, God's word, is by definition nothing but the revelation, that is, the self-manifestation, of God. An existing God means a manifest, revealed and related God. The process of manifestation is the process by which God 'comes into being' (at least in the perspective of the being to which he relates).

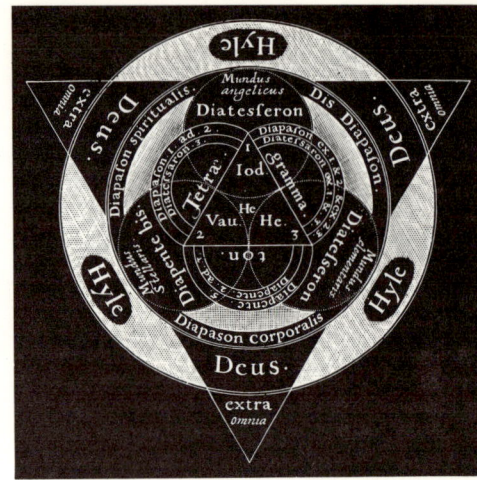

Opposite The Cabala's central doctrine deals with the unfolding of the hidden and unknowable God into the 'fullness' of the manifest God, known by his works: a diagram of the universe by the 17th century author Robert Fludd, with the links between the hidden God and the world. Many modern occultists have been powerfully influenced by the Cabala

The theory of emanation from God is a way of providing links between the many different phenomena of the world and the spiritual One, in which all things have their source. But the Cabalists use the theory of emanation not so much for this purpose but rather to account for the procession of the fullness of the Divine Being from the Hiddenness of the Divine Non-Being or Nothingness.

The Ten Sefiroth

The *pleroma* or dynamic 'fullness' of the Life Divine is described as a complex organism consisting of ten emanations, potencies or focal points, called sefiroth. These potencies are not ten gods, but ten aspects, stages or manifestations of the Living Deity. The 'World of Emanation' or 'World of the Sefiroth' is not the universe but the godhead in its 'existent' aspect. The dynamic interrelation of the ten sefiroth pictured in the three lines of the sefirotic Tree (the right side is male, the left female, and the middle line mediates between them and harmonizes them) make up the dramatic inner-life of the godhead which, in spite of its complexities, is essentially one.

Orthodox critics held the dualism between the hidden and the manifest God, as well as the doctrine of sefiroth, to be departures from strict Jewish monotheism. The Cabalists, who had some of the greatest luminaries of orthodox Jewish learning in their camp, replied that they were speaking of a profound mystery, and that the mystical understanding of the Divine Unity was precisely their main concern. In fact, the emphasis on this essential Unity grew more insistent as by the sheer inherent power of the cabalistic symbolism the various sefiroth became more and more personified.

The Cabala's picture of the divine totality as an emanated 'fullness' of ten sefiroth is reminiscent of the great Gnostic systems of earlier centuries. But whereas the Gnostic pleroma or 'fullness', the realm of the divine,

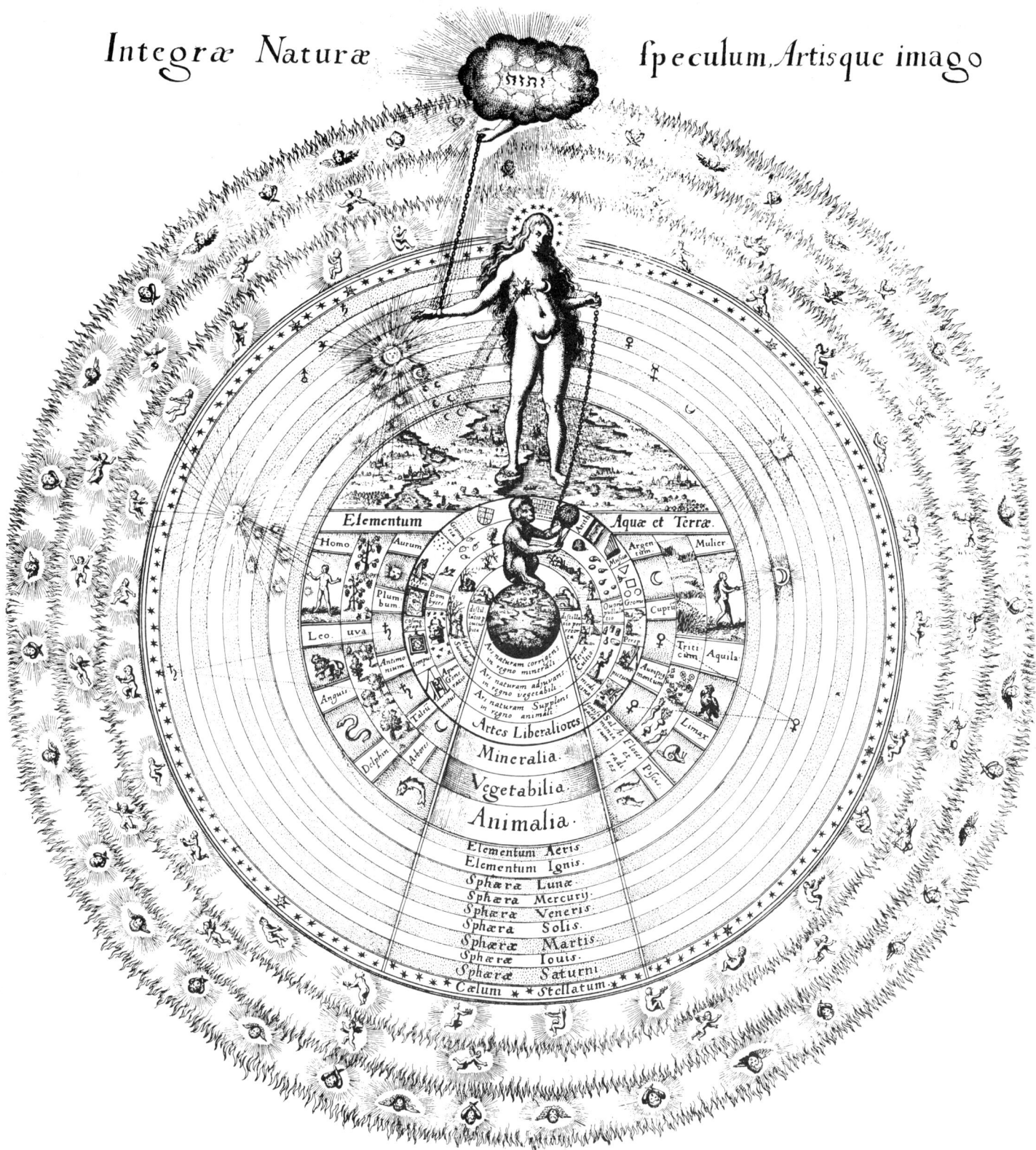

consisted of hundreds of divine *aeons* or powers, the cabalistic 'World of the Sefiroth' is reduced to a manageable ten. Moreover the Gnostic aeons are a rather chaotic and disorderly lot: they ascend and descend in almost anarchic freedom, whereas the cabalistic sefiroth are ordered in a strict hierarchy.

The notion of the cosmos as a series of descending emanations from a divine source is a familiar Neoplatonic motif. Medieval Arab philosophy was markedly Neoplatonic and there is definite evidence of specific Neoplatonic influences on the early Spanish Cabalists. The classical doctrine of the sefiroth is therefore an intriguing combination of Gnostic and Neoplatonic motifs. The cosmos as a hierarchial structure of successive emanations – this is Neoplatonic.

But the idea that this emanated cosmos is divine or, to be more exact, constitutes the fullness of the divine realm and that the entities making it up are divine forces, is thoroughly Gnostic.

Later cabalistic cosmology spoke of four words. These are, in descending order; *Asiluth*, the divine world of the sefiroth; *Beriah*, the sub-divine sphere, the world of the Divine Throne and the angels; *Yetsirah,* the world of the heavenly spheres down to that of the moon; and finally *Asiyyah*, the sub-lunar universe. This fourfold division is prefigured in the realm of the sefiroth, since the sefirotic Tree can be divided into four tiers corresponding to the four 'worlds'. The image of the sefirotic realm as a tree already occurs in the first cabalistic text to have

survived, the 12th century *Bahir*. The tree is, of course, growing downwards and its roots are above.

The supreme and central mystery of the Cabala is the Holy Union or 'sacred marriage' between the two aspects of the Divine, or in other words the unification of God. The greatest catastrophe that the Cabalist can imagine is the destruction of the unity within the godhead, the separation of the Shekhinah from her husband. This was precisely the tragic consequence of Adam's original sin in The Garden of Eden.

It is thus really the fate of God that is at the core of religion, and man's efforts, both in good works and in mystical contemplation, should be directed to the one end of promoting the wholeness of God.

SATANISM

The root ideas of Satanism go far back to the Gnostic sects. Far more people have been accused of worshipping the Devil than have ever actually done so, but they saw the world about them as profoundly evil, as the real hell, and life on earth as a sentence served in a prison. If the world is evil, then the power which made it and rules it must be evil too, and some of the Gnostics identified this evil power as the God of the Jews, who is described as creating the world in the book of Genesis and whose behaviour in the Old Testament they found impossible to reconcile with Christian principles. The good God, they said, lives far away in some distant heaven and we on earth are in bondage to the evil Yahweh.

The God of this World

They could draw some support for this opinion from the New Testament. In the story of the temptation in the wilderness, the Devil offers Jesus 'all the kingdoms of the world and the glory of them' (Matthew, chapter 4), with the clear implication that the gift is his to make. In St John's gospel (12.31) the Devil is called 'the ruler of this world', and St Paul calls him 'the god of this world' (2 Corinthians 4.4). And the belief that this evil god of the world was Yahweh could have been supported from another passage in St John (8.44), where Jesus tells the Jews that their Father is not God but the Devil.

Gnostics generally regarded Jesus as a Saviour sent by the good God to rescue men from enslavement to evil, but the identification of Yahweh as the evil power naturally turned the Old Testament upside down. Patriarchs and prophets and servants of Yahweh turned into villains, and Cain, Esau, the Sodomites and other opponents of Yahweh became heroes. The serpent of Eden was now a messenger from the good God, sent to bring Adam and Eve the knowledge of good and evil so that their eyes would be opened to the evil nature of Yahweh's creation. Some Gnostics, or so their Christian antagonists said, attacked Jesus as the evil Son of the evil Father and glorified Judas Iscariot for betraying him.

If God the Father was an evil deity, then it could be deduced that the Ten Commandments, and the other moral rules laid down by him were also evil, intended to keep men in subjection to him. Some Gnostics led austere lives of self-denial to disentangle themselves from the wicked world, but others were accused of attempting to escape from bondage to evil by breaking all conventional moral rules.

Gnostic ideas were kept alive in the East by obscure sects and were eventually transmitted into western Europe by way of the Bogomils and Cathars. The Cathars identified the God of the Old Testament as the Devil, the lord of this world which he had created, the master of the human body and of all material and temporal things. They attacked the Roman Catholic Church because it worshipped a being they regarded as Satan, and because they considered it stained with the worldliness and materialism inevitable in the service of the Evil One. But the Church reversed the accusation and branded the Cathars as Satanists.

Perhaps some of the Cathars did reach the conclusion that if the God of Catholics was really the Devil, then perhaps the Devil of the Catholics was the true God. Certainly, the Church maintained that they did. In the following centuries the same accusation was made against other heretical groups, including the Waldensians, the Luciferans in the 13th century, and the Knights Templar in the 14th. A pattern of 'Satanist' belief and behaviour was built up, whether or not any real Satanism was involved, its essential ingredients being worship of the Devil and the reversal of Christian values. A Satanist was one who renounced Christ and his Church, and blasphemously maltreated its sacred objects, symbols and ceremonies; who

The Black Mass is a sacrament of matter and the flesh, instead of spirit, and an adoration of the power opposed to Christianity: celebrating it on the body of a naked woman is a comparatively modern refinement

adored the Devil in the form of a man or a goat or some other animal; who sang and danced in the Devil's honour and obscenely kissed his person; and who revelled in child-slaughter and cannibalism, indiscriminate sexual orgies, perversion, homosexuality and every species of crime and abomination. This same pattern of accusations was brought against the witches.

The heart and centre of the persecution of witches was that they were Satanists, that they had rejected the rightful God and given their allegiance to his arch-opponent, and that in their 'sabbaths' or meetings they worshipped the ruler of evil, carnality and filth. Some of those accused as witches do seem to have taken the Devil for their god, worshipping him as an equal opponent of the Christian God, over whom he would eventually triumph. They looked to Satan for power and pleasure in this world and for a happy future in the next, and they vilified Christ as a traitor and a cheat, who had made promises which he did not keep, and who had gone away to live in heaven while Satan remained with his faithful on earth. The fierce hatred and contempt felt for Christianity comes out in many of the confessions extorted from witches and in accounts of the Black Mass, which they were accused of performing at the sabbath, in adoration of the Devil, as a blasphemous degradation of Christian ritual and as a celebration of the flesh and matter, as against the spirit.

In modern times Satanism appears more often in print than in real life. There is a vivid account of the Black Mass in J. K. Huysmans's novel *Là-Bas*, probably drawn from life. In his *History of Witchcraft and Demonology* Montague Summers quoted from an Italian newspaper a description of a Satanic chapel discovered in the Palazzo Borghese in 1895. 'The walls were hung all round from ceiling to floor with heavy curtains of silk damask, scarlet and black, excluding the light: at the further end there stretched a large tapestry upon which was woven in more than life-size a figure of Lucifer, colossal, triumphant, dominating the whole. Exactly beneath an altar had been built, amply furnished for the liturgy of hell: candles, vessels, rituals, missal, nothing was lacking. Cushioned prie-dieus (kneeling desks) and luxurious chairs, crimson and gold, were set in order for the assistants; the chamber being lit by electricity . . . arrayed so as to glare from an enormous eye.'

A few Satanist groups still exist, here and there, and the survival of Gnostic ideas is illustrated by a set of questions and answers issued by one of them, styling itself Our Lady of Endor Coven, The Ophite Cultus Sathanas. 'Satanism,' it says, 'is the position opposed to the worship of the force that brought the cosmos into existence as mind and matter out of the realm of pure spirit', in other words, opposed to the worship of the Gnostic evil world-maker, the Christian God the Father. Cain 'celebrated the First Satanic Mass' and Satanism 'has no conception of sin, but rather puts ignorance (the lack of the Gnosis) in the place of sin'. Members of less unorthodox faiths may be relieved to hear that Satanists hold aloof from the world ecumenical movement.

34

THE ROSY CROSS

It is generally supposed that the Rosicrucians were members of a German mystical or occult order that suddenly became active during the second decade of the 17th century, but could nevertheless trace its origins back to the early part of the 15th century. It is widely thought, too, that the Rosicrucians possessed important and arcane wisdom that has been transmitted to their spiritual heirs and successors. Thus even today there are people who claim some form of Rosicrucian 'adeptship'.

One of the most interesting features of the Rosicrucian legend is the persistence with which it has survived, particularly in circles identified with occultism. The mythical Christian Rosenkreuz (literally 'Rosy Cross') represents a forerunner of the 'Secret Chiefs' who added lustre to Baron von Hund's Masonic Rite of the Strict Observance (Germany, late 18th century). They never existed but there were many who believed in them. Again, a century later there were Madame Blavatsky's invisible 'Mahatmas', whose letters to her arrived literally out of thin air. They were also representatives of the 'Secret Chiefs' tradition. There is, too, a parallel between the Rosicrucian legend, with its small community of secret but somehow occultly powerful brethren, and the Masters of a far more recent and equally unidentifiable 'Great White Lodge', who are also said to be the guardians of hidden knowledge.

The Christian Rosenkreuz legend has now been in existence for more than 350 years. In the process of time, however, the main details of the legend, more especially its original form, have been largely forgotten and the word 'Rosicrucian' is associated with arcane or occult teachings.

The substance of the Rosicrucian legend originated in three short books that were published anonymously between 1614 and 1616. The first, which was no more than a slim pamphlet, was printed at Kassel in Germany in 1614. Its title in an abbreviated form was *Fama Fraternitatis* and it purported to come from a hitherto unknown Rosicrucian order or brotherhood. It contained no information whatever about the order's chiefs and where they might be found.

A brief introduction announced the reason for the publication. Its unknown author

La Vièrge aux Lilas, 1897, by the Belgian painter Carlos Schwabe, who exhibited at the Salons de la Rose Croix. The Madonna and Child are shown in white robes, for purity, with white clouds and white lilies, which are traditional symbols of the purity of the Virgin Mary. The rose is another traditional emblem of Mary and rose and cross together can stand for the Mother and Christ, for the fount of earthly life and the fount of spiritual life. The founder's aim was 'to restore the cult of the Ideal in all its splendour, with Tradition as its base and Beauty as its means': 'all humorous things' were banned from the Salons

hoped for a 'general reformation' of the world and mankind by means of a harmonious fusion of the two major achievements of the past century: the Reformation, and advances in scientific knowledge. The *Fama* was in some respects a Utopian tract, but its message was presented so obscurely that its meaning was very difficult to understand.

It begins with the story of Christian Rosenkreuz's travels in search of knowledge and true wisdom and ends with an account of the order that commemorated his name.

The *Fama* was soon followed by the *Confessio Fraternitatis R.C.* Indeed, its publication had already been announced in the *Fama*. It appeared to be by the same anonymous author and was printed at Kassel in Latin and German in 1615. It contained no expansion of the story of Father Christian Rosenkreuz but did mention that he had been born in 1378. Since he is supposed to have lived until the age of 106, and to have reappeared again 120 years later, it will be noted that the date of his expected return coincided with the publication of the *Fama*.

The *Confessio* contained 37 'reasons of our purpose and intention', meaning the brotherhood's policy, and invited its readers to join the Rosicrucian 'movement' but did not state how this could be achieved. It proclaimed its antagonism to the papacy, Islam, and the pretensions of quack alchemists. The brotherhood's aims were stated vaguely, rather than precisely, but the reader would have gathered that it was opposed to sectarianism and political strife.

The third and last of the three original Rosicrucian books was the *Chymische Hochzeit Christiani Rosenkreutz,* which was published at Strassburg in 1616 with three further editions during the same year. The first English version, *The Hermetick Romance: or the Chymical Wedding,* appeared in 1690. The word 'Chemical' should be construed in a vaguely alchemical sense.

This 'hermetic romance' presents a delightful fairy story, liberally packed with allegorical and symbolical detail. Its ultimate meaning is nowhere very clear and a detailed textual analysis presents the student with some considerable difficulties.

Puzzling Purpose

The problem of the authorship of the three tracts described above did not begin to attract the attention of modern scholarship until about 50 years ago and then, as might be expected, in Germany.

It has been established that the author of the *Chymische Hochzeit* was Johann Valentin Andreae (1586–1654), a young man when he published the book. Later he became a well-known Württemberg theologian whose pedagogic and pastoral writings were highly esteemed. Towards the end of his life he admitted that he had written *The Hermetick Romance* and, with evident embarrassment, tried to convey the impression that the book was a youthful folly. It is likely that he was also the author of the *Fama* and *Confessio.*

All three books originated in a small circle that was close to Christoph Besold (1577–1638), professor of law at the university of Tübingen. Andreae was both his pupil and his close friend. Besold's learning was

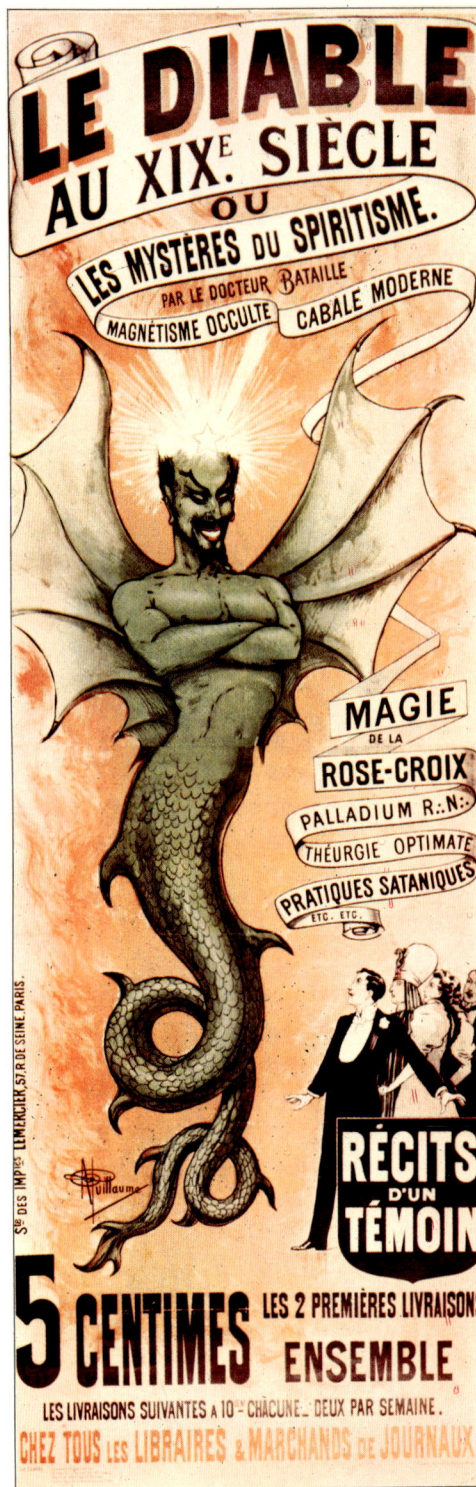

The variety of ideas and traditions sometimes associated with the Rosicrucians is suggested by this advertisement for a book on The Devil in the 19th century, *purporting to deal with modern Cabala, occult magnetism, theurgy and Satanism, as well as Rosicrucian magic*

immense: he had a detailed knowledge of Islamic culture and philosophy, could read Arabic and Hebrew, and at the same time knew the works of all the great humanists and Neoplatonists of the more recent Renaissance period. German scholars have pointed to Besold's influence in relation to the texts of the *Fama* and the *Chymische Hochzeit.*

While there is no quarrel about Andreae's literary and intellectual sources, there has

been much argument about his intentions. Is he to be considered a satirist, a moralist, a social reformer or perhaps a Pansophist, that is, a white magician? The latter was the view held by W. E. Peuckert, the late, distinguished Göttingen historian.

In the circles that provided a reading public for these books during the period 1614–c 1620 their effect was nothing less than sensational. There were, of course, many who wished to join the Rosicrucian brotherhood. Unable to identify a single person who belonged to it, let alone the slightest clue that would reveal where its 'headquarters' might be found, they printed pamphlets, mostly in the shape of letters, which, it was hoped, would eventually find their way to someone 'in authority'. Some of these announced that their respective writers were already members of the fraternity. This secondary Rosicrucian literature is very extensive.

Next there were those who did not claim any personal connection with the fraternity but nevertheless enthusiastically defended its aims, in so far as these were understood. Among them, for example, was the English alchemical writer Robert Fludd. Descartes, the French philosopher, who was in Germany in 1619, did his best to find a genuine Rosicrucian but failed and hence adopted a sceptical attitude.

Link With Freemasonry

About 1620 interest in the Rosicrucian 'phenomenon' began to decline in Germany and the movement, if it can be described as such, began to go underground. If these strange stories were remembered at all, then it was only by those who were still preoccupied with alchemy. In German occult circles there was a lively concern with alchemy until the end of the 18th century.

In 1710 something came to life which vaguely depended upon the Rosicrucian legend. It was in fact pre-Masonic but its name was later inherited by a German Masonic group. This was the Order of the Gold and Rosy Cross, the invention of Sigmund Richter, who called himself Sincerus Renatus, and who published at Breslau a tract with the title *The Perfect and True Perfection of the Philosopher's Stone by the Brotherhood of the Gold and Rosy Cross.* The order was supposed to be divided into two branches, the Rosy Cross and the Golden Cross, with a total membership of 63 Adepti. It was essentially an alchemical fraternity. If it ever existed, except in Richter's imagination, it soon disappeared without trace.

From this time onwards all the groups, fraternities and associations that have incorporated such words as Rosicrucian, Rozenkreuz or Rosenkreuzer, Rose Cross, Rosy Cross, Rose-Croix, and so on, in their titles have, with one exception, completely ignored the alleged erstwhile existence of Christian Rosenkreuz and his order. The story had been forgotten and the name alone survived.

Indeed, the only fraternity which actually revived and, indeed, 're-lived' the legend in its rituals was the Hermetic Order of the Golden Dawn, the most renowned magical society of modern times. The Golden Dawn, however, was not Masonic, although its founders were enthusiastic Freemasons.

THE GOLDEN DAWN

The Hermetic Society of the Golden Dawn or Stella Matutina was formed in 1887 by three members of the Rosicrucian Society in England, which had been founded in 1866. The Order had 11 grades or degrees, subdivided into three groups: the Golden Dawn in the Outer, with five degrees, and the Stella Matutina comprising the Rosea Rubiae and Aurea Crucis, each of three degrees. In addition the Silver Star, or Argenteum Astrum (three degrees) was said to consist of 'Secret Chiefs'.

René Guénon in *Le Théosophisme* (1921) wrote: 'The English secret society of the Order of the Golden Dawn in the Outer is a society of occultists studying the highest practical magic, somewhat akin to Rosicrucianism. Men and women are admitted on equal terms. There are three principal officers, Imperator, Praemonstrator and Cancellarius.' The grades, besides that of Neophyte, were four (corresponding to the four letters of the Tetragrammaton or personal name of Yahweh in the Old Testament): Zelator, Theoreticus, Practicus and Philosophus; also a sub-grade, the Portal, leading from the Golden Dawn to the Rosea Rubiae and Aurea Crucis, the Inner Order.

The story of the founding of the Order follows the mysterious pattern characteristic of the Rosicrucians. In 1880 an Anglican clergyman, the Rev. A. F. A. Woodford, bought some cipher manuscripts from a bookstall in Farringdon Street in London which he showed to two Masonic and Rosicrucian colleagues, Dr Woodman and Dr Wynn Westcott, an antiquarian, scholar and London coroner, both Masons of high standing and learned in the Cabala. Accompanying the manuscripts was a letter in German, saying that whoever cared to decipher the text should communicate with Sapiens Donabitur Astris (S.D.A.) through a Fräulein Anna Sprengel, and would receive further information. The manuscripts were duly deciphered; they were found to consist of notes and rough diagrams for the five rituals of the Outer Order (grades 0 = 0 to 4 = 7) together with certain lectures on elementary occult and cabalistic knowledge.

S.D.A. then instructed Westcott and Woodman to elaborate the rituals. This was done by another Freemason, a Scot, Samuel Liddell Mathers (who later, under the influ-

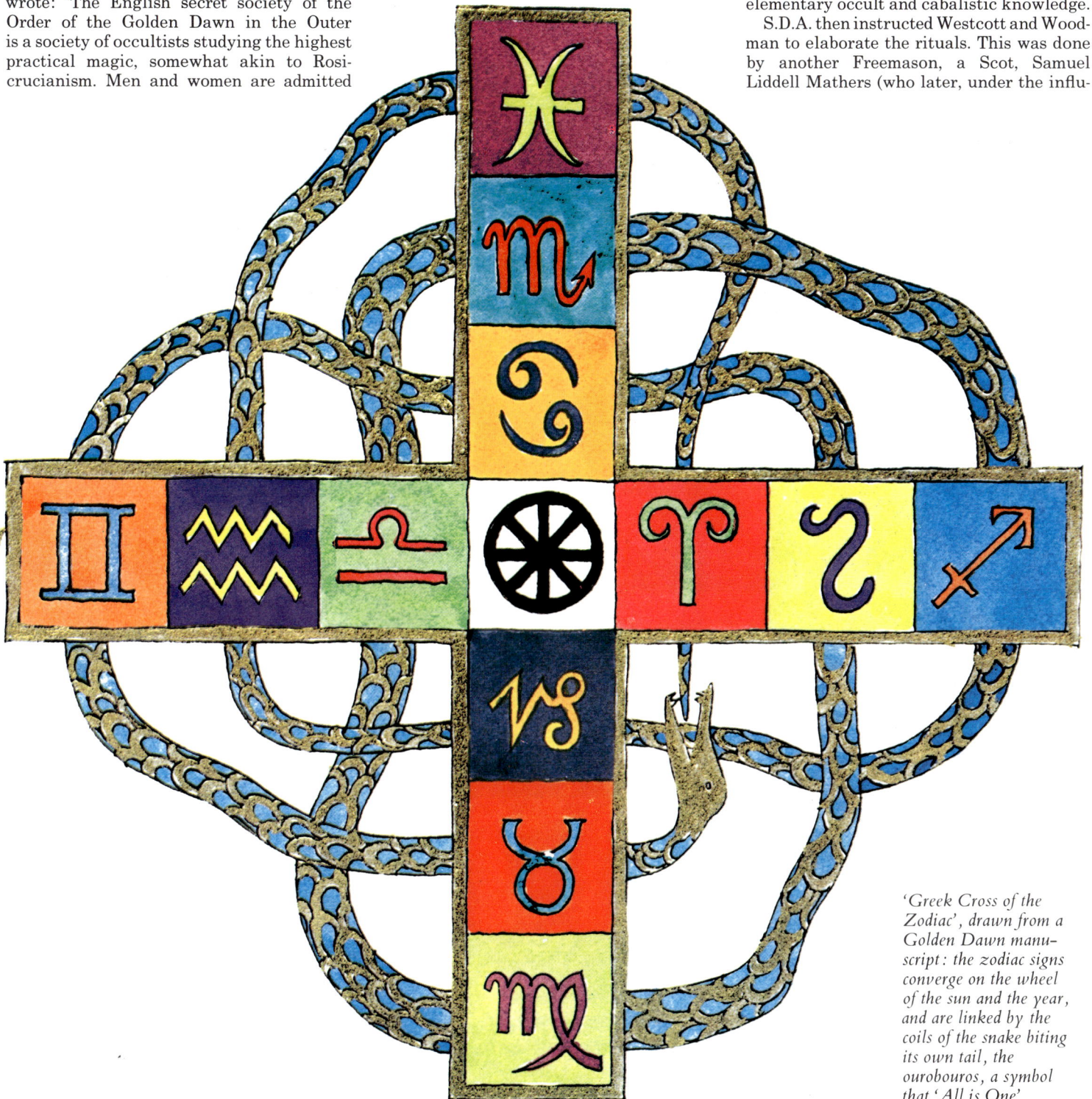

Kenneth Grant

'Greek Cross of the Zodiac', drawn from a Golden Dawn manuscript: the zodiac signs converge on the wheel of the sun and the year, and are linked by the coils of the snake biting its own tail, the ourobouros, a symbol that 'All is One'

ence of the Celtic movement, called himself MacGregor, and later le Comte de Glenstrae), assisted by Dr Westcott. The poet W. B. Yeats, who was initiated into the Order 'in a Charlotte Street studio' in 'May or June 1887', had met Mathers while both were working in the British Museum Reading Room: 'a man of thirty-six or thirty-seven, in a brown velveteen coat, with a gaunt resolute face, and who seemed, before I heard his name, or knew the nature of his studies, a figure of romance'. Yeats, who became a prominent member of the Order, and Imperator of the London lodge in 1901, helped Mathers in the writing of the rituals. These were published in America by Dr Israel Regardie, a member of the Order in its later days. The main body of the ritual consists, according to Regardie, of 'the sonorous and resonant versicles of the Chaldean Oracles – the translation, I believe, of Dr Westcott.' There is also a strong influence, especially in the rituals of the Outer, of the Egyptian Book of the Dead, and – doubtless through the influence of Yeats, who was editing the works of Blake at the time – marked traces of Blake's 'Prophetic Books'.

The Golden Dawn's rituals were written by W. B. Yeats and MacGregor Mathers. Yeats became Imperator of the London lodge after the expulsion of Mathers, who is seen here celebrating a Mass of Isis, and who claimed to be in touch with 'Secret Chiefs' who met him on the astral plane

Apart from the cipher manuscripts and other Hermetic literature found in libraries both in England and on the Continent by Mathers, most of the early teaching was received by Mrs Mathers clairaudiently.

Subversive Powers

Mathers had trouble with his 'black' *enfant terrible*, Crowley, who in 1905 broke away to found his own Order, the Argenteum Astrum (A∴A∴) or Silver Star. The Golden Dawn had at no time practised any form of sexual magic but Cowley, identifying himself with the Antichrist under the sign of the Great Beast 666 of the Apocalypse, made sexual rituals central to his Order. Mathers died in 1917, broken, some say, by Crowley, whose stronger personality proved too much for him and who stole many of the rituals which were in fact Mathers's work. After the death of Mathers the Ahathoor lodge was closed. According to an article on the Golden Dawn by Gerald Yorke, 'the A∴A∴ survives in New York, the Stella Matutina though dormant is not quite defunct, and the Golden Dawn in its original form is no more'. A member of the Golden Dawn, 'Dion Fortune', whose real name was Violet Firth, founded the Society of the Inner Light, which is still in existence.

The Great Work

Gerald Yorke says that, 'In the main the brethren fell by the wayside.' Dr Israel Regardie, on the other hand, considers that, 'there can be little or no doubt that the Golden Dawn is, or rather was until very recently, the sole repository of magical knowledge, the only Order of real worth that the West of our time has known.'

Magic was indeed only one aspect of the work of the Golden Dawn. The original intention of the Order was 'to prosecute the Great Work: which is to obtain control of the nature and power of my own being'. According to some of the texts the purpose was even more specifically Christian: 'To establish closer and more personal relations with the Lord Jesus, the Master of Masters, is and ever must be the ultimate object of all the teaching of our Order'. There was at one time in the Society a strongly Anglo-Catholic bias; besides the scholar Charles Williams, a number of members of the Anglican Society of the Resurrection were members, and even, briefly, Evelyn Underhill, the writer on mysticism. Lectures and papers were circulated expounding the Catholic doctrines of the Apostolic Succession, the seven Sacraments, the Assumption and the Immaculate Conception of the Blessed Virgin, or teaching the three grades of prayer. None of these papers is included in Israel Regardie's four volume publication of the rituals; which gives in this respect a one-sided impression.

The studies and practices of the Adepti centred round the cabalistic Tree of the ten Sefiroth; especially as taught by the Christian cabalist tradition. Mathers, quoting from Eliphas Levi's *Histoire de Magie* wrote that, 'the absolute hieroglyphic science had for its basis an alphabet of which all the gods were letters, and all the letters ideas, all the ideas numbers, and all the numbers perfect signs'. Astrology and geomancy, scrying and travel on the astral planes were taught, besides the theory of alchemy. Every adept had to prepare his own magical apparatus: cup, wand, dagger and pentacle, together with an elaborate symbolic Rosy Cross. He must also consecrate a sword. Ceremonies were performed in robes whose colour would vary according to both the grade and the nature of the work.

Three varieties of magic were taught: the Clavicula of Solomon the King, the Sacred Magic of Abramelin the Mage, and the Enochian system with its peculiar alphabet and language as revealed by Dr John Dee, Queen Elizabeth's astrologer. Mathers was industrious in translating cabalistic literature into English; *The Key of Solomon the King* (1889), *The Kabbalah Unveiled* (1889) and *Abra-Melin the Mage* (1898).

The central rituals are based upon the descriptions, in the Rosicrucian *Fama Fraternitatis,* of the Vault of the Adepti; translated by A. E. Waite in his *Real History of the Rosicrucians.* This consists of a symbolic enactment of the uncorrupted body of 'our father Christian Rosencreuz', symbolic of the buried sleeping higher Self. In the words of Dr Regardie, 'the whole concatenation of symbols is an elaborate and dramatic portrayal of the central theme of the Great Work. In a few words, it depicts the spiritual rebirth or redemption of the candidate, his resurrection from the dark tomb of mortality through the power of the Holy Spirit.'

The Golden Dawn can therefore be seen as one of a number of manifestations of 'the revolt of soul against intellect'.

FREEMASONRY

All Freemasonry in existence today can be traced, through one channel or another, to the Grand Lodge of England constituted in 1717. A 'Noble Brother' as Grand Master presented himself in the person of the Duke of Montague in 1721, since when the office of Grand Master has always been held by one of noble or royal birth. The present Grand Master is H.R.H. the Duke of Kent.

There was a rapid expansion of interest in Freemasonry during the 1720s. A list of Lodges published in 1725 includes 64 names. The first Provincial Grand Masters, namely those for North and South Wales, were appointed in 1726. The first overseas Lodges were constituted in Bengal, Gibraltar and Madrid in 1728.

One of the most surprising features of Speculative Freemasonry's early history is the Craft's vigorous and speedy expansion in Europe. An English Lodge was founded at Paris in 1732 and three years later Freemasonry had reached Portugal, Holland and Sweden. The first German Lodge was established at Hamburg in 1737. During the next decade the Craft took root in many other European centres, although not without encountering, here and there, official hostility. The first Papal Bull against Freemasonry (*In Eminenti*) was proclaimed in 1738 by Clement XII.

Freemasons meet in a specially furnished Lodge room. The Worshipful Master, the Wardens and other officers of the Lodge sit in their appointed places. In the ante-room adjoining the Lodge room a functionary known as the Tyler keeps guard to forbid the entry of strangers. First it is necessary to 'open' the Lodge in whichever degree is being 'worked'. A dialogue is held, in the form of questions and answers, between the Worshipful Master and various officers of the Lodge. Its time-honoured purpose is to remind the participants of the symbolical or allegorical nature of the ceremony they are performing.

When an initiation ceremony takes place the Lodge is opened in the First Degree. Outside in the ante-room the candidate is prepared by the Tyler. His collar, tie and jacket are removed and he lays aside his money: with this demonstration that the Lodge accepts him even in penury, he accepts the same obligation towards his fellow Masons. He is then led into the room blindfolded. The Tyler presents him to the Master and in reply to the question 'Whom have you there?' replies: 'A poor Candidate in a state of darkness.' The implication is that the darkness is spiritual but that he will be shown Light.

In the course of the ceremony the candidate swears a solemn oath not to reveal Freemasonry's secrets which, once again, are all symbolical. The blindfold is then removed. He is also shown certain grips and signs, a survival of the old Operative Masonry, and told certain words which refer to the symbolic building of King Solomon's temple.

He is presented with the First Degree Mason's working tools, and the Master explains their significance: the 24-inch gauge represents the 24 hours of the day, to be divided between prayer, work, refreshment and helping a friend; the gavel represents

Masonic aprons are decorated with symbols and emblems Left *A calico apron illustrating the story of the Garden of Eden* Right *An apron from the English Lodge known as the 'Antient' Lodge*

the power of conscience; the chisel represents the advantages of education. Finally the Master explains the symbolism of the First Degree tracing board, a rectangular plank containing a painted representation of the symbols appropriate to the First Degree. The Lodge is then 'closed' in the First Degree according to the appropriate ritual.

In due course the Entered Apprentice will be advanced, normally at intervals of about three months in each case, to the Second Degree (Fellow Craft) and finally to the Third Degree (Master Mason). In each case there is a specific ritual and the disclosure of more information. As a Master Mason the new Brother has nominally reached the end of the road although he can proceed further to the Royal Arch, which can roughly be described as an extension of Craft Masonry, and may later elect to ask for membership of the other available degrees and Orders. This is entirely a matter of choice.

The three Craft Degrees, then, form the basis of the whole Masonic system as practised in English-speaking countries. Together with the Royal Arch they form the sum total of Freemasonry as officially recognized by English Grand Lodge. However, for those who are interested there are certain 'Higher Degrees', including Mark Masonry, the Knights Templar, and the Rose-Croix.

THEOSOPHY

The German orientalist Friedrich Max Müller (1823–1900) defined theosophy as 'expressing the highest conception of God within the reach of the human mind, and the perception of the eternal oneness of human and divine nature.' The emphasis is on the intuitive, inner nature of the knowledge, something not experienced through facts open to ordinary intelligence.

It is an ancient conception, particularly in India, where the philosophical schools of Vedanta and Sankhya, and the Yoga *Upanishads* teach it. At Alexandria the philosopher Philo Judaeus (1st century AD) joined the ideas of Plato with Judaism in a theosophic system. It persisted in the Cabala and Neoplatonism, and adherents of the system appear down through the centuries. Paracelsus, Giordano Bruno, Jacob Boehme, Emmanuel Swedenborg, John Tauler and Meister Eckhardt – all taught the essential basis of theosophy.

In modern times the name is associated with the system set out in the 19th century in her books by H. P. Blavatsky. She stated that she had received these doctrines from Indian teachers or masters who had reached a higher plane of being and of spiritual development. Her experiences and witness to occult feats made her salon a magnet for a wide variety of people, who usually found her in possession of out-of-the-way facts in their own special subjects. The Theosophical Society, which she founded in conjunction with Henry S. Olcott and W. Q. Judge, exercised an influence on many notable people, either by its books, or by recruiting them as members. A copy of Blavatsky's *The Voice of Silence* was on Lord Tennyson's bedside table when he died. Sir William Crookes, chemist and psychic researcher, was a member; so were Thomas Alva Edison, the inventor, and W. B. Yeats, the poet. Lord Crawford, the astronomer, was a frequent visitor in London, and the student Mahatma Gandhi made his first acquaintance with the *Gita* among the theosophists. Rudolf Steiner, editor of Goethe and founder of Anthroposophy, was for a time at the head of the German section of the society.

When Annie Besant was criticized for her political activity in India, she explained, in 1929: 'What I say of the Inner Government of the World I speak from personal knowledge, for I have studied and practised Raja Yoga steadily during 40 years. . . . the Freedom of India within the great Federation of Free Nations linked by the British Crown is a condition essential to the Great Plan which must ultimately succeed.'

In 1934 Dr Arundale, then President of the Society, stated what he called the marks theosophy makes upon the chart of Life: '(1) Life is essentially one and universal; (2) Life is within a great evolutionary process whereby an infinitude of life-units move from lowliest unconsciousness through innumerable stages of unfolding to heights of self-consciousness; (3) This irresistible movement is under beneficent and immutable law, order and purpose; (4) That all good and ill fortune, individual or collective are signs of this evolutionary principle at work; (5) Each life-unit can hasten or retard the pace of its own evolutionary process, through understanding or through ignorance.'

Dr Arundale married an Indian lady, Shrimati Rukmini Devi, who did important work in the revival of the classical Indian dance, Indian art, and the education of women. As President he did not travel as widely and frequently as others, but that was partly owing to the Second World War. He did give a great deal of attention to the movement in Australia, with good results. His books on special subjects like *Nirvana, Kundalini, You* (some critics said it should be 'Me') and *Mount Everest, its Spiritual Significance*, were intended to stimulate the intuition of the reader. This applied still more strongly to his large book on symbolism, *The Lotus Fire*, which most people found too difficult.

Jiddu Krishnamurti

In the early 1900s some European male residents of the Theosophical Society's headquarters used to swim of a morning in the Adyar river. Two young Indian brothers used to watch them and then were given swimming lessons. C. W. Leadbeater had noticed the exceptional aura of the older boy, and it occurred to him that it would be interesting to look at the previous lives of an ordinary Indian boy like this and see what his history was. The boys were two of

a rather large family who lived in the village on the estate, sons of a minor local official, G. Narayaniah. Ernest Wood claimed to have suggested to Leadbeater that he look up the past lives of Krishnamurti and Nityananda, and that this was done with the father's permission. Wood's idea was that most Indians he knew abhorred the suggestion that they might be reborn in the West, and he wondered if experience in different races was the general rule. Leadbeater found to his surprise that the boy had had previous lives of great significance, and he commented, 'surely he is not here by accident'.

An offer was made to the father that Mrs Annie Besant would undertake the education and development of Krishnamurti and Nityananda, and he signed a statement before witnesses that he had no objection to the boys being taken to England to continue their education. However, pressure from orthodox Hindu friends and relatives made the father change his mind, and he sued for the restoration of the boys; and the court ruled that they should be returned to the father by May, 1913. Mrs Besant appealed first to the High Court, Madras, where she lost, and then to the Privy Council in London. There the case was reviewed with the welfare of the boys as the first priority. The boys had stated that they wished the benefits of an English education and did not wish to return to India. The Council overruled the two previous decisions, allowing the father, if he so wished, to make application in England for restoration regarding the guardianship, custody and maintenance of his children.

In 1910 Dr G. S. Arundale had formed among the boys of the Central Hindu College a private association called 'The Order of the Rising Sun of India'. He meant it to include those of his pupils who believed that the coming of a great Teacher was near. This Order was opened to the public in 1911, at the instance of Mrs Besant, and

Founded by H. P. Blavatsky, in conjunction with Henry S. Olcott and W. Q. Judge, the Theosophical Society influenced many eminent figures including Mahatma Gandhi, the inventor Thomas Edison and W. B. Yeats Below left Mme Blavatsky, and (left to right) Dr G. S. Arundale, C. Jinarajadasa and N. Sri Ram, successive presidents of the Society

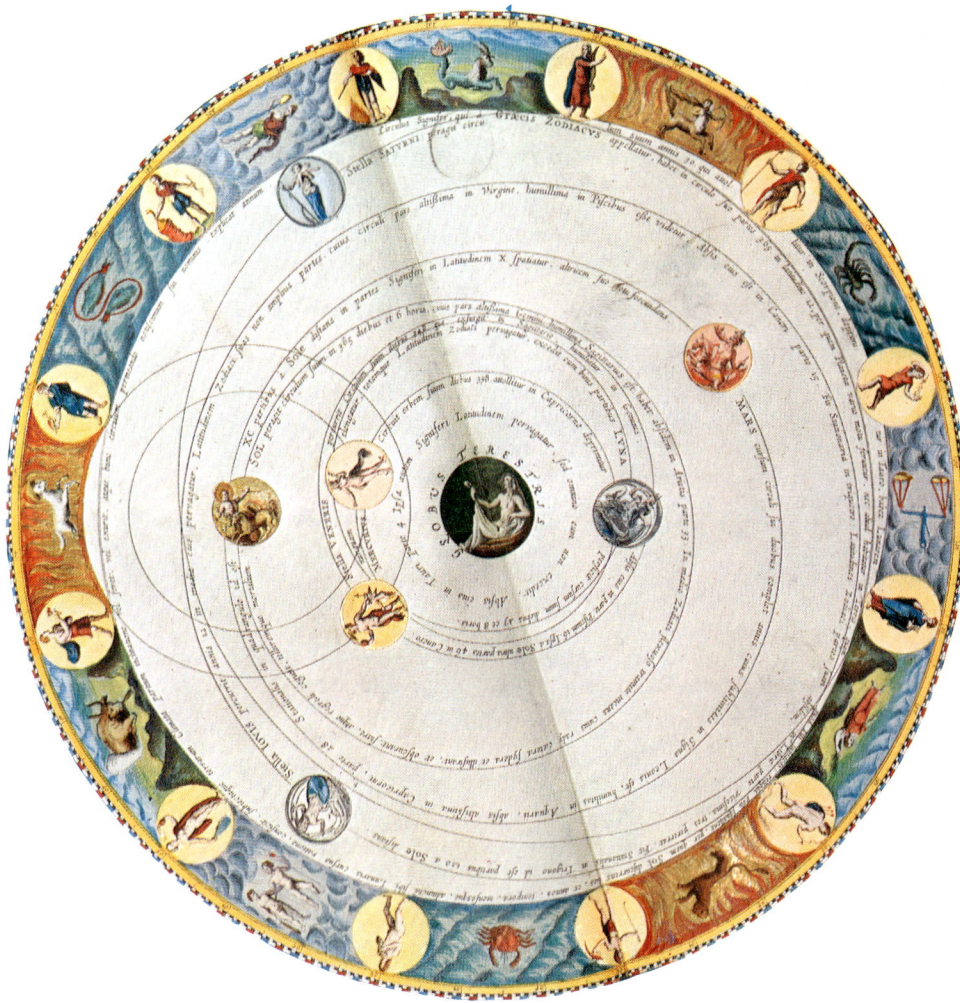

different from what was expected of him, yet Bishop Leadbeater, using his psychic faculties "picked a winner" in a lad of about 12, described by Professor Wood as "a very frail little boy, extremely weak . . . He was bullied and beaten to such an extent that it seemed the boy might fade away from this life and die." '

The prehistory of mankind goes back, in the theosophical system, not tens of thousands, but millions of years. Seven great human types will develop during the earth's present cycle of activity, and we are already well through the fifth type. But there are natural phenomena which shut off the great races from each other – ice ages, subsidence into the ocean, earthquakes and volcanic storms. These catastrophic events are initiated and controlled by non-human intelligences under the command of the Planetary Logos. Hence the last word does not lie with man, who thinks he is now powerful enough to devastate his home in space.

In 1925, when the Order of the Star in the East was flourishing world-wide, its membership exceeded 100,000 or more than twice that of the Theosophical Society. The Theosophical membership figures (with some returns awaited) given in the General Report for 1966 were 26,487 in 49 countries. The three largest totals were India, 7664; United States of America, 4054; and England, 2252.

VIBRATION

In the past a few rationalists have gone so far as to allege that all those who claimed to have experienced 'occult phenomena' were, quite literally, mad. Today, few would openly admit to such an extreme point of view, but it is true that occultists and schizophrenics have always shared a tendency to attempt to explain the interior experiences they have undergone in terms of the generally accepted beliefs of the societies in which they lived. Thus in the 17th and 18th centuries a schizophrenic would usually attribute his peculiar mental state either to the activities of spirits and witches or to the punishment of a jealous Calvinistic deity.

With the decline of popular belief in witchcraft such rationalizations were replaced by others of a more 'scientific' type, and the schizophrenic tended to blame his condition on the activities of evilly disposed individuals broadcasting 'death rays' or mysterious 'telepathic radiations'. The recent occult revival has brought signs of a reversion to earlier modes of explanation and a surprisingly large number of seriously disturbed patients in mental hospitals claim to be the victims of either black magic or 'astral attacks'.

Like the schizophrenic, the occultist of the last century attempted to explain his beliefs and experiences in the light of the science of his own day; the astral light of Eliphas Levi, for example, showed much more resemblance to the luminiferous ether of 19th century physics than to the astral light of Paracelsus. Similarly, the promi-

shortly afterwards she altered its name to 'The Order of the Star in the East', and put Krishnamurti at its head. The Order brought out a magazine called *The Herald of the Star*, and through sympathetic members of the Theosophical Society it spread rapidly in many countries, despite the fact that many members strongly opposed its intrusion upon the time and resources of its followers.

Much newspaper publicity was focused upon Krishnamurti, who was concluded to be a 'Messiah'. This effectively prevented him being sent to an English university, as it seemed certain his life would be made intolerable. His first venture into print was while still a boy, a booklet in simple English titled *At the Feet of the Master*, in which he recorded the instructions said to have been given him in sleep by an adept. Later he tried to express his mystical feelings in collections of poems, and wrote editorials for the magazine of the Order.

However, Krishnamurti became increasingly impatient of being associated with theosophists. He had his own individual outlook and message. In 1929 he dissolved the Order of the Star in the East, and returned Castle Eerde and its grounds to Baron van Pallandt, who had wanted him, or a group on his behalf, to take it over. In the following years he made his base at Ojai

in California, and there and elsewhere held seminars of talks and question and answer meetings. Many books, revised from these occasions, were published. He became a friend of Aldous Huxley and other original thinkers. From time to time he visited Europe and India.

In 1927 he had a profound experience, and on 2 August he said: 'I could not have said last year, as I can say now, that I am the Teacher; for had I said it then it would have been insincere, it would have been untrue. But now I can say it. I have become one with the Beloved, I have been made simple. As I have changed, as I have found my end, which is the end for all . . . and because I have affection – and without affection you cannot attain the end . . . because I have suffered and seen and found all, naturally it is my duty . . . my pleasure, my dharma, to give it to those who have not . . . I am not going to be bound by anyone; I am going on my way, because that is the only way. I have found what I wanted. I have been united with my Beloved, and my Beloved and I will wander together the face of the earth.'

One cannot but agree with the English theosophist T. H. Redfern when he says: 'The strange and puzzling thing is that although his work has turned out much nence which the concept of vibration assumed in the occult theorizing of the last quarter of the 19th century owed much to the importance of vibrational frequency in the wave theory of light. Spiritualists took over the idea and explained the invisibility of the spirit world (supposed to interpenetrate the ordinary world of matter) to ordinary individuals as being the result of varying 'rates of vibration'. Mediums, so it was claimed, were those individuals who were able partially to adjust their vibrational rates to those of the spirit world.

Madame Blavatsky and her theosophical following were particularly prone to use vibration as an explanation of supernormal events. They held that there existed a mysterious 'inter-etheric force' which could be controlled by the use of the vibrations of sound and would ultimately provide mankind with a free source of energy, enabling a complete control over its environment.

The theosophists seem to have derived this idea from a charlatan named John Worrell Keely, 'inventor' of the notorious Keely motor, of which its creator wrote: 'In the conception of any machine heretofore constructed, the medium for inducing a neutral centre has never been found. If it had, the difficulties of perpetual-motion seekers would have ended, and this problem would have become an established and operating fact. It would only require an introductory impulse of a few pounds, on such a device, to cause it to run for centuries. In the conception of my vibratory engine, I did not seek to attain perpetual motion but a circuit is formed that actually has a neutral centre,

DE ARITHMETICA MVSICA.

Regula

A diagram from Utriusque Cosmi Historia *by Robert Fludd, concerned with the universe as a harmony of musical vibrations. The different spheres which make up the macrocosm are shown to produce a universal harmony*

which is in a condition to be vivified by my vibratory ether, and, while under operation by said substance, is really a machine that is virtually independent of the mass (or globe), and it is the wonderful velocity of the vibratory circuit which makes it so. Still, with all its perfection, it requires to be fed with the vibratory ether to make it an independent motor . . .'

Madame Blavatsky appears to have been much impressed by Keely. In the *Secret Doctrine* she referred to him as 'a natural-born magician' and quoted with approval a description of him as being 'great . . . in soul, wise . . . in mind, and sublime . . . in courage . . . the greatest discoverer and inventor in the world . . .' He was, in reality, a fraud who managed for many years to enjoy a comfortable existence on the money he had extracted from those gullible enough to invest in his 'Vibrational Self-Motor'. After his death it was discovered that the working model of his motor which, seemingly set in motion by the vibration of a violin string, had so impressed visitors to his laboratory was in reality powered by a secret supply of compressed air. In spite of this fiasco theosophists and other occultists continued to attach great importance to 'vibrational energy', and to the Keely motor; even today there are those who defend Keely as a great occultist and physicist.

Music of the Universe

In the present century vibration has ceased to occupy an important place in the theoretical framework of most occult systems and its place has been taken by other, more fashionable, scientific (or pseudo-scientific) concepts. Thus some 19th century astrologers attempted to provide a rationale for their art by arguing that each planet had its own vibrational frequency which, transmitted by radiation through the ether, blended with the vibrations of the other planets to influence the child at birth; today such theories have been largely abandoned by astrologers in favour of Jungian 'synchronicity' – the belief that everything done at a certain moment of time has the qualities of that moment of time.

Nevertheless, vibrational theories have survived, and indeed have been developed much further in attempts to provide a semi-physical explanation for the phenomena of dowsing and radiesthesia. Such explanations often involve a belief that the vibrational frequencies of the ordinary musical scale have an occult significance of cosmic importance. Dr H. Tomlinson, an Australian radiesthetic and homoeopathic practitioner, has claimed that: '. . . the notes of the tonic sol-fa system are a universal constant . . . The universe visible to man can be likened to a web of tiny interlacing octaves of vibrations. These octaves are of two sorts, ascending and descending. A descending octave is progress from matter of higher vibrating rate to matter of lower vibratory rate . . . An ascending octave is progress from denser matter to more spiritual matter . . . The diviner . . . is operating in a web of interlacing celestial octaves . . . Every substance, when tested by radiesthetic methods, can be found to react to one of the notes of the octave . . .'

Trembling With Energy

At the present day, those occultists who are devotees of either the original Golden Dawn magical system or of one or other of its many derivatives – mostly greatly inferior to the original – give widely varying descriptions of both what is actually done and what is subjectively experienced when a Divine Name is vibrated. The best descriptions – which ultimately seem to derive from Aleister Crowley – take it for granted that the experiences undergone are subjective in nature but that, nevertheless, a *psychologically* real vibration is felt. One occultist has described himself as having his consciousness so filled with the spiritual essence of the Divine Name he is vibrating that not only his body but 'the universe itself seems to be shaking, trembling and vibrating with the energy of the God-name invoked'.

MEDITATION

Once regarded almost exclusively as a pre-occupation of mystics, saints and hermits, meditation is today an established feature of several popular cults. What it is all about, what it does, and how it is achieved, are matters of considerable interest to a growing number of people today.

Though common to Hinduism, Buddhism and Islam, meditation has not played a particularly prominent role in the Christian tradition. Now, as a result of an unprecedented upsurge of interest in achieving states of mind in which the consciousness is expanded by various means, meditation is being rediscovered as a useful plumb-line to the deeps of the mind.

But why meditate? In a busy world is the time spent pondering on abstractions worth anything at all? Is it not just a futile pursuit, at best another 'opiate' with no practical benefit to recommend it? For the majority, the occasional periods of introspection are of little help. Men only become more confused by what emerges from their deeper reflections. Instead of the restorative relief they seek from the muddled complexity of their lives, they find themselves thinking about their problems more than ever.

Union With the Absolute

Perhaps the most detailed and systematic presentation of meditative techniques can be found in Hindu writings, as exemplified in yoga. The aim of yoga is 'union' with the Absolute, achieved by progression through eight stages of development. The first two pertain to external and internal 'ethics', with stress on non-injury and the elimination of negative emotions like anger, acquisitiveness, lust, greed, and the practice of equanimity and peace of mind. After these two ethical prerequisites we come to the third stage, namely, bodily postures, to inure the physical frame to the various positions assumed during meditation, some of which are extremely difficult. Next comes breath control, control of the *prana*, which is held to be one

Yoga practiser during meditation: statuette of a deity sitting in the lotus position. The most common of the positions, this has been found to be the simplest for people accustomed to sitting on the ground, for it obviates any danger of the student falling over during trance

of the basic potencies of the universe. The air we breathe contains it, and the yogi practitioner subtilizes the air for its prana content and sends it streaming through his subtle body. This is followed by control of the senses, that is, withdrawing attention from all external distractions, or, as it is called, 'silencing the traffic of the senses'. By the time this stage is reached the body should be properly conditioned, the emotions under control, and all the mental faculties ready to be directed to a single goal.

The sixth stage is devoted to concentration (*dharana*) or holding the mind firm and steady. Here the student concentrates on a spot on a blank surface such as a wall; a point of light; the flame of a candle; a flower; the picture of a deity such as Krishna or Shiva; a letter of the alphabet.

The seventh stage of yoga concerns contemplation (*dhyana*), a turning within of the consciousness, a focusing of the mental faculties inwards. The eighth and last stage, called *samadhi*, is a stage of super-consciousness, which is the supreme goal of yogic meditation.

Because of its stringency yoga can be a disheartening course for the average practitioner. The most that is generally attempted are elementary postures like the head-stand and simple exercises in breath control. Recent exponents have evolved their own variations on the theme, such as Transcendental Meditation, tailored to the needs of an age which demands instant results. Most of these variations entirely bypass ascetic doctrines and world-abnegation, and permit and indeed encourage a two-way movement between spirituality and worldly life.

DRUGS

The religious use of drugs usually accompanies the practice of shamanism, though shamanism often does without drugs. Shamanism is a technique by which a man, and sometimes a woman, prepares himself by singing, dancing, training and long periods of seclusion during which he meditates, for an influx of untoward inspiration that can carry him into the world of spirits where events on earth are ordained and carried out. It is often a hereditary calling, but may equally well be embraced by those who have either a surplus of mental energy or who have suffered from what we would call a nervous complaint of some severity. Such unsatisfied or unbalanced states of mind are continually looking for a resolution of their frustrations and ambitions, and they do so by using traditional methods which articulate their powers coherently.

The purpose of a ritual setting for the taking of a drug is to prevent madness, by directing the energies which the drug releases into a number of specific channels, and to put paradise into relation with objects in the outside world by establishing a dogmatic plan within the imagination, through which social events can be seen as psychological ones, psychological as physical ones, and physical ones as spiritual.

By such a method even opium, the grandmother of all narcotics, has occasionally been used not merely to enjoy its sumptuous and pearly visions but to carry out a conscious intention. Such is the habit of shamans in parts of Southeast Asia, who take opium to increase the ecstatic effects of dancing and through them send their spirits upon a supernatural adventure for the curing of illness or the foretelling of the future.

Wherever a drug is used by a religion to gain a view and foretaste of divinity, it is treated as though it were a god itself. 'We have drunk Soma, we have become immortals, we have arrived at the light, we have reached the gods: what power has malevolence over us now, what can the perfidy of mortals do to us, O Immortal?' So runs one of the hymns of the *Rig Veda*, one of the sacred texts of the East. Opium has been called the hand of God and anchor of salvation, though Cocteau has remarked that it resembles religion as an illusionist resembles Jesus. Tobacco has been called the blessed plant, honour of the earth and gift from Olympus, and both wine and beer have been similarly praised down the centuries. 'Our glass was the full moon, the wine is the sun.'

A drug is nothing unless it kindles the spirit in a man, though this spirit may be thought of as divine or demoniacal according to predilection. Whichever it may be, the spirit is not man's possession but a gift made to him, and as a gift it has a nature and a morality of its own which must be both wrestled with and obeyed if it is not to bring harm to its host. Every religion has its own way of experiencing and ordering this power, and their often stringent ritual requirements are the product of a long experience in bringing the spirit in touch with the world of men. The religious taking of drugs is one particular example of this: it says plainly enough that amateurism in these matters does little but create a problem, and that if the mind is to reach beyond itself through drugs it must be placed in the service of an idea and a method that makes for wisdom and communion, not folly and isolation.

Shamans in parts of Southeast Asia take opium to increase the ecstatic effects of dancing; but the drug is a soporific, and the devotee usually soon reaches a passive state where 'one no longer dreams, one is dreamed'

Spiritualism

THE HUMAN PERSONALITY SURVIVES

The term Spiritualism has been used to refer to two distinct types of ideas. In the 18th and 19th centuries it referred to those philosophical theories which held that spirit was the ultimate reality. Today the term is used to denote a movement which is characterized by two major beliefs: that the human personality, in some form, survives the death of the body, and secondly that it is possible to communicate with the spirits of the dead. During the 19th century the critics and opponents of modern Spiritualism used the word Spiritism to describe the movement.

A belief in spirits is not restricted to modern Spiritualists, indeed as the anthropologist Sir Edward Tylor suggested in his study of *Primitive Culture* (1871), a belief in spirits is a universal feature of human societies. This is linked with a belief in life after death and that spirits may be contacted by the living. Amongst the earliest forms of religious specialists were the shamans and spirit mediums who in different ways were concerned with the contact between the 'spirit' world and the human world.

It has been claimed that Christianity itself originated as a 'spiritualist' movement and that Jesus himself was a highly-developed medium. Spiritualists have argued that such an interpretation enables us to understand the 'miraculous' elements in the biblical accounts of the life of Jesus. There is also evidence which indicates that mediumship was practised in the early Christian Church, but it had certainly ceased to be a regular feature of Christian practice before the 3rd century AD, although the Church continued to recognize the possibility of occasional communications with saints and angels.

The Reformation led to what the sociologist Max Weber described as 'disenchantment', a growing disbelief in the supernatural. By the 18th century rationalism was triumphant amongst the educated classes in Western Europe but while rationalism was still growing, a reaction against the extreme forms of materialism was already appearing. Within Christianity this reaction took the form of the development of mystical movements, such as the Quakers and the Quietists, and of 'enthusiastic' movements such as Methodism. But the sources of modern Spiritualism are to be found outside the Christian tradition, in the work of the alchemists, in the theories of Paracelsus, of Franz Mesmer and Emmanuel Swedenborg in ideas derived from eastern religions and from contact with the shamanistic practices of the North American Indians.

The modern Spiritualist movement arose in America in 1848 as a result of the publicity given to the events that occurred in the home of the Fox family in Hydesville, a small hamlet in New York state. The Fox family moved into the house in December 1847, and for the next three months they were disturbed by strange noises that frequently kept them awake at night. The family consisted of John Fox, his wife and two young daughters. Margaretta and Kate. On Friday 31 March 1848 the family retired to bed early. Mrs Fox described the events of that night in the following statement:

It was very early when we went to bed on this night – hardly dark. I had been so broken of rest I was almost sick – I had just lain down when it commenced as usual – the children, who slept in the other bed in the room, heard the rapping, and tried to make similar sounds by snapping their fingers.

My youngest child, Cathie, said: 'Mr Split-foot, do as I do', clapping her hands. The sound instantly followed her with the same number of raps. When she stopped the sound ceased for a short time.

Then Margaretta said, in sport: 'Now do just as I do. Count one, two, three, four, striking one hand against the other at the same time' – and the raps came as before. She was afraid to repeat them.

I then thought I could put a test that no one in the place could answer. I asked the 'noise' to rap my different children's ages successively.

Instantly, each one of my children's ages was given correctly, pausing between them sufficiently long enough to individualise them until the seventh – at which a longer pause was made, and then three more emphatic raps were given, corresponding to the age of the little one that died, which was my youngest child.

I then asked: 'Is this a human being that answers my questions correctly?'

There was no rap.

I asked: 'Is it a spirit? If it is, make two raps.'

Two sounds were given as soon as the request was made.

In this way Mrs Fox and her daughters believed they had discovered a means of communication with a spirit who claimed to

have been murdered in the house. Sir Arthur Conan Doyle in his *History of Spiritualism* (1926) says that subsequent excavations on the site disclosed human remains.

The Fox family were now plagued not only by spirit noises, but by sensation seekers, and Mrs Fox and the girls went to live with her married daughter in Rochester. Their psychic abilities continued and around them developed the first Spiritualist circle. In 1849 the girls gave a first public demonstration in Rochester and followed this up with demonstrations in many other towns in the eastern states. Their activities created a sensation in the popular Press, and their popularity was not affected by pronouncements made by three professors from Buffalo University, following an investigation in 1851, that the raps were produced by movements of the knee-joints, or by the subsequent alleged confession by Kate that they were produced by cracking her toes.

'Spirit rapping' rapidly became a craze in the United States, but in the early stages Spiritualism was as much a popular scientific movement as a religious movement. People who had attended a mediumistic demonstration, or had read about such events, held seances in their own homes attended by relations and friends. They were often motivated by curiosity and the spirit of scientific enquiry. They met in an attempt to test the claims of Spiritualists, they continued to meet if they felt that such claims were being confirmed by their experiences within the circle, and it was on the basis of such successful groups that permanent organizations, societies and churches began to develop and flourish.

The National Union

The Spiritualist movement was introduced to Britain in 1852 when Mrs Hayden, an American medium, gave demonstrations. She was followed by other mediums and, as in America, a short-lived craze swept the country. The early days in Britain were similar to those in America, the movement of that period consisting of 'home circles', either of friends who met to experiment or of followers who gathered together, and met round a successful medium.

Science or Religion

Spiritualist meetings soon began to develop a ritual which included music, hymn singing, prayer and Bible reading. Such ritual is claimed to create an atmosphere conducive to the appearance of psychic phenomena and to the prevention of the disruption of the seance by evil spirits. By the 1870s many societies were adopting the title of churches.

Non-Christian Spiritualists frequently held that Spiritualism was a new religion which would ultimately replace Christianity, while others saw Spiritualism as the basis of all religion. The Christian Churches as a whole attacked Spiritualism, arguing that communication with the dead was forbidden by the authority of the Bible, and that the spirit communicators were evil entities dispatched by the Devil to mislead men. The Roman Catholic Church has maintained this attitude, as have such sects as Jehovah's Witnesses and the Pentecostal movement, but the 'Free Churches' and the Anglicans

46

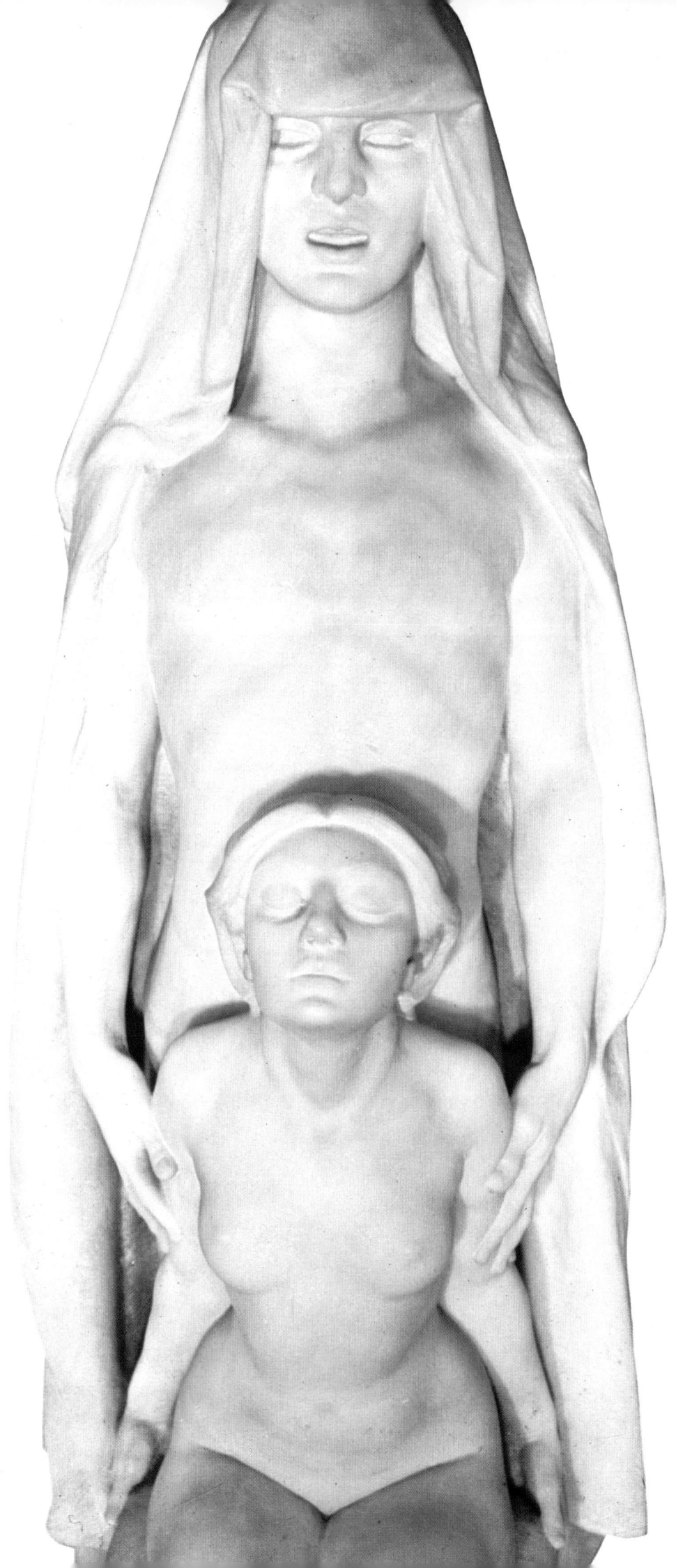

John Moses

John Moss

Harry Price Library

Opposite A medium and her spirit guide, a statue by G. H. Paulin. The key role in the Spiritualist movement is played by the medium, through whom the spirit world communicates with the material world: in some cases messages from the dead come through a spirit 'guide' or 'control' whose personality temporarily replaces the medium's normal personality, and whose function is to protect the medium and to regulate the attempts made by the departed to communicate through her Above A medium in trance: though fraudulent mediums flourished in the earlier days of the Spiritualist movement, there have always been genuine mediums, and Spirit-ualists are convinced that communications coming through them from the spirits of the dead constitute conclusive proof that human beings survive death Below Photograph by A. Martin, of Denver, Colorado, showing Houdini, the famous escape artist and fierce opponent of Spiritualist mediums, with spirit forms

have moved towards a more tolerant position, reflected in the establishment of the Churches' Fellowship for Psychical Study in 1953. Christian Spiritualists have always argued that they were attempting to restore to the Church those practices which were commonly accepted by the early Christians.

Until the middle of the 20th century Britain and the U.S.A. were the main centres of Spiritualism. In recent years the movement has grown most rapidly in Latin America, particularly in Brazil, where there are said to be at least two million Spiritualists. The movement in Brazil is divided into two broad groups, the Western type based on the teaching of Kardec and largely supported by the middle-class, and native Spiritualism or Spiritism which is derived largely from African and American-Indian influences and is practised generally by the poorer classes.

The Seven Principles

Spiritualism is a movement and not an organization. It consists not only of international and national associations but of many independent local societies and of numerous 'home circles' and individuals who are unattached to any formal organization. You do not have to join any organization to be a Spiritualist. There is no agreement on a Spiritualist creed of beliefs,

beyond the two broad beliefs already mentioned. Spiritualist beliefs are the result of messages received from the spirits through a medium, and the teachings of the spirits display wide differences. Spiritualists explain that spirits are human beings who have survived death; transition to the afterlife does not immediately make a man wise; he takes with him the ideas he had in life, and continues to hold to these beliefs at least during his stay in the lower planes of the afterlife. Spirits who have moved upwards after death, to increasingly high planes of existence, find it more difficult to communicate through mediums, so that communications usually come from the recently dead and those who have made little progress in the afterlife. It is not surprising therefore to find a wide diversity of belief held by Spiritualists. In Europe and Latin America, where the teachings of the French Spiritualist Alan Kardec predominate, most Spiritualists believe in reincarnation, in England and America few Spiritualists do. Some Spiritualists are agnostic, since there appears to be no greater proof of the existence of God in the lowest levels of the spirit world than can be discovered and accepted on earth.

If there is no Spiritualist creed neither is there a Spiritualist bible. The most widely accepted book is *Spirit Teachings*, a series of communications from the spirit world trans-

47

mitted through the automatic writing mediumship of Rev. W. Stainton Moses.

A widely accepted credal statement is to be found in the Seven Principles subscribed to by all members of the Spiritualists' National Union, which were derived from a spirit communication received through the medium Emma Hardinge-Britten. The principles are: the fatherhood of God; the brotherhood of man; the communion of spirits and the ministry of angels; the continuous existence of the human soul; personal responsibility; compensation and retribution hereafter for all the good and evil deeds done on earth; eternal progress open to every human soul.

The S.N.U., which is the largest of the two national organizations in Britain, has about 460 affiliated churches with some 15,000 members and represents the non-Christian element in Spiritualism. The other organization, the Greater World Christian Spiritualist League, with over 200 churches represents the specifically Christian influence in the Spiritualist movement. There are also many churches not affiliated to either of these organizations offering a variety of beliefs and practices.

While it is difficult to generalize about Spiritualist beliefs, most Spiritualists in Britain and America would probably accept the following beliefs. Man is an immortal being composed of two elements, a body and a soul or spirit, and on death the spirit leaves the body and enters a phase of existence in a 'spiritual plane'. The universe consists of seven such planes of existence, of which the material (earth) is the lowest. After death most souls awake into the second plane, known to many as the Summerland, a level of existence in which life is not unlike that on earth except for the absence of pain and suffering. In this plane, as on earth, each soul has the opportunity for spiritual development which opens up the possibility of ascent to high planes.

Every individual has the opportunity of rising through the ascending order of spiritual levels until he reaches the seventh heaven, in which he will finally be united with God and all the great souls who have preceded him. Great souls such as Jesus are said to have risen directly to the seventh heaven, but just as goodness leads to spiritual advancement, so evil leads to decline; men are not punished, they punish themselves by opting for a course of action which prevents their spiritual development.

Spirit and Matter

From the early days Spiritualism has involved phenomena in which material objects have been moved by what many have claimed to be supernatural forces. As early as 1849 there is the record of a table being levitated six inches. The first instance of the levitation of a human being, a Mr Gordon, was reported in the journal *Spirit World* in February 1851. Materialization of a spirit and the 'apport' or mysterious appearance of a physical object were also early forms of manifestations. At some seances coloured lights appeared which floated round the room, and at others musical instruments were mysteriously played.

Spirit photography was first practised by William Mumler, a Boston photographer, in 1862, but his work was soon exposed as fraudulent. Frederick Hudson was the first spirit photographer in Britain, but he was exposed by the well-known Spiritualist writer W. H. Harrison in *The Spiritualist* in 1872. The most famous spirit photographer was William Hope (died 1933) who worked with the Crewe circle: his work was also exposed, but he found a faithful champion in Sir Arthur Conan Doyle.

There appears to have been a decline in physical mediumship since the Second World War, which cynics have attributed to the greater ease of detecting fraud by modern scientific methods. From the first Spiritualists practised 'spirit healing' and this has become an increasingly important part of their work.

The key role in the Spiritualist movement is played by the medium, who is quite literally the medium through which the 'spirit world' communicates with the material world. In theory all men are potential mediums, but it is clear that while some people are endowed with psychic abilities which may appear spontaneously, others require years of training before they can make use of their abilities. Many of the most gifted mediums report that they had spontaneous psychic experiences when they were children. The claims of Spiritualists have frequently been investigated by critics and during the 19th century psychic phenomena were subject to rigorous study by a series of eminent scientists. Some were convinced that not all Spiritualist manifestations could be explained by theories of fraud or illusion, but in spite of a considerable body of accumulated evidence most scientists have remained unconvinced by the Spiritualist interpretation.

If psychic phenomena are a universal feature of human life, why did the modern Spiritualist movement arise in the U.S.A. and Britain in the 19th century? Sociologists attempt to explain the rise (or decline) of social movements in terms of the conditions affecting the lives of the members of a society, in terms of the processes going on within the society and of the changes in the structure of that society.

Sociology of Spiritualism

Modern Spiritualism is one of a particular type of religious movements known to sociologists as cults. Such movements are characterized by two general features: they are outside the major religious tradition of the society in which they originate (as already mentioned Spiritualism owes more to non-Christian than to Christian sources), and they are attempts to solve the problems of individuals, particularly those problems that arise out of man's attempts to understand the world in which he lives, to give meaning to his life and to experiences of a psychic or mystical nature. Spiritualism certainly offers man a new view of the universe and man's place in it and is particularly concerned with the place of psychic experiences in human life.

Cults seem to arise in the greatest profusion, and to gain the most adherents, when a society is disorganized by rapid changes. In such circumstances the old religious traditions are challenged and men find the old views of life no longer satisfying. American society in the middle of the 19th century was going through a period of particularly rapid change as the result of the influx of immigrants, mainly from Europe, as well as the early effects of the industrial revolution. In Britain the industrial revolution was changing the traditional way of life; in particular this was the period of rapid urban expansion, and Spiritualism was from the first predominantly an urban religion.

The rationalism of the 18th century intellectual was beginning to spread more widely through society and following such publicists as Thomas Paine men began to demand proof of religious claims. While not claiming to offer proof of the existence of God, Spiritualism did claim to provide proof not only of the survival of the human soul beyond death but also of the soul's ability to communicate with those on earth after its decease.

A Philosophy of Life

Many of the early adherents to Spiritualism were agnostics or atheists, men who had ceased to find Christianity credible but who nevertheless sought a philosophy of life which went beyond scientific materialism while remaining consistent with science. Spiritualism was at first closely connected with psychical research though the two movements gradually drifted apart. In common with many modern cults, such as the Flying Saucer movement, Spiritualism started as an attempt to study phenomena which were not being seriously studied by orthodox science and indeed which did not 'fit' the established scientific theories of the time. In each case the movements developed into religions, because they offered solutions which were not only intellectually but emotionally satisfactory to certain key problems in the lives of individuals. The 19th century was obsessed with death but many people were losing faith in the Christian explanation, as a result of the growth of belief in science. Death was a major source of tension in the lives of such persons, who were not satisfied with faith but needed proof of the survival of the soul after death. Spiritualism was attractive because it offered evidence of survival.

It was during the First World War and in the following years that the movement experienced its greatest growth, thus reflecting the tension created by the high death rate. In the second half of the 20th century death has ceased to be such an obsession and many people are more concerned with a search for the meaning of life; this has meant on the one hand that the Spiritualist movement has ceased to grow, and on the other that within the movement there is less concern with proofs of survival and a greater interest in the philosophy of Spiritualism for its own sake.

Spiritualism aroused violent antagonism and criticism, concentrating particularly on the physical phenomena occurring at seances, which opponents claimed were faked: the famous conjurer J. N. Maskelyne put on long-running shows (above) to demonstrate his ability to duplicate Spiritualist phenomena Below A 'rapping hand', used at fraudulent seances and probably controlled pneumatically through rubber tubing

Between the First and Second Parts of the Entertainment

MR. CHARLES WOODMAN

Will introduce his wonderful Musical Novelties.

Exposition of Spiritualism (so-called)

LIGHT AND DARK SEANCE EXTRAORDINARY.

Mr MASKELYNE briefly opens the subject, requests the audience to elect a Committee to examine the Cabinet, the Stage, and everything that may be considered auxiliary in producing the manifestations.

After the light in the Hall has been subdued the spiritualists' most favourite spirit-form of

JOHN KING,

appears rising from the stage, and distributes amongst the audience, flowers from the spirit garden.

SELF-LEVITATION AND OTHER MANIFESTATIONS.

MR COOKE FLOATS INTO THE HALL, TAKING WITH HIM THE CABINET IN WHICH HE IS SECURED.

Luminous musical instruments are distinctly seen moving about the room and the audience generally participate in the peculiar pleasures of the Dark Seance.

ZOE !

In preparation, and shortly to be presented. Mr MASKELYNE'S new Writing and Sketching Automaton, ZOE, Psycho's mysterious lady companion.

Price 6d.—A Book containing a full description of the Entertainment, and brief biography of Mr MASKELYNE can be had in the Hall.
Price 1s.—Spiritualism (Raps for the Rappers), being a short account of the Rise and Progress of Modern Spiritualism, with exposures of the frauds of so-called Spirit Media, by JOHN NEVIL MASKELYNE, can also be obtained of the attendants.

MESSRS.

MASKELYNE AND COOKE

THE ROYAL

Illusionists and Antispiritualists.

EGYPTIAN LARGE HALL,

PICCADILLY.

DAILY AT THREE and EIGHT O'CLOCK.

FOURTH YEAR IN LONDON.

Fauteuils, 5s.   Stalls, 3s.   Area, 2s.   Balcony, 1s.

Seats can be booked at any time during the day, at the Box Office, free of charge.

Messrs. MASKELYNE & COOKE had the distinguished honour of a Royal Command to perform before H.R.H. the Prince of Wales, at Sandringham, on Monday, January 11th, 1875.

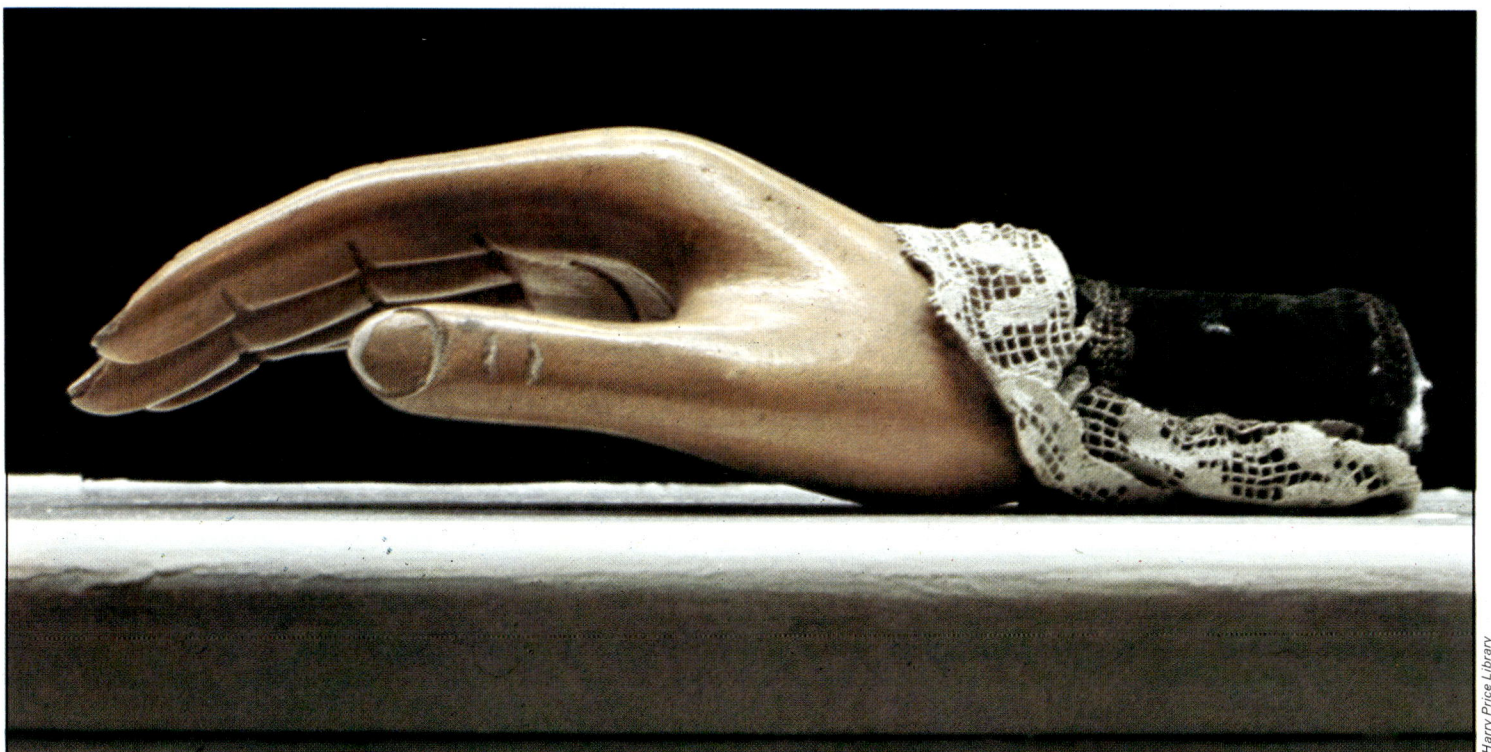

W. MORTON, Manager.

MEDIUMS

Medium is the name given by Spiritualists to a person whom they believe is able to act as a medium of communication between the living and the dead.

Mediumship divides roughly into two types, physical and mental. A mental medium is a person who claims to be able, in certain states of consciousness, to see and talk with the dead, to transmit messages from them to the living and even, at times, to hand over his own body to discarnate (or disembodied) persons who can then communicate directly with the living. From the evidential angle this claim provokes two main questions: firstly, what alternative mundane sources can be found for statements purporting to come from the dead? And secondly, are there any occasions on record where all such alternative sources appear to be ruled out and a discarnate source for a particular statement seems overwhelmingly likely?

Looking at mediumship simply as a psychological phenomenon, the questions it calls for are different: for instance, what is the psychological process involved in such experiences? What brings them about? Why does a person become a medium? How does mediumship relate to other psychological states? It should perhaps be said that some persons who are mediumistically gifted do not always believe that the communications they receive necessarily come from the dead, and a more neutral name for mediums which includes such people, and is often used, is 'sensitive'. In our culture more women than men are mediums, so from now on they will be referred to here as feminine.

Increasing Dissociation

The first impression gained by a neutral observer when watching an honest medium at work is likely to be that the verbal or written utterances she makes to her sitters (a sitter is the name usually given to a person who visits mediums) are welling up from subconscious levels of her own psyche. Very often these utterances show every sign of having originated within her psyche, but not always; on occasion a good medium will impart relevant and specific information to an unknown sitter which she apparently could not have obtained by normal means, and which is too detailed to be reasonably attributed to a series of lucky guesses. In fact it gives the impression that at the least she has made subconscious contact with events distant in time or space, or time and space, in some unknown and possibly extrasensory fashion.

There are many stages of mediumship

and each successive stage seems to imply an increasing degree of dissociation, in which communication with the subconscious gets progressively easier. When dissociation is slight and a medium not far from her normal waking state, she usually behaves as if fleetingly aware of various discarnate presences whom she describes as friends or relatives of persons present to whom they wish messages to be given. As a rule these messages are vague and they could apply to any one of a number of people. Some mediums can induce a state of dissociation so deep that it reaches trance level and at this point their normal personality is replaced by quite a different one, whom Spiritualists accept as a discarnate human being who has taken over the medium's body and whom they call a 'control'. Variants of this phenomenon have, of course, been known throughout history, but the control is not always looked on as human. For the Witch of Endor it was a familiar spirit, for the Cumaean Sybil it was the god Apollo, for Neoplatonists a beneficent daemon, for the early Christians, as a rule, a devil, and in Voodoo today it is thought to be a god.

On the whole modern psychologists tend to look on 'controls' as split-off facets of the medium's own personality and point out that similar 'splits' can occur apart from mediumship and may be hysterical symptoms or dramatizations of repressed tendencies. But one should perhaps bear in mind that the dissociation of mediumship does not seem very different in kind from that experienced by the rest of us. We all go into daydreams in which the outer world is forgotten. We all find that a forgotten name or tune, or even the solution to a problem which consciously we have failed to find, will float into our minds unexpectedly from 'nowhere'. And reports by creative persons of unexpected 'upwellings' of material from the subconscious are legion.

Many such creative upwellings take the form of images and symbols, in much the same way as mediums often claim to receive their information. Sometimes, for instance, new ideas emerge in visual symbols, as on the occasion when the chemist, Friedrich August Kekule, while dozing by the fire, had a vision of a snake eating its own tail which led him to envisage the circular form of the benzene molecule. Or new ideas may come in the form of automatic speech. Dante declared that as he was pondering how to begin a poem, 'my tongue spoke as though by its own impulse'. Other poets and writers may feel as if a work were directly dictated to them. Blake claimed this of a major poem and said that he could praise it because 'I dare not pretend to be other than the secretary'.

But it is not necessary to be a genius or a medium to bring up material from the subconscious, independently of the conscious mind. A number of people can do it by automatic writing, but what they write is usually, though not always, fragmentary, incoherent and of little interest. Others, from medicine-men to palmists, do it by some such technique as 'reading' cards, hands, bones, tea-leaves and so on; others again by the use of dowsing twig or pendulum. Subconscious material can also emerge through collective action, such as spelling out words

on a ouija board or making a table tilt when a group of people place their fingers on them.

It will be noticed that all these procedures have one thing in common with control mediumship; any information given appears to the performer to come from a source exterior to himself. He 'sees' it in the cards or the bones or the hand. The pendulum or the dowsing twig moves independently of his conscious will. Each owner of the fingers which rest on a ouija board or table can assume that if any pushing, conscious or unconscious, is being done, it is by one of his co-performers, not himself. All such exteriorizations, however foolish they seem, may in fact serve a useful purpose by releasing the conscious mind of the performer from a sense of responsibility for what is said. This would reduce tension and in this way, perhaps, facilitate contact with the subconscious level of the psyche which appears to be able to receive what, for want of a better term, may be called extra-sensory 'signals'.

The quality of mediumistic utterances varies enormously, and to some extent in relation to the intellectual level of the medium. They are usually banal and fragmentary and in most cases seem almost like the product of a kind of dream state; nor need they be true to fact. One well-meaning trance medium implored a lady repeatedly on behalf of her dead husband to cease excessive mourning for his loss, and she was not deterred by assurances that he was alive and well. To her trance personality all greyhaired women must, so it seemed, be sorrowing widows. But although mediocre and even dishonest mediums exist, this does not alter the fact that on occasion a good one appears to make meaningful contact in some unknown way with remote events and personalities, and, on the face of it, even at times seems to be able to communicate with the dead.

'Like Diving into Dark Fog'

Before seeking to discover what in fact happens on such occasions, one must be clear as to what appears to happen. Take for example a sitting with a trance medium. It usually opens with the medium remaining quietly seated in a chair for a short time with her eyes closed. Then, as a rule, she begins to breathe heavily, perhaps gives a groan or two and falls into a deep though restless sleep. Shortly afterwards she wakes up as the control, whose voice, mannerisms and whole personality seem quite different from her normal one. Controls range from childish characters of either sex to 'Red Indian' chiefs, Arabian physicians and Chinese sages – but they are all liable to make childish mistakes about the countries in which they claim to have lived on earth. Most mediums have only one control, but others have two or even three. One of the regular controls turns up at every sitting, the claim being that its task is to safeguard the medium's welfare and to regulate the many attempts made by discarnate spirits to communicate through her. Even so, a purported intruding 'spirit' sometimes manages to break in, and occasionally makes unexpected statements which are found to relate to a sitter who does not happen to be present at the time.

As a rule the control begins by reporting the presence of discarnate 'communicators' who wish him to transmit messages from them. Sometimes sitters say that they recognize these communicators and sometimes they do not. The communicators are usually given a name such as John or Mary, though occasionally a good medium will get hold of an improbable name which is correct. Sometimes, with a familiar sitter, the control will allow a communicator, as he puts it, to take over the medium's body directly, and when this happens a second marked change may come about in her voice, speech and vocabulary; there have even been occasions when reliable and intelligent sitters felt that the personality who purported to talk through a medium's lips had mannerisms resembling those of the deceased friend or relative it claimed to be.

These communicators often complain that the process of making contact with mundane conditions through an unfamiliar body is hard, painful and depressing – one compared it to diving into a dark fog – and they account for the triviality of many communications by saying that to get through more than distorted fragments is extremely difficult. Nevertheless, and in spite of the mass of inapposite and dream-like material which even the best mediums are liable to produce, at times a communicator's performance is too lifelike and convincing for a dispassionate inquirer to feel comfortable about rejecting its authenticity out of hand. Something which is not cheating and appears inexplicable on any known hypothesis is certainly going on. Even so, it is obvious that all thinkable alternative explanations to communication with the discarnate must be considered with great care.

It has often been observed that an entranced medium will serve up, as coming from the discarnate, snippets of information which could, unconsciously as well as consciously, have been guessed or inferred from a sitter's behaviour, age, sex, wedding ring or unwisely revealing remarks – but no more.

Many, but not all controls, will fish or grope for information from the sitter, which is natural enough, but inexperienced sitters are liable to give away more than they realize and then take it as coming from the discarnate when it is returned to them later. It should also, in fairness, be said that some sceptical sitters are so determined to give away nothing that they create an atmosphere as cold and silent as a winter's night at the North Pole, and this is unlikely to encourage any type of skill or sensitivity. The conscious self of an honest medium should not be blamed for the deception or evasiveness of the trance-personality, for even if she realizes what has been said, which she usually does not, she may have no idea that its source was her own subconscious observation or influence. Mediums do not know the actual source of what floats into their minds, however much they believe in the validity of their own interpretation of it.

A medium's ignorance of the source of her information is shown by another possible alternative to certain apparent contacts with the dead – unconscious memory. There are in fact many hints that the subconscious never forgets. If so, a medium's statements can never provide watertight evidence, even of mundane ESP, unless it is certain that she could not have had normal access to the information she imparts.

The phenomena produced by physical mediums often took the form of materializations, figures which ranged from scarcely visible wisps to fully formed and clothed bodies that apparently grew out of ectoplasm Below left *The face of Raymond Lodge (actual photograph inset) son of Sir Oliver Lodge, a pioneer of psychical research, appears in the ectoplasm issuing from a medium's nose* Centre *Katie King was a feminine spirit allegedly materialized by the medium Florence Cook* Right *Photograph of ectoplasm exuding from a medium's ear*

Subconscious Histrionics

When trying to assess the authenticity of a purported communicator, a further complication is that in all human beings, not mediums alone, the subconscious frequently acts as a great dramatizer of all types of circumstances. Dreams make that clear enough.

But whatever the real nature of controls or communicators and however much a medium may subconsciously dramatize, the fact still remains that on occasion she appears to obtain information by some unknown and apparently extra-sensory means. What alternatives are there to the belief that this information has been given her by the discarnate? Single 'hits' can in theory be attributed to a lucky coincidence, but when a complicated series of similar apt statements are repeated by several mediums independently, this explanation appears fanciful. Excluding, then, chance coincidence and knowledge obtained by recognized sensory means, the simplest paranormal explanation would seem to be telepathy from somebody present at the sitting; the next, telepathy from some distant living person. A further paranormal, but still mundane, alternative is that the medium could have perceived clairvoyantly some document of which the existence was not known at the time, such as a letter written by a dead person, which was only found after the sitting (as in Mrs Leonard's book tests). That telepathy and precognition do occur has been experimentally demonstrated to the satisfaction of a number of eminent scientists, and the indignant denial of others.

Continuing Sense of Purpose

Mediumship can produce great puzzles, including some which actually suggest continuing intention on the part of individuals who have survived bodily death. In some of these cases, the only alternative explanation, apart from collective cheating or a fantastic series of chance coincidences,

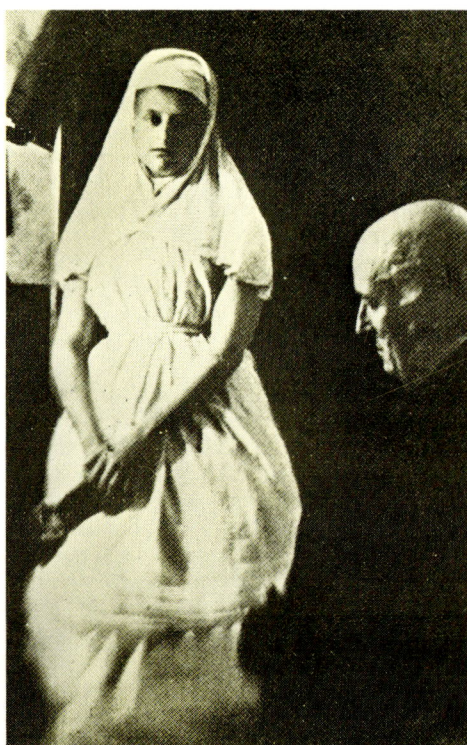

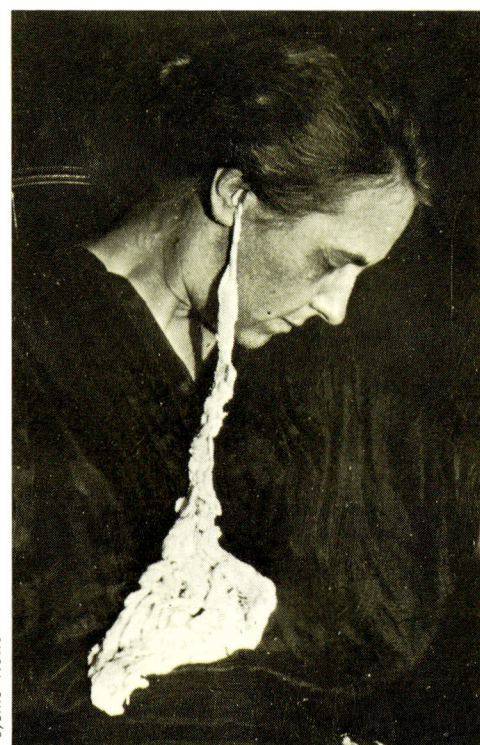

Psychic News

Psychic News

University of London/Harry Price Library

seems to be that several mediums have performed the extraordinary feat of collecting snippets of information telepathically from various living persons whom they did not know, and then combining and dramatizing their contents into wishes which have been expressed by a discarnate spirit.

It will be obvious that it must be very rare for such cases to occur in apparently watertight conditions, because most sittings with mediums are not undertaken by investigators who have taken precautions against all sources of leakage, but by bereaved persons who are usually ready to jump at the slightest hint that they can communicate with those they have loved and lost. Fortunately a few exceptionally gifted mediums, particularly Mrs Piper, Mrs Leonard, and Mrs Willett, have provided a number of such cases, since they allowed themselves to be studied over long periods by expert investigators. To the neutral observer their work makes it clear that there is something, produced in all honesty, to be explained.

Supernatural Crosswords

There is a complicated series of mediumistic utterances known as the Society for Psychical Research cross-correspondences. As more of these were written than spoken, for convenience they are usually all referred to as scripts. They were produced over a period of about 30 years by some educated amateur English sensitives and one professional American medium, Mrs Piper – about 12 in all. Some of the sensitives were widely separated (Mrs Fleming, for instance, Rudyard Kipling's sister, lived in India) and some of them never met each other; yet their scripts, which ran into thousands, showed every sign of being interrelated. The story is long and complicated, and without details loses much of its impressiveness, but no description of mediumship would be complete without some indication of its elaborate interrelationships.

The first cross-correspondence scripts were automatically written in 1901 by Mrs Verrall, a Cambridge Lecturer in Classics, shortly after the death of the last of three distinguished Cambridge scholars, Henry Sidgwick, Edmund Gurney and Frederic Myers, who had all been founder members of the S.P.R. and who were all deeply concerned to establish whether or not some component of a human being could survive the death of his body. Mrs Verrall's scripts were followed by others, mainly written by women who were not classical scholars, yet many of them referred to abstruse classical subjects about which few people except erudite scholars would ever have heard. The scripts were usually signed 'Myers' or 'Gurney'.

They were fragmentary and apparently meaningless when taken separately, and it was only after it occurred to an investigator at the Society's headquarters to try to fit them together that it was found that the fragments were apparently complementary and that when they were fitted together coherent meanings emerged. Sometimes a clue as to what such a meaning would be was given in one script in advance. Eventually a group of expert scholars, in particular the second Lord Balfour, who studied the scripts over many years, were driven to the conclusion that the elaborate verbal puzzles they contained showed every sign of having been designed by somebody. The question was, by

Voices speaking from 'nowhere' and raps and bangs on floors and tables are other phenomena that have occurred during physical seances Below left *Ectoplasmic hand produced by Margery Crandon, a famous medium during the 1920s; the controversy that developed around the physical phenomena she produced deeply divided the SPR in the United States* Centre *Mme Eugénie Picquart, a French medium, impersonating Mephistopheles* Right *Medium tied to a chair; trumpets and various musical instruments are part of the physical medium's stock-in-trade*

whom? An intriguing aspect of this story is that the scripts took an enthusiastic part in investigating themselves. For one thing they insisted that the various automatists must not see each other's work, for they claimed that the verbal puzzles the scripts contained had been designed by the surviving Myers and his friends as evidence of their continued existence and power to plan. There was in fact an excellent reason for such a circuitous procedure. During their lives the founders of S.P.R. had learnt the hard way that to demonstrate survival by means of mediumship – or indeed by any other means – is extremely difficult. For a purported communicator merely to announce his identity is obviously no proof at all. To remind the sitter of past events is little better, for even when the medium could not have heard of them by sensory means, she could, in theory, have discovered them telepathically from any living person to whom they were known. But here, claimed the scripts, was evidence of many complicated designs which were apparently not known to any living person. This raised the question: where could they have come from except the dead?

The alternatives to this claim seem just about as startling as the claim itself. One is that all the elaborate patterns and interrelationships came about by chance. A second is that investigators such as Lord Balfour, and sensitives such as Mrs Verrall, Dame Edith Lyttelton, Mrs Coombe-Tennant (Mrs Willett), and other equally well known and respected figures had got together to perpetrate a long-term fraud, which took a lot of time and trouble and brought them no gain but rather, mockery. A third alternative is that the whole plan might have originated in the subconscious mind of that sternly upright scholar Mrs Verrall, and that over many years she had led a *subconscious* telepathic class of other equally upright women, some of whom she had never met, to make fools, not only of their friends and the public,

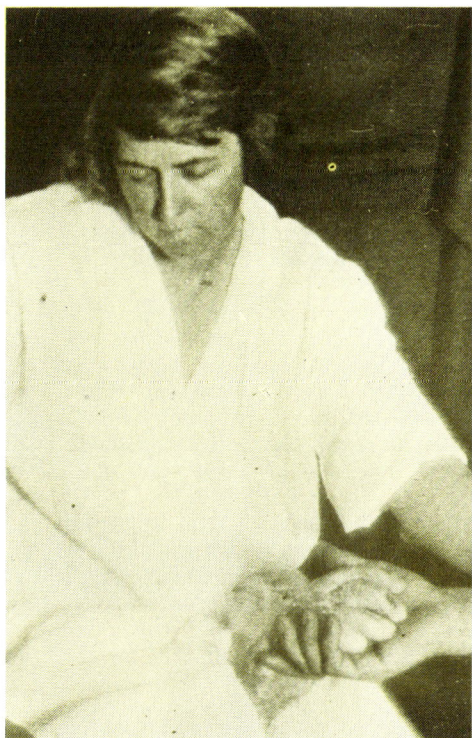

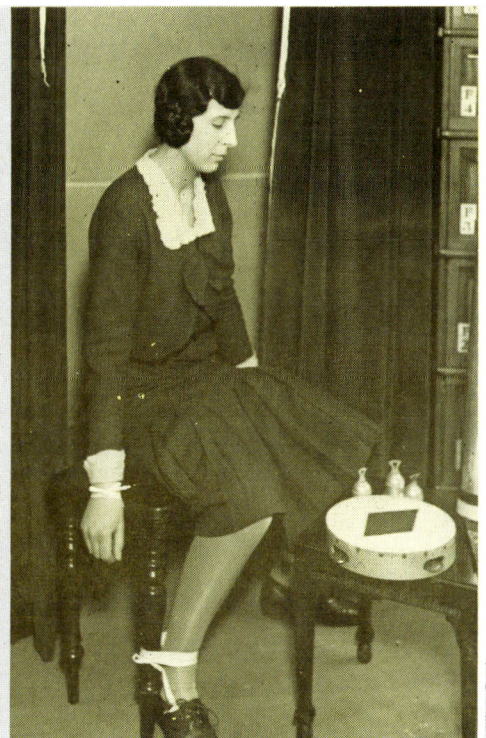

53

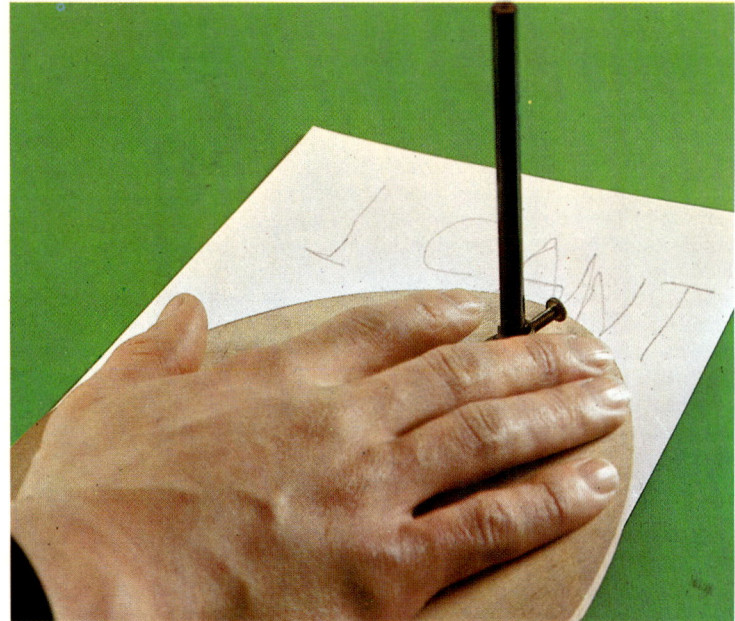

Chris Barker

The simplest form of ouija board, an upturned glass in the centre of a circle of letters (left)*, and a planchette* (right)*: both devices seem to open up 'shortcuts from subconscious to conscious' and can be upsetting or frightening if 'censored' material comes through*

but also of their own conscious selves. One weakness in this explanation is that the script puzzles went on after her death, when no one seemed to be left with her knowledge of the classics, personal contact with the dead scholars, and interest in the subject of survival, to carry on such an elaborate hoax.

The present position regarding the evidence for survival provided by mediumship appears to be something like this: it is extremely hard to ascribe the best material provided by the best mediums to chance, or fraud, or to information obtained by sensory means and subconsciously remembered. If these explanations are excluded there seem to be two alternatives: either mediums can obtain information from the discarnate, as they themselves believe, or they get it by means of ESP of mundane events, which is more efficient and widely ranging than has ever been observed in other situations and which they then dramatize subconsciously to fit a particular case.

Some aspects of the psychology of mediumship may have been glimpsed in the foregoing sketch of the evidence it claims to provide for survival, but one further aspect should be mentioned as it gives an interesting clue to the oddities and limitations of both mediumistic utterances and certain spontaneous ESP-type experiences. In both cases, information which has not come through one of the known senses appears to have been received at a subconscious level, and it has often been noticed that subconscious material, whether it has originated in an individual's own psyche or has penetrated it from outside, sometimes has difficulty in rising to the surface in a straightforward manner. It seems as if some kind of censorship has to be evaded. A similar impression is often given by dreams. Hence, information which appears to have

reached the subconscious in some paranormal fashion from an exterior source, whether mundane or not, is liable to emerge disguised or distorted, or obliquely by means of an associated idea or a symbol. Then it will have to be interpreted, and here both medium and sitter can make mistakes.

Thinking in Pictures

A few examples may clarify the pattern. Take the following case of associated ideas leading towards an item which helped to identify a purported communicator. Topsy, the control of a well-known medium, Mrs Warren Elliot, who allowed her work to be studied by serious investigators, seemed to be groping for the identifying fact that in life a certain communicator had much enjoyed rice pudding. She spoke of India, then of some hot place with dark people, then of palms, then bananas, and finally she said, 'He laughs and shows Topsy a lot of rice. There must be a joke about rice – lots and lots of rice – more rice, never tired.'

Conversely, associated ideas in a sitter's mind may lead a medium along a trail towards no particular goal. After a small dinner, at which three scientists were guests, a medium who was known to none of them was brought in to demonstrate his gift of ESP. On this occasion he made no claim to communicate with the dead, but merely to perceive images which he left to them to interpret. His first image was of one man hastily putting in order a mass of sheets of typescript. This was a bull's eye, for, unknown to anyone present, the day before one of them had been hurriedly putting together the untidy scattered sheets of the carbon copy of the manuscript of a book, because his publisher had unexpectedly telephoned for a second copy to be sent urgently. From this impression the medium passed on to two incidents mentioned in the book, an old manor house connected with one of them, three pictures in that house, including a Romney, in which one of them had delighted as a child, and so on. None of these linked items were in his conscious thoughts, but all were correct.

A medium's impressions frequently emerge by means of symbols and these often take the form of visual images, which is natural enough as the subconscious, like primitive man, seems to think in images rather than in the verbalizations of the highly educated. Topsy once deduced, for instance, that a couple had been 'nearly married and then not married', because a communicator had shown her a wedding dress and then let it fall. Similarly one of the cross-correspondence sensitives, Dame Edith Lyttelton, told me that she had become aware of her pianist grandson's death in action by 'seeing' his grand piano covered with a Union Jack.

Mrs Leonard's control, Feda, whose personality, like Topsy's, was that of an artless young girl, said that she got her information in several different ways. She might seem to herself to hear words or other sounds, or to see written words or imitative or symbolic pictures. She said that impressions came more easily in the form of symbolic visual images than in words but, partaking of Mrs Leonard's extreme honesty, she admitted that she often found it difficult to interpret them. She sometimes claimed to have feelings of, say, roughness or coldness. Incidentally, some mediums seem to pick up the type of pain a purported communicator had suffered from in life, and actually experience the pain themselves.

Both the cross-correspondence communicators and Feda's insisted that from their point of view communication with the living was very difficult. Professor Broad has summarized the description by Feda's communicators of the various methods they could use to convey information to her. One was by actually speaking to her, the other by telepathy, and of this, they said there were several modes. Suppose, for instance, that they wanted telepathically to convey the idea 'horse'. The simplest way was to create an auditory or visual image of the word in Feda's mind; or an image of the horse itself; or a symbolic image of, say, a jockey with a whip. Or they might convey the idea without an image of any kind. One of them drew an interesting distinction between himself projecting an idea or image into Feda's mind and her playing the active role and reading his. In that case she might take up some quite unimportant thought which had nothing to do with what he was trying to communicate.

An important factor in mediumship is the relation between individual mediums and sitters. Some sitters evoke interesting material from a medium, others by their chilling attitude will reduce her to a state of numbed inhibition. But even with good sitters, one will stimulate one medium more than another, and another sitter will do the reverse. A third, however open-minded and sympathetic at a conscious level, will never get any results at all. It is as if there were some subconscious interaction between medium and sitter of which, so far, nothing is understood.

Mediumship has received less psychological study than might have been expected, seeing that it is a phenomenon which arises in all cultures. This may be due in part to distaste for the credulity with which much of it is surrounded and to the prevalence of fraudulent and mediocre mediums, and in part to the widespread acceptance today that survival after death is out of the question. Yet, even if that were so, good mediumship would merit study for the interesting sidelights it appears to throw, not only on subconscious levels of human personality, but also on the subconscious interactions which take place between the living.

The writing not infrequently develops a 'character' of its own, professing beliefs and opinions which differ from the automatist's and sometimes it may display a fluency in composition greatly exceeding his.

The majority of published automatic scripts fall into one or two classes. The first class consists of moral and religious precepts, and accounts of the nature of the next world and of life in it, purportedly coming from deceased persons. The religious teachings and the accounts of the next world vary very much in detail from one automatist to another, but on the whole the general resemblances outweigh the individual differences, and the similarities of tone are often striking. As the American philosopher William James remarked, automatic scripts and utterances abound 'in a curiously vague optimistic philosophy-and-water, in which phrases about spirit, harmony, beauty, law, development, etc., keep recurring. It seems exactly as if one author composed more than half of the trance messages.'

The second category consists of historical romances narrated from the standpoint of some deceased person possessing first hand information or enhanced knowledge of the events and periods concerned. Some of the more interesting of these writings are those of Hélène Smith (in T. Flournoy, *From India to the Planet Mars*, 1900); of Mrs J. H. Curran (in W. F. Prince, *The Case of Patience Worth*, 1927); and of Geraldine Cummins (*The Scripts of Cleophas*, 1928 and *When Nero was Dictator*, 1939). There is no doubt that these and similar writings

AUTOMATIC ART

The term 'automatic' applied to writing, painting and drawing means the production of work not consciously directed by the person whose hand executed it. It belongs to, and cannot be sharply separated from, a whole range of phenomena commonly regarded by psychologists as manifestations of layers of the personality which are subconscious or dissociated, cut off from the conscious mind. This includes hysterical tics, loss of memory, sleep-walking, multiple personality, 'speaking in tongues', prophecy, and mediumship in trance.

Sometimes automatic writing develops as one hysterical symptom among others, or is induced by a psychotherapist as a means of reaching dissociated memories; but often it has been deliberately cultivated by normal people. The method adopted is usually to sit in some peaceful place holding a pencil to a piece of paper, and occupying the mind with irrelevant thoughts or with a book. A certain degree of suggestibility and a willing suspension of disbelief are probably essential prerequisites of success.

It is quite impossible to generalize about the automatist's state of mind during the production of automatic writing and drawings. Some go into a deep trance and are quite oblivious of their surroundings; some are drowsy but partially aware of what is going on; some are awake but abstracted; and some are fully conscious and may read or talk normally. Some automatists are aware of the movements of the hand and of what it is writing or drawing; some are conscious but quite insensible of what is written or drawn; and some are unaware even that their hands are moving.

In their early stages automatic writing and drawing are generally very crude and monotonous; they may begin with incessant repetition of the same figure or letter, and they often proceed no further than the production of a few empty phrases or irregular shapes. But in a few cases the automatist comes in time to exhibit skill or knowledge beyond his ordinary capacities. Automatic writing has been known to report events forgotten or unnoticed by the waking self, to produce fragments of languages not consciously known to the writer, and to exhibit what look like flashes of telepathy.

'Automatic' painting by Mrs Alaric Watts, a late 19th century amateur artist who found that when sketching her pencil would begin to move by itself. When painting, she prepared colours on her palette and let her hand be 'guided' to choose them

Layton-Sun

sometimes display knowledge, dramatic flair or literary gifts in excess of those which the automatist ordinarily possesses.

A distinction can be made between cases of automatic drawing and painting, and cases of 'psychic art' in which a clairvoyant or sensitive, gifted in the use of crayon or brush, has sketched some spirit or other-worldly scene allegedly revealed to him by his supernormal faculties. Many of William Blake's pictures belong in this class. The most noted British 'psychic artist' of recent years has been Frank Leah. However, it seems possible that no sharp line can be drawn between automatic drawing and painting and the 'psychic' drawing and painting of clairvoyants; for many 'psychic artists' would claim not merely to discern the subjects of their sketches by some form of non-sensory perception, but to receive inspiration and help from departed spirits (often those of famous artists) in the actual execution of their pictures, Madge Gill, an uneducated East London housewife, whose drawings have recently received some notice (she died in 1961), worked in a state of semi-trance, and said that she 'felt impelled to execute drawings on a large scale . . . I am undoubtedly guided by an unseen force'.

If the concordance between the writings of the various automatists are not to be set down to the plans and activities of deceased persons we are forced to make some very remarkable assumptions. The alternatives to a Spiritualist interpretation of certain automatic writings are themselves not easy to swallow; for the possibility of deliberate fraud can be canvassed in only a very small number of cases. But what makes the Spiritualist interpretation unacceptable to many researchers is the fact that the best cases are commonly found inextricably entangled with the worst. The most convincing of an automatist's 'communicators' will guarantee the credentials of the most implausible ones; and this fact opens up problems of an unapproachable complexity.

and the study of cures is by no means the same thing, and that spontaneous recovery may be one of the reasons why no rational theory of healing exists. It is difficult to define a boundary between paranormal healing and orthodox medical practice; a doctor giving a patient a placebo (a pill or other medicine which is a 'dummy' and which has no known chemical action) in the hope and expectation that the sufferer will benefit by being humoured in this way is a good physician; the faith healer may *believe* that he is doing something positive and his actions and his belief may also serve as a placebo; the patient feels better.

The methods of orthodox medicine change continuously. Mesmer's 'unorthodox' activities were investigated in 1784 by a commission of physicians and scientists, including Benjamin Franklin, and their unfavourable conclusions forced him to retire 30 years before his death in 1815 at the age of 80. By the 1850s some of his methods, under the name of hypnotism, were again considered seriously and as a result of Professor J. M. Charcot's work had become respectable by the end of the century.

The concepts of the unconscious mind elaborated by the Freud-Adler-Jung group were embellished by discoveries with the aid of hypnosis of mental processes hitherto unrecognized. The relevance of the patient-doctor relationship has received increased recognition and in this sense some of the faith healing methods are being incorporated into orthodox medical practice.

The methods by which unorthodox healers work may be loosely categorized into three groups. Firstly, there are 'magical' methods not based on observable and constant cause and effect but adopted as a result of falling into the old trap of *post hoc propter hoc* (after this, therefore because of this). These methods include the practices of early historical times – for example the use of charms and talismans as a form of protection.

The second group contains the vast array of methods involving touch – among them

FAITH HEALING

Faith healers claim to have, usually in the absence of medical knowledge or skills, the gift of healing; treatment methods vary with the individual healer but in general are not those appropriate to orthodox medical practice. Attitudes about the faith aspect (that is, belief held in the absence of, or in spite of, logical argument based on available facts) of faith healing vary so widely that it is not even possible to establish that such belief is an essential element in the process either for the healer or for the patient. Noel Bayon and Maurice Colinon worked experimentally as healers during recent years without the slightest faith in their powers, but both achieved considerable reputations.

The words 'illness' and 'disease' arouse widely differing subjective and objective responses. Dr A. E. Clark-Kennedy gives a good working definition: 'A disease . . . so far as definition is possible, is that condition of man, woman or child of a certain psychomatic constitution, and at a certain stage of his or her life, when a pathological process of body or mind is leading to alteration of structure or disturbance of function, with the result that he or she sooner or later starts to complain of symptons, or signs are discovered on examination, most diseases being due to to complicated interaction between

genetic weakness, the adverse factors to which a man is exposed in his environment, and the psychosomatic machinery of his individual constitution. No two cases, therefore, are ever quite the same, although certain types of reaction are common, justifying the abstract conception of the real existence of disease, apart from the individual patients who actually suffer from them.'

Another authority, Professor Emilio Servadio, suggests that the study of healing

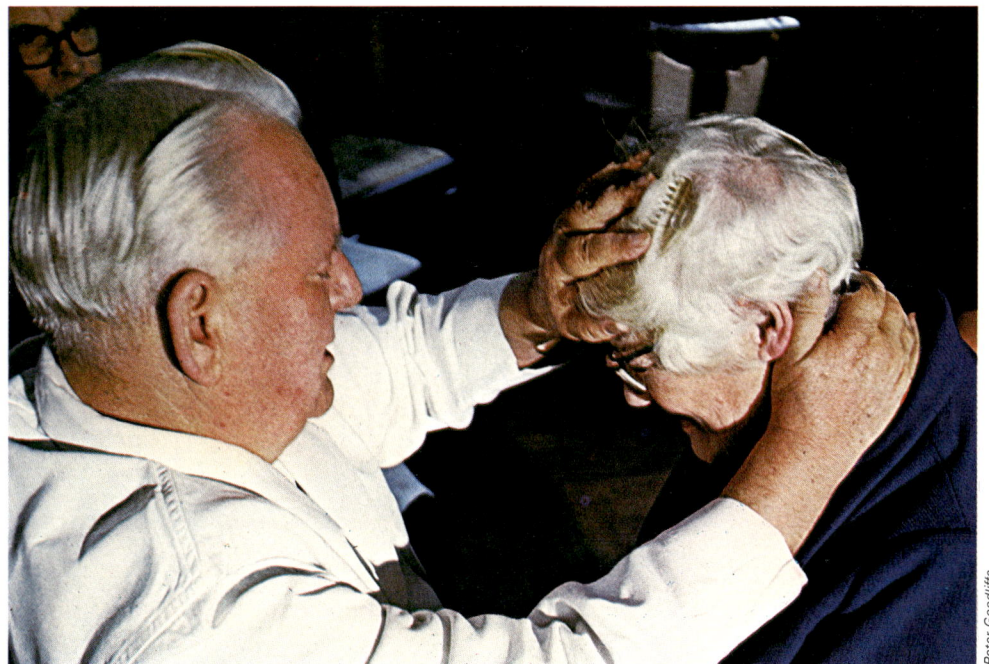

Peter Goodliffe

anointing with oil, 'stroking', the method used for his cures by Valentine Greatrakes (1629–1683), the laying on of hands and, according to Plutarch (c 46–120 AD), the highly individual method of laying on of toes which is recorded as having been practised by Pyrrhus, who was the king of the Molossians.

The final group consists of those methods by which the patient has no physical object to reassure him and does not gain the comfort of touch. These include exorcism, commands to be well and merely being stared at, as advocated by the zouave Henri Jacob. Indeed, the sufferer may not be physically close to the healer, or even aware of his existence, as happens in some of the forms of absent healing.

The will to health may finally express itself in the patient who has failed to gain relief in the usual medical environment; and even though such a patient may say that he does not believe in faith healing, he has, usually unconsciously, reached the point at which he *must* become well, and this is the time when the healer may contribute to the reversal of a psychologically-based illness or to the mental well-being of a patient suffering from organic disease.

According to the magnetists, a sick person was someone whose contact with the magnetic fluid that fills the universe had been obstructed, and he could be cured if he obtained a fresh supply. Patients undergoing treatment at a 'magnetic dispensary': 18th century etching

MAGNETISM

The term 'animal magnetism' was coined in c 1766 by F. A. Mesmer to denote a supposed fluid or force, pervading the universe, but especially concentrated in animal nervous systems and magnets. It was not identical with electromagnetism but possessed certain analogies to it.

The general idea was not new, but Mesmer gave it some distinctive twists. He was led to postulate the existence of this fluid by observing that the movements of the planets and other heavenly bodies produced fluctuations in the course of diseases, and that magnets or the hands of a vigorous person might exercise a striking therapeutic effect when applied to the body of someone who was ill. He thought that the fluid had properties resembling those of electromagnetism because it could apparently be stored in objects submitted to 'magnetization' and transmitted from these to other objects or to the bodies of patients; and because it apparently possessed polarity, some parts of the body, and certain people and objects, exerting a counter active influence upon positively magnetized persons and things.

Some writers, especially in Germany where a new period of literary romanticism was beginning, took a very exalted view of the supposed fluid.

Dr J. H. Jung-Stilling, whose well-known work, *Theory of the Science of Spirits,* was first published in 1808, regarded it as a halfway house between spirit and matter, to be equated with the ether of physicists. He believed that it was especially concentrated in the human organism, and was the medium through which the rational element in man, his 'spirit', could control the body. Disturbances of this ether, such as those produced by a mesmerist, could affect the spirit, perhaps partially freeing it from the body, and so releasing its inherent clairvoyant faculties. Jung-Stilling called the union of a rational element, or spirit, with a particular portion of etheric fluid the 'soul', and it is the soul, not just the spirit, that survives death. Similar doctrines have been propounded by many modern Spiritualists.

In the late 1840s the whole subject of animal magnetism received a boost from the apparently related findings of a noted Austrian chemist, Baron K. von Reichenbach (1788–1869), whose important study *Physico-Physiological Researches* was translated into English in 1850.

He believed he had shown that certain sensitive persons, especially spontaneous cataleptics and somnambules, could, if kept in the dark for upwards of an hour, perceive

characteristic lights emanating from magnets, crystals, metals, the human body, stars, planets, and other objects; and could also feel sensations of heat or cold in connection with the lights. To account for these phenomena, Reichenbach postulated a quasi-magnetic emanation or fluid, which he called 'Odyle' or 'Od Force'.

He conceived this force as radiating outwards, but in very different degrees, from all objects and also to be generated by heat, light, electricity, friction and all kinds of chemical change. Odyle exhibits polarity. The negative pole of a magnet appears blue, and induces a feeling of coldness, whilst the positive pole appears red and causes a feeling of warmth. The right hand is odylically negative and the left positive, the sun negative and the moon positive. Uncharged bodies are capable of being charged if they are brought into contact with a charged body.

Healing by Touch

The magnetic movement in Britain and the United States subsided rapidly after the 1850s, because its impetus and personnel were absorbed into the newly founded Spiritualist movement. In France, however, during the later 19th and early 20th centuries, a number of people continued to believe that there was a residue of phenomena which were not clearly intelligible or explicable in terms of suggestion, but which indicated quite strongly that some kind of emanation from the human organism took place.

The only modern experiments which might in any way be used to support the views of the animal magnetists are some quite recent ones by G. H. Elguin and others, in which human agents have produced beneficial results on lesions in animals without actually touching them. In these experiments there were of course untreated 'control' groups; and animals are presumed to be immune to suggestion.

B. Grad and other investigators have reported somewhat comparable findings in experiments on the growth of seedlings. But it is hardly necessary to remark that experiments such as these must be assessed with extreme caution at this stage.

POSSESSION

For thousands of years, all forms of madness, of grossly abnormal behaviour and, sometimes, of physical disease have been explained in terms of spirit possession. The spirit might be an evil one, a morally neutral one, a good spirit or a god. Various Christian groups have felt, as Wesley did at first, that 'enthusiastic' behaviour was a sign of possession by the Holy Ghost. In other societies

Madness, abnormal behaviour of various kinds, and the ability to fall into an ecstatic state have been attributed to spirit possession all over the world. In West Pakistan a youth drinks the blood of a goat after becoming 'possessed'

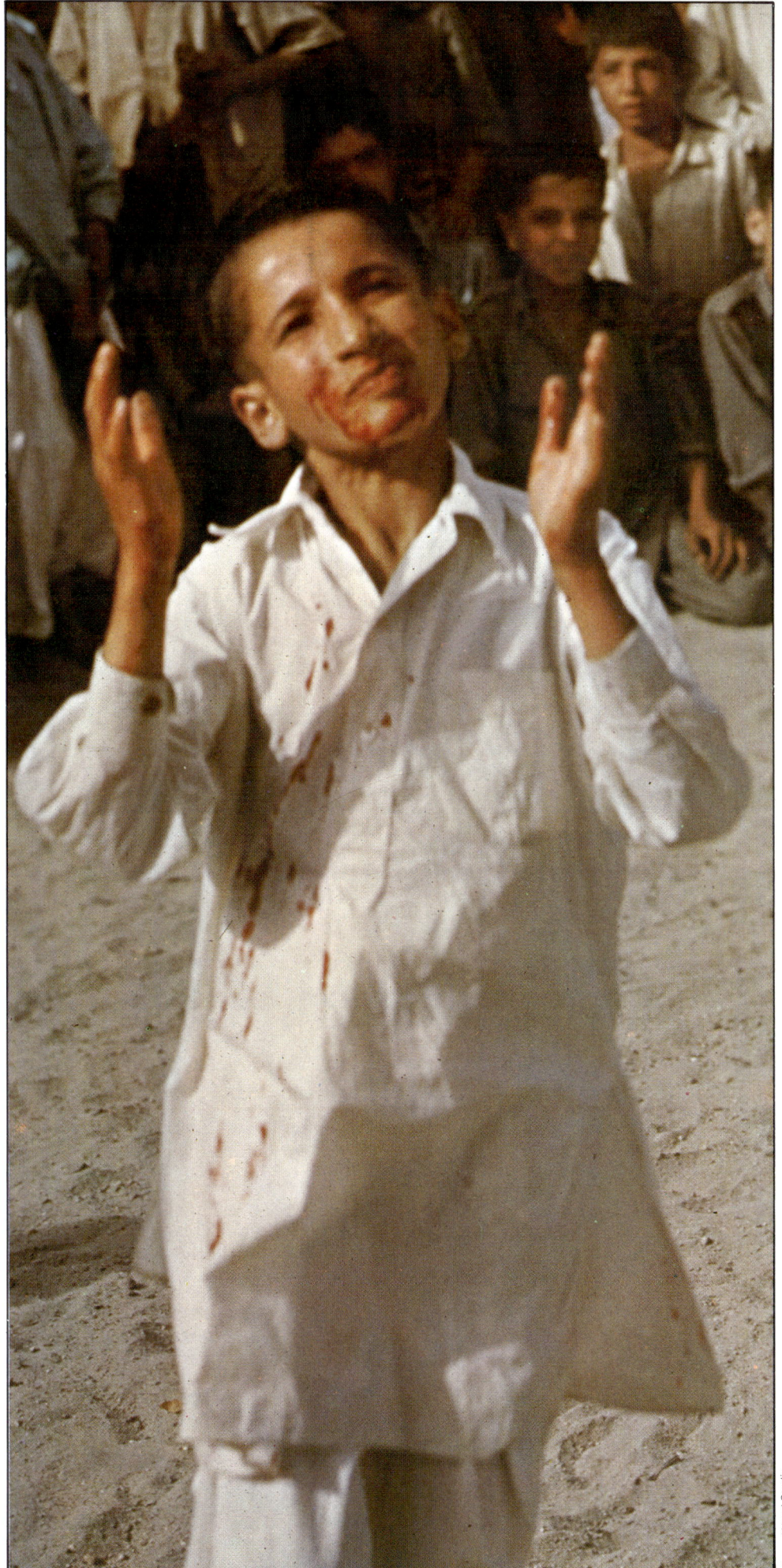

Roger Wood Studio

there has been the belief in 'holy madness' or the belief that a magician or shaman can become possessed by a god or a spirit, can convey the god's words to his worshippers and can heal the sick. Many of these cures work, probably because of the patients' heightened suggestibility.

In Ethiopia, for example, people are sometimes believed to be possessed by spirits called 'zars'. Patients are treated by a 'doctor' who is himself zar-possessed but who has 'come to terms' with his zar. He, or she, sometimes goes into a state of trance, in which his own zar takes control of him, and then tries to discover the identity of the patient's zar so as to negotiate with it. He speaks in the special language of zars, a jumbled tongue based on Amharic and recalling the phenomenon of 'speaking in tongues'. He persuades the zar, by promising it the gifts which it demands through the mouth of the patient, to turn itself into a kindly and helpful guardian spirit.

In Haiti the main purpose of Voodoo ceremonies is for one or more of the worshippers to become possessed by a *loa*, a god or spirit which 'rides' him as if he was a horse but which is also inside his head. As in many other parts of the world, drumming and dancing help to induce the experience. When the loa enters a man, he behaves in its characteristic manner and speaks with its voice, sometimes in the loa language, which is a jumble of muddled words.

Possession by a god or by the ghost of someone who has died is common in India. Two anthropologists who investigated a case at a village near Delhi commented that 'spirit possession, like hysteria, has two conditions: a basic condition due to the individual's intra-psychic tension and a precipitating condition due to an event or situation involving unusual stress or emotion.' The young woman who was possessed, shivered and complained of feeling cold. Presently she sat up and started to jerk violently. The ghost, which had now entered her, spoke through her mouth and her assembled relatives had a long conversation with it. They were mainly concerned to establish its identity, and the emphasis on discovering the name of the possessing spirit, so as to gain a measure of power over it, is a common feature of exorcism procedures all over the world.

Mircea Eliade has described how a Siberian shaman restores the soul of a sick patient, which has escaped from his body. After drumming for a long time, the shaman calls on various spirits to come and stand near him. After more drumming, he goes to the door and breathes deeply, to swallow the spirits he has summoned, who now speak through his mouth. Then he lies on the ground, face down and motionless, for he has left his body and is travelling in the spirit world. Eventually he returns, bringing with him the fugitive soul which he has rescued from the 'kingdom of shadows' and which he restores to the patient's body.

Streaming in Like Light

Drugs and sex have both been used to induce the experience of possession and to gain personal contact with the divine. Here is John Addington Symonds, the 19th century art critic, describing his sensations under chloroform: 'I thought I was near death; when suddenly my soul became aware of God, who was manifestly dealing with me, handling me, so to speak in an intensely personal present reality. I felt him streaming in like light upon me . . . I cannot describe the ecstasy I felt.'

The magician Aleister Crowley experimented liberally with both drugs and sex as gateways to communication with spirits. To take only one example from many, here is his account of the results of an operation of sex-magic with a woman named Mary d'Este Sturges in 1911, 'At about midnight she was in a state of excitement, exhaustion and hysteria . . . one little removed from an amorously infuriated lioness . . . suddenly and without warning (this) gave place to a profound calm hardly distinguishable from the prophetic trance and she began to describe what she was seeing . . . (she) had seen in a dream the head of five White Brothers . . . The person now appeared again to her. He was an old man with a long white beard.'

The evidence increasingly suggests that cases like this have nothing to do with spirits of any kind but have their causes in the human brain, and particularly in greatly increased brain suggestibility in states of emotional excitement and upheaval. If this is true, the implications go far beyond the field of possession, and may throw much light on the phenomena of conversion and faith, the mystical experience of being 'one' with God, ecstatic and 'enthusiastic' behaviour, 'speaking in tongues', mediumistic communications with the dead, trance and semi-trance states, 'astral travel', spiritual healing and other supposedly supernatural manifestations.

The number of gods, spirits or devils which have been believed to seize control of human personalities has been legion. What is particularly interesting about so many accounts of possession and exorcism is their marked similarity to modern psychiatric cases.

HYSTERICAL POSSESSION AND WITCHCRAFT

Much has been written in the last 50 years on the psychology of the witch. It seems undeniable, on the evidence of trials and personal testimonies, that in every era a number of the people who were accused of witchcraft did believe themselves to be witches. Isabel Gowdie, whose spontaneous confession in 1662 amazed and discomforted her contemporaries, is a classic example of this type.

On the basis of this and comparable cases there is now a substantial modern literature which treats the witch as a mental case, a person suffering from a classic psychosis, often associated with senility, characterized by delusions as to her own importance and powers. While there is undoubtedly much truth in this view, it seems important to realize that the insanity was by no means one-sided. Frequently as much emotional abnormality, irrationality and sheer ill-will was displayed by the witch-hunters and the witches' 'victims' as by the witches.

Seen in the context of their own time, not all witches were grossly abnormal nor were all the 'bewitched' constitutionally inadequate or hysterical. Nor indeed were all the judges sadistic and neurotic: many were averagely decent, Christian men of their time, doing what they believed to be their duty. Nevertheless it is undeniable that the rigid, tendentious nature of Church law on witchcraft during the centuries of persecution, with the tendency to regard many circumstantial facts as automatic evidence of sorcery and to consider an accused witch guilty unless proved innocent, rather than the other way round, did load the dice consistently against the accused. This provided the opportunity for the abnormally impressionable or paranoid person to give full rein to his or her imagination.

In every era there are a substantial number of people who are ready, indeed eager, to believe themselves harmed or threatened. The paranoiac who today believes that 'they' (the police, the government, the Jews, the Blacks, the Communists, the Arabs) are conspiring against him or his society, is the same man as the suspicious citizen of past centuries who accused witches. The focus of paranoia changes with regimes and fashions in belief, but the type of emotion remains constant. Moreover most paranoiacs display a dreary lack of originality. The repetitive accusations against witches in the past ('they're cursing my pigs – blighting my crops – laming me') are paralleled today by accusations such as 'they're trying to kill me by radar' (or 'by electricity'), which are familiar to every mental health officer.

Unchanging, too, is the paranoid tendency to ascribe the evil not just to one individual's malevolence but to an organized conspiracy of ill-doers; hence the collective prejudice against a mythical 'secret society' – of witches, or Jews, or coloured people. The belief that the scapegoat-group are physically different in some way from ordinary people, and that they are plotting to multiply their number and gain control over society also seems to be constant. The probable explanation for this apparent flaw in the argument is that the accuser, having made

In many parts of the world drumming and dancing help to induce a state of possession Above During a Ghanaian festival held annually in a medicine-man's camp, a woman dances frenziedly until she finally falls into his arms Below Yoruba worshippers of Sopono, the god who is deemed to inflict smallpox, dance themselves into a possessed state

John Moss

Philip Daly

a particular group into his collective scapegoat, has to justify his persecution of its individual and apparently defenceless members by making out that there is some widespread organization behind them. The judges who followed the dictates of the *Malleus Maleficarum* (1487) and similar manuals would no doubt have found it difficult to condemn many of the simple old hags dragged before them unless they had fixed in their minds the idea that it was the whole secret society of witchcraft they were attacking, not just this individual.

Self-induced Symptoms

It may be felt that accusations made by individual paranoid schizophrenics can hardly account for the large-scale witch persecutions that took place, especially on the Continent, in the 15th and 16th centuries. In fact, though such clinical paranoia may have been relatively rare, even one isolated case in a town could (and still can) serve to excite the milder, more generalized but equally irrational paranoid tendencies and prejudices found among otherwise sane members of the community. Therefore, although there are probably only a few people in a community at any one time who are convinced that they themselves have been singled out by the scapegoat for evil attentions, there are many more who will concede the possibility of such things happening.

There is also another form of unbalanced behaviour which is in itself less ominous than paranoia but which can be just as devastating in its social effect if it is not recognized for what it is. This is characterized by the production of hysterical ailments, usually believed by the subject himself to be genuine. The prime reason for them seems to be a desire to attract attention and sympathy, but often an accusation is thrown in to substantiate the hysteric's case. The accusation is therefore not an essential part of the syndrome, but when it is made, and believed, the effect is the same as with the primary accusations of the paranoiac.

In short, while the paranoiac develops a rooted distrust of one particular person or group, and only then invents his injuries, often fantastic ones, the hysteric reverses the process. He – or, perhaps more typically, she – produces symptoms of injury, often in great variety and abundance, and only then casts around for a scapegoat on which the blame can convincingly be laid. Usually this process seems to be unconscious, but it also seems possible that in many cases the hysteric does know, at some level, that her afflictions are self-induced, and therefore finds it particularly necessary to have a good story about their origins. There is no doubt that both types of person, the paranoiac and the hysteric, made a substantial contribution to the history of witch-persecution.

Very little was generally known or accepted about the working of the human mind in the Middle Ages or, indeed, until the 19th century. At various times individual physicians and scholars preached what we should now regard as sound sense: Agrippa (1486–1535) was one and he narrowly escaped being branded as a witch himself for his pains. His pupil the Dutchman Johannes Wier or Weyer was another, and so were the 16th century English squire Sir Reginald Scot and, slightly later, an English doctor named John Cotta. Other writers, such as James I of England in his *Daemonologie* (1597) and Joseph Glanvil in his *Saducimus Triumphantus* (1681), while subscribing in the main to popular prejudice on the subject of witchcraft, were sufficiently intelligent to discount certain aspects of it, or to point out rampant abuses. Glanvil, who was in principle a persecutor of witches, admitted that it was 'very improbable that the devil who is a wise and mighty spirit would be at the beck of a poor hag, and have so little to do as to attend to the errands and impotent lusts of a silly old woman.'

But such flashes of reason have to be set against a background of radical ignorance and prejudice. The ancient belief in possession by devils was entrenched in Christian thought; the madman in the New Testament whose 'devil' Christ was supposed to have cast out was the prototype for an interminable series of lunatics in the 16th and 17th centuries whose madness was blamed on the evil attentions of a witch. Inevitably, if society has this basic concept of 'bewitching', the supposed signs of it are taken at their face value without further examination. There was little realization, in the centuries of persecution, that vomiting, pains, disturbance of the menses, impotence, paralysis and indeed 'wasting disease' and fits, could be psychosomatic or hysterical ailments, having their root in the sufferer's own fear or in desire for attention rather than in any organic interference on the part of another.

Hysteria Due to Repression

One of the oldest charges against witches was that they caused impotence, either (in the most ancient accusations) by stealing the male organ, or by 'impeding the conjugal action of men and women' in some less drastic way. This may be taken as simply one manifestation of the general link between witchcraft and sterility, the distortion of the original fertility cults into a 'black' form. It may also be considered as evidence for an important psychological source of witch-fear, the rejection of the mother figure and the buried, infantile fear that the mother is all-powerful and has the power to castrate. The sexual roots both of certain forms of witch activity and of witch-phobia are obvious, but as time went by the emphasis within this psycho-sexual area changed.

The male accusing the witch of stealing his masculinity largely disappears, and instead there appear in the records numerous women displaying what to modern eyes seem clear symptoms of hysteria due to sexual repression. These they frequently blamed on male demons and, ultimately, on a specific witch, male or female, who was said either to be wishing the demons onto them or, if a man, 'possessing' them, in two senses, in spirit form. The earliest such recorded case occurred among a group of nuns at Cambrai, in France in 1491, shortly after the *Malleus Maleficarum* and the Bull of Pope Innocent VII had alerted the gullible public to the dangers of witchcraft all round them. The nuns had fits in which they showed superhuman strength, barked like dogs and foretold the future. Eventually the nun who had first begun to have fits and who was therefore the ringleader of the hysteria, was 'unmasked' as a witch herself.

This was by no means the last occasion on which a 'witch's victim' was finally declared to be a witch herself, and this illustrates the confusion that existed on the whole subject of possession. Literally, the root of the word 'possess' implies that the person is actually being inhabited by an alien spirit sitting within it, as distinct from 'obsessed', the linguistic root of which means 'sitting *by*'. Since witches were commonly regarded as being 'possessed by the Devil', in the sense of owned by him, and also as having intercourse either with him or with 'possessing' demons in the forms of incubi and succubi, the assertion that one was 'possessed' could be rather double-edged.

Involuntary Possession

At the same time, since it was also believed that witches could 'shift shape', go forth in spectral form and send their own spirits or those of attendant demons out to inhabit hapless bodies, a plea that one was possessed could also be regarded as a protestation of innocence. 'Involuntary possession' could therefore be a legal defence and a let-out; it was used as such by Johannes Wier when defending accused witches. This doctor of medicine, who has been called 'the founder of modern psychiatry', was a pious man who subscribed to the established belief in devils but at the same time displayed an admirable insight, common sense and frequently courage, in judging particular cases, rejecting hearsay evidence and carefully scrutinizing notions of bewitchment. 'The uninformed and unskilled physicians,' he wrote in his book *De Praestigiis Daemonum*, 'relegate all the incurable diseases, or all the diseases the remedy for which they overlook, to witchcraft . . . In all such cases a good doctor is to be consulted because nothing is more important than to make the clinical situations as clear as daylight, for in no domain of human life are human passions so freely at play as in this one, these passions being superstition, rage, hate and malice.'

In 1712, Jane Wenham was the last to be convicted for witchcraft in England, though a witch was burnt in Scotland some years later. A pamphlet war raged around her in true 18th century style and she was reprieved.

It is the treatment of the maid that is most interesting from a modern point of view. A doctor examined this girl, and ordered that she wash her hands and face twice a day, and that she be confined under observation. Her keeper was to be 'a lusty young fellow'. This was done. The fits and other inconveniences ceased forthwith, and the lusty young fellow later married her. Light, it seems, had at last broken on the true nature of possession and the real needs of many of the possessed.

In every era there have always been a substantial number of people who are prepared to believe in a mythical 'secret society' conspiring against them. In the past this delusion resulted in the persecution of witches; in the 20th century Jews were victims of the same kind of prejudice: Dutch poster advertising an anti-semitic film in the 1940s

MIRACLES

The ancient Greek world ascribed healing functions to no less than 38 gods or heroes. The hero Amphiaraus, regarded as a great man whose benign spirit survived death, had a temple by a sacred spring at Oropus in Boeotia, in central Greece. Patients underwent purification and fasting, and then slept in the temple: the practice called incubation. Cures resulted if the patient had a favourable dream. At length the healing cult of the hero Asclepios surpassed all others; he was revered as a god and his shrines appeared throughout the Mediterranean region. As with Amphiaraus, Asclepios's patients undertook incubation after elaborate preparations. A patient often dreamt that the god examined him, made a diagnosis and prescribed a treatment. Sometimes in the dream the god would heal the patient then and there, perhaps by surgery.

Inscribed on the stonework of the temples were accounts of many cures, some so remarkable as to be indeed miraculous, if true, but their veracity is suspect. However, many cures were perfectly genuine according to the testimony of great physicians like Galen (c 130–200 AD). The priests may have edited or heightened some of the descriptions but there is no real evidence that they employed systematic fraud, such as appearing disguised as Asclepios. The genuine cures can be explained in normal ways. Some patients would have recovered in the ordinary course of events. Belief in the god and expectancy can account for the regularity of the dreams. But the most interesting and significant cures were those of ailments with a strong psychological component, which today are called hysterical or psychosomatic. For example, a man with paralysed fingers, very sceptical of the inscriptions, dreamt that Asclepios stepped on his hand and straightened it. On waking he found himself cured of his ailment.

Releasing the Unconscious

Healing at Christian churches may have followed with continuity from pagan days, the shrines often being converted to churches. In early days incubation was still practised, but gave way to the cult of relics, not necessarily those of official saints. The tomb of the Jansenist Deacon François de Pâris at Saint Médard in Paris in the 18th century yielded cures of great scientific interest because the symptoms before and after cure were carefully recorded by a lawyer, Carré de Montgeron; his descriptions suggest that

15th century Flemish illustration of Christ feeding the 5000: the two miracles of feeding the 4000 and 5000 (Mark, chapters 6 and 8) are increasingly interpreted in terms of 'spiritual feeding'. Jesus himself is described in the gospels as despising mere wonder-working to impress, and his numerous healing miracles are said to have accompanied the cure of patients' spiritual illnesses through faith

hysterical ailments comprised the majority of cures. Moreover the cures were not instantaneous but rather progressed by stages in accordance with the physiological laws well-known at the time.

Hysteria can take the form of 'the Hystericks' as known to our ancestors, or other types of hysterical fit, but can also manifest a bewildering range of other symptoms: deafness, mutism, partial or complete blindness, anaesthetic patches on the skin, paralysis of hand, arm or leg, permanent contraction of muscles, wry-neck, ill-defined aches and pains and, strangest of all, astasia in which the patient has his full strength when lying down, but falls as soon as he tries to stand. There is no physical cause for hysteria but the patient is not shamming. He is genuinely ill and ignorant of the cause of his illness, which is psychological, and therefore locked away without access in the unconscious part of his mind.

Suggestion and Faith

Modern treatment employs psychological means to enable the patient to discover the subconscious origin of his condition, and also tries to relieve those pressures of everyday life which contribute to his illness. Hypnotism is often efficacious, because it is

Medieval stained glass window, showing the prophet Elijah praying to God to restore a widow's dead son to life (I Kings, chapter 17): the fact that so many reported marvels are healings has concentrated attention on possible psychological factors in 'miracles'

a condition in which the patient may be susceptible to remedial suggestion. 'Suggestion' is a difficult term to define precisely or completely understand. Sometimes suggestion received consciously is effective but generally it works in ways as yet unknown. To be successful in healing it must stimulate some unconscious layer of the mind.

In Catholic countries intercessors sometimes make the pilgrimage that the patient is too weak to undertake on his own behalf. Interestingly enough Mark said that in his own country (where 'the prophet is not honoured') Jesus 'could work no miracle there'.

Studies of the miracles at Lourdes show that where sufficient data are available, the cures appear to fall into the regular pattern of healings by suggestion. About one case a year, admittedly, remains puzzling. But medicine is an incomplete science and even hospital physicians are sometimes puzzled by spontaneous remissions. There may be true miracles of healing, but as yet they cannot be proved.

THE SAINTS

If healing miracles are omitted as essentially psychological, the curious physical phenomena reported variously of some mystics include: stigmatization, *incendium amoris* ('flames of love'), incombustibility, fragrance,

bodily elongation, and *inedia*, the ability to survive without food. Physiological peculiarities alleged of the mystic's mortal remains comprise the ability to bleed, incorruptibility and absence of rigor mortis. Levitation, irradiance, telekinesis and 'miracles of abundance' may also be classified as physical phenomena.

The tests of evidence in this field are the same as those in psychical research or in historical studies. Eyewitness depositions are preferred to hearsay evidence, and should be recorded soon after the event with circumstantial detail. The value of depositions made at processes for beatification or canonization is often, but not always, reduced by the lapse of time between the death of the candidate and the inquiry. Because of these or other uncertainties we cannot readily form a judgement concerning the status of fragrance, *incendium amoris*, bodily incorruption and so on, telekinesis or miracles of abundance. But with levitation, irradiance and stigmatization the evidential position is distinctly better.

If supernatural intervention be discounted, stigmatization cannot be explained naturalistically in purely organic terms such as haemophiliac bleeding because of the specific location of the stigmata. Analysis shows that in stigmatic bleeding actual blood is exuded, which further distinguishes the condition from haemathidrosis, which is characterized by red perspiration due to the presence of the bacterium *micrococcus prodigiosus*. The naturalistic explanation of stigmatization therefore sees the stigmata as the result of autosuggestion on the part of the stigmatics who, almost without exception, have been given to brooding intensely on the manifold physical sufferings of Christ.

This theory is well supported by the fact that many stigmatics show undoubted signs of having suffered from hysteria at some time in their lives. 'Hysteria' is employed in the technical sense to designate an illness that can take a bewildering variety of forms: temporary blindness, deafness, paralysis, losses of sensibility in the skin, or excessive sensibility; comas, fainting fits, spasms; miscellaneous aches and pains, and so on. Some stigmatics like Elena Ajello are described as manifesting hysterical symptoms. Others like Teresa Neumann and Berthe Mrazek (a friend of Nurse Edith Cavell who was shot by the Germans in 1915) suffer from mysterious paralyses of sudden onset, relieved by equally mysterious cures, which almost infallibly may be ascribed to hysteria.

A hysterical illness has no organic cause, and is psychological in origin. But the patient is not shamming; he is really ill and is the victim of a complex and mainly unconscious process of auto-suggestion. When hysteria is found in a stigmatic it is a good indication of a high degree of auto-suggestibility. The naturalistic theory of stigmatization ascribes it to auto-suggestion affecting blood flow and tissues, in persons endowed with unusual suggestibility and an obsession with the sufferings of Jesus. This is not quite the same as ascribing stigmatization directly to hysteria, which would go beyond the facts, as there are stigmatics like Father Pio Forgione (1887–1968), of the Capuchin monastery of San Rotundo near Foggia in Italy, who cannot at the present time be classified as hysterical. The link between hysteria and stigmatization is merely that each is a possible result, in appropriate conditions, of a temperament potentially auto-suggestible in certain ways.

Moist wounds appeared

Advocates of the supernatural origin of stigmata have stressed the rather minor character of the effects such as blisters, rashes and eczemas, produced on the skin by suggestion under hypnotism. But this does not do full justice to Dr Adolph Lechler's results with 'Elizabeth', an Austrian peasant girl who was both very devout and under treatment for hysteria. On Good Friday 1931 she was deeply affected by seeing a film of the suffering and death of Christ, and (significantly) complained of pain in feet and hands. That evening Dr Lechler gave her the hypnotic suggestion that wounds would develop at the site of the pains. Moist wounds appeared during the night. Further suggestion deepened them, and resulted also in tears of blood, and inflammation and sagging of the shoulder; a remarkable case.

It would be unwise to speculate overmuch on incombustibility or immunity to fire because little of this nature has been asserted since the 16th century, when it was said that Venerable Domenica del Paradiso (1473–1553) could carry live charcoal in her hands. Numerous incidents of this sort were reported of St Francis of Paola (1416–1507), such as putting his hands into boiling oil or mending hot lime-kilns. St Catherine of Siena (1347–1389) and her clothes are said to have been miraculously preserved from scorching when she lay for an appreciable time in contact with the kitchen fire, in an ecstasy. Father Thurston has attempted to erect some parallels between mystic incombustibility and the practice of fire-walking, as well as the feats of the 19th century medium Daniel Dunglas Home, but the subject seems at present beyond the reach of critical analysis.

Allegations of distortion or elongation of the mystic's person would seem on the face of it to be too grotesque for pious hagiographers to insert them into the record as conventional indications of sanctity. But there are no recent instances. Also, even if the veracity of the witnesses is accepted, there is in some cases a doubt as to whether the more understandable and better authenticated phenomenon of levitation has not been mistaken for elongation. Thus the fellow nuns of sister Veronica Laparelli (1537–1620) measured her height with a yardstick and found that during her prolonged ecstasies she seemed to be some 10 inches taller than usual. But on one occasion Mother Plautilla Semboli put her hand under Veronica's robe and 'found she was lifted up above the ground'.

Cases are often hailed as miraculous where the individual, almost invariably a woman, apparently survives for months and years on no food and little drink. It is not fully understood why inedics can survive for such long periods and it would be foolish to underestimate residual difficulties of naturalistic explanation. But there is no obvious feature by which inedia in the devout differs from anorexia in hysterical persons. Religious

inedics usually show other signs of hysteria; female stigmatics are almost invariably inedics also.

As pointed out by Father Thurston, a surprisingly high proportion of saints have been exhumed *after* beatification and their bodies discovered to be in a remarkably good state of preservation. In only a few cases has beatification or canonization been authorized on the basis of apparent incorruptibility of the remains. The body of St Bernadette of Lourdes (1844–79) was found to be incorrupt in 1909, though the face was brown and the eyes sunken, but only bones were revealed when St Thérèse of Lisieu (1863–97) was disinterred.

If there is no circulation of air the decay of a corpse can be hindered. Dry conditions favour mummification even if there has

St Catherine of Siena: she was said to have suffered the pain of the stigmata while she was undergoing mystical experience at Pisa; detail from a painting by Sodoma

been no embalmment. Moisture sometimes produces saponification, in which the internal tissues are converted into a kind of ammoniacal soap, called *adipocere*, or *gras de cadavre*, and the skin becomes like that of a mummy. The body of Blessed Marie Pelletier was found in this condition in 1903 when exhumed 35 years after death. But when Blessed Anna Maria Taigi (1769–1837) was exhumed in 1868, the surgeon reported that the corpse resembled that of a person only three days dead. The skin was soft and discharged an inoffensive somewhat aromatic fluid, recalling the balsam or oil which have been reported of the bodies of holy persons on other occasions. The absence of rigor mortis has often been commented upon, but might just possibly occur naturally in aged inedics who have had a tranquil death. Liquidity of the blood and bleeding from incisions long after death have also been alleged. At present it seems impossible to say whether or not naturalistic explanations are potentially available, or whether attitudes of mind during life can bequeath unusual biochemical features to the remains.

Lifted Up by Ecstasy

The term telekinesis is applied to the spontaneous flight of the host (the wafer of consecrated bread in the Mass) to the mouth of a divinely-favoured recipient. An aspirant to a reputation of sanctity might fraudulently conceal a wafer in his mouth prior to announcing the miracle, as seems to have been done by Vittoria Bondi in the 18th century. However, when the Curé of Ars said that the host once detached itself from his fingers and placed itself upon the tongue of a communicant we cannot doubt his veracity, although the possibility of a hallucination or a false memory remains. It is also possible that the Curé produced the 'miracle' himself by unconscious psychokinesis, having been for many years the centre of poltergeist activity. The case of St Joseph Mary Dessu (Joseph of Copertino, 1603–63) is adequate to prove the occurrence of levitation. He gained such fame in the district of Copertino in southern Italy for his goodwill, piety and holiness that he was examined by the Inquisition of Naples but acquitted of the charge of deceiving the populace by false miracles.

The majority of eyewitness accounts concerning other mystics (and there are many relating to widely different times and places) affirm that the mystic is suspended about six inches above the ground while in ecstasy and at length makes a gentle landing. The levitating mystic may be preaching like St Alphonsus Liguori (1696–1787) and St Andrew Fournet or praying like St Teresa of Avila and the great theologian Francis Suarez (1548–1617). The evidence is not conclusive but it strongly suggests that levitation occurs only in ecstasy. In 24 cases out of the 155 listed by Leroy the face or figure of the levitating ecstatic has been said to give off or be bathed in a mysterious radiance. Sometimes this light is said to emanate from a sacred image or crucifix, but in other cases there is no obvious source. Levitation (including radiance) is the one mystic phenomenon requiring us to postulate either a supernatural explanation or the existence of natural forces unknown to physics.

SPEAKING-IN-TONGUES

Speaking in tongues, or glossolalia, is best known as the practice of Pentecostalists but it is very much older than the Pentecostalist movement and, in recent years, the incidence of glossolalic experience within

The Descent of the Holy Spirit, by Pinturicchio; Acts, chapter 2, describes the experience of Christ's disciples at Pentecost, when they 'began to speak in other tongues, as the Spirit gave them utterance'

Christendom has extended far beyond the boundaries of the various Pentecostal denominations and sects. Although there is some evidence of glossolalia in the Old Testament and in ancient Egypt, and reports of it in China and among various tribes in Africa and Burma, it is in Christianity that speaking in tongues is best recorded and has been of most significance doctrinally.

The nature and purpose of speaking in unknown tongues has been disputed, but Paul appears to have regarded the use of unknown tongues at Corinth as ecstatic utterance that was not to be understood except by divine inspiration. On the other hand, the scriptures make clear that when the apostles spoke with tongues at Pentecost, the Jews who had gathered, and who spoke many different languages, all heard them each in his own native language. However, some have regarded that incident as a miracle of hearing rather than of speech.

Tarrying Meetings

A considerable number of Protestant sects have experienced glossolalia at different times. The most celebrated are the Camisards, among whom a number of children suddenly broke out into speeches in eloquent French that was considered far

beyond their natural capacity. In the 1780s, Mother Ann Lee, who had become the leader of a small religious group in Lancashire known as Shakers, whose origin is traced to the missionary activities of refugee Camisards, spoke in a number of apparently recognizable languages.

The Pentecostal denominations, which trace their beginning to the American meetings at which Barratt experienced glossolalia, were not, however, the first Christian denominations to incorporate the gift of tongues in their regular worship. In 1830 a reputedly dying woman in Scotland was reported to have spoken in unknown tongues and to have instantly recovered her health. The news fired the interest of a group of devout Christians gathered round Edward Irving, a celebrated Presbyterian preacher, who soon after established his own Catholic and Apostolic Church, in which glossolalia became a dominant feature. For the Irvingites, tongues were a distinct sign of the nearness of the coming of Christ, and they devoted themselves to warning the established Churches of the need to accept Irvingite teaching and organization before it was too late. Tongues had also broken out spontaneously in a church in southern Germany, and this congregation joined the Catholic and Apostolic Church, which enjoyed rapid growth, in particular in the United States and Britain. Tongues continued as part of its devotional practice until, disappointed in the falsification of the prophecies on which the Church was based, the movement declined in the 20th century.

TRANCES

Quite ordinary words are often used by occultists and magicians in a sense different from their everyday meaning. In the case of the word trance, however, there is no such semantic divergence and a majority of occultists would have no quarrel with the dictionary definition: 'state suggesting that the soul has passed out of the body; ecstasy, rapture, extreme exaltation'.

It is the combination of a grossly abnormal state of mind with the continuation of conventional behaviour patterns – and even comprehensible speech – that probably gave rise to the idea that the soul had temporarily left the body. Once this theory had been accepted, it was an easy step to the concept that the soulless body could be used by non-human entities, and therefore that the entranced person could become, quite literally, a mouthpiece of the gods.

In many societies the use of such a divine mouthpiece became an established part of the prevailing religious culture; in ancient Greece the Delphic Oracle was consulted not only by citizens of the Greek city-states but by representatives of colonies as far away as Spain, and wherever Hellenic culture was dominant the Delphic Oracle was held in veneration. In pre-Communist Tibet, not only did every major monastery have an individual oracle, but the Dalai Lama and

his government had their own state oracle.

Such official oracles did not, of course, have their trance states induced by anything so crude as a blow on the head; in Tibet the oracles almost all appeared to have been epileptics, looked upon as people in whom trance could be particularly easily induced, but rhythmic drumming, dancing and (possibly but not certainly) psychedelic drugs were used to achieve the desired disassociation of consciousness. At Delphi, the oracle inhaled the smoke of burning laurel leaves. This would have contained both a small amount of hydrocyanic acid and a certain amount of complex alkaloids, and it is probable that inhaled in sufficient quantity it produced a state of cerebral intoxication highly conducive to trance and other abnormal mental states. In any case, however, it seems likely that as in Tibet, oracles were chosen for their inherent ability to achieve a voluntary disassociation of consciousness.

There is no doubt that trance is most easily attained by the use of such drugs as LSD and *anhalonium* (mescaline), but while the states of consciousness attained in this way seem fundamentally identical with the

Left The Diolas of Senegal celebrate major festivals with several days of dancing which culminates in a state of collective trance Below The solitary trance of a yogi; the attainment of samadhi demands extraordinary discipline in order to achieve the desired total control over all mental and physical faculties

René Burri/Magnum

Magnum

trances of the mystic and the magician, their effects do not seem to be either as permanent or as profound as those produced by more physically and emotionally demanding techniques, such as those of the *Spiritual Exercises* of St Ignatius Loyola or the frenzied dancing of Haitian Voodoo. In the trance experienced by participants in Voodoo rites the entranced worshipper is not just the mouthpiece of the god but actually becomes the god.

The White Darkness

Voodoo is a synthetic religion, a blend of elements derived from West African religious cults, popular Catholicism and the debased ceremonial magic of the printed grimoires (textbooks of ritual magic) of 18th century France. Its central religious rite is the invocation of the *loa* (gods) by drums, dance and sacrifice, and these invocations normally end in the entrancement and possession ('mounting') of one or more of the participants in the ceremony by the particular loa invoked – each loa has its own particular dance pattern and drum rhythm. Sometimes, however, an unwanted loa makes a spontaneous appearance but in this case it is made clear to it that it is not welcome and the possessed worshipper comes out of his trance fairly quickly.

In the last analysis, all trance, whether mediumistic, drug-induced or the result of mystical, magical or Voodoo techniques, is identical; that is to say, a part of consciousness is split off or disassociated from the whole. Nevertheless, most of those who have experienced trance have been unable to communicate to others even a faint idea of the nature of the subjective experience they have undergone. Fortunately, the late Maya Deren, who was herself frequently possessed by the goddess Erzulie (the Haitian Venus), has left us a clear description of the processes of Voodoo trance, and when due allowance has been made for the cultural variations between Haiti and, say, Tibet, her account throws a great deal of light on the nature of trance in general.

Maya Deren, a maker of avant-garde films with a particular interest in choreography, first visited Haiti in 1947 with the object of filming Haitian dance forms. She began to attend Voodoo rituals, soon realized that the dance could not be separated from the mythology, the rapture from the religion, joined the dance and was entranced and 'mounted' by the loa Erzulie. She described her experience of entrancement as being 'the white darkness' – a contradiction in terms that is reminiscent of the paradoxes used by mystics of all ages in an attempt to communicate the incommunicable. She wrote: 'Resting . . . I felt a strange numbness . . . I say numbness, but that is inaccurate . . . To be precise I must call it a white darkness, its whiteness a glory and its darkness terror. It is the terror which has the greater force . . . The white darkness starts to shoot up . . . My skull is a drum . . . This sound will drown me . . . The white darkness moves up the veins of my leg like a swift tide rising, rising; is a great force which I cannot sustain or contain, which, surely, will burst my skin. It is too much, too bright, too white for me; this is its darkness. "Mercy!" I scream within

me. I hear it echoed by the voices, shrill and unearthly: "Erzulie". The bright darkness floods through my body, reaches my head, engulfs me. I am sucked down and exploded upward at once. That is all.'

The Magical Method

Western magicians have a number of ways of inducing trance, and all of them show some similarity with the techniques of Voodoo, although they do not usually involve the complete cessation of normal consciousness: in some little corner of his mind the magician retains his individuality and can observe the actions performed by the disassociated aspects of his own consciousness.

One of these methods involves the per-

formance of a mystery play (Aleister Crowley particularly recommended the *Bacchae* of Euripides for this purpose) with the actors so strongly identifying themselves with the characters they play that they become those characters. At the Abbey of Thelema in Sicily, Crowley and his disciples performed such a magical version of Oscar Wilde's *Salome*, seemingly with considerable success. Years earlier, Crowley had stage-managed the public performance of a series of dramatic rituals incorporating music and dance, the *Rites of Eleusis*, during which the poet Victor Neuburg became entranced and, according to Crowley, literally inspired.

Other Western methods of achieving trance and possession are the processes of

invocation and evocation. Here the idea is to achieve 'one-pointedness' by surrounding the practitioners with the symbols of the force invoked, and to achieve the frenzied psychic escape – a form of trance – by 'enflaming oneself with prayer' and chanting the barbarous words of evocation. Once this suspension of everyday consciousness has been achieved, the god invoked is enabled to manifest himself in one or more of the practitioners. In a variant version of this system, sex, sometimes deviant sex, is used to induce trance.

The word trance is also used in a secondary sense by Western occultists; in this sense it is approximately equivalent to the word 'rapture', and reference is made to the 'Trance of Wonder', the 'Trance of Indifference' and even the 'Trance of Sorrow'. During such a trance, ordinary consciousness is not in any way interrupted; the occultist is able to carry on a conversation to go about his ordinary business, while at the same time undergoing the extraordinary subjective experiences associated with, for example, the Trance of Wonder. In this meaning of the word, every authentic occult operation partakes of the character of trance. Aleister Crowley wrote that: 'The essence of the idea of Trance is indeed contained in that of Magick, which is pre-eminently the transcendental Science and Art. Its method is, in one chief sense, Love, the very key of Trance; and, in another, the passing beyond normal conditions . . . Nor need any man fear to state boldly that every Magical Operation soever is only complete when it is characterised (in one sense or another) by the occurrence of Trance. It was ill done to restrict the use of the word to the supersession of dualistic human consciousness by the impersonal and monistic state of Samadhi . . . it is the first necessity as it is the last attainment of Trance to abolish every form and every order of dividuality.'

When in deep trance and the mouthpiece of a 'guide' or other supposedly discaranate communicator, the mental state of the medium seems remarkably similar to that of a Voodoo devotee who has been mounted by one of the loa. He, or she, appears to be the vehicle of a distinct personality.

One of the main differences between Spiritualistic and Voodoo possession is that the latter almost always follows a highly conventional pattern, the loa using the entranced worshipper's body in the way that it is expected to use it.

The same is true of the trances experienced by devotees of Yoga. While it may seem that there is an enormous gulf between the silent entrancement of a yogi experiencing Samadhi and the behaviour of the medium possessed by her spirit guide, there is considerable evidence to show that on a physiological and psychological level they are undergoing the same experience.

Finally, we come back to our dictionary definition of trance – and we find it not so much a definition as a description. For today we are only a very little nearer to comprehending the real nature of trance (and its first cousin, hypnotic trance) than were our ancestors. It is true that there are a multitude of psychological explanations – Freudian, Jungian, Behaviourist – of the phenomenon, but the very fact that so many conflicting hypotheses can be defended so vigorously by men of real intellectual integrity is an indication that we are still far from understanding what trance really is.

Opposite *In trance, 'a part of the consciousness is split off and disassociated from the whole': the condition has long been valued because it puts man in touch with planes of experience beyond his normal grasp. Techniques of trance include rhythmic drumming and chanting, as in the Jamaican Pocomania cult* (above), *or the dangerous use of drugs* (below)

Above *Illustration from the* Projection of the Astral Body *by Sylvan Muldoon and H. C. Carrington (Rider, 1929), showing the astral body leaving the physical body: the experience can be deliberately induced, though the connecting 'cord', on which Muldoon placed great emphasis, does not appear in many people's descriptions of their experiences*

OUT-OF-THE-BODY EXPERIENCES

An out-of-the-body experience is one in which the subject appears to view the external world from some position other than that of his physical body. The following is an example:

. . . It was summer time, the day bright and sunny and I wore a dress and blazer. I was walking along Brentwood High Street in Essex and there were people shopping and walking near me. As far as I can remember I was thinking of nothing in particular when suddenly I was about 15 ft. above myself and I watched myself walking towards a cinema called the Palace which was a short distance ahead of me, I noticed the people walking round me. I supposed I watched myself walk about 30 or 40 steps and then I was back 'inside' myself again. I felt in no way different and just went on walking along the High St.

The whole incident must only have taken a few seconds . . .

Experiences of this kind seem to be relatively common.

Out-of-the-body experiences may be of two kinds, firstly, 'parasomatic', in which the subject appears to be located in a duplicate body more or less resembling his physical body, and secondly, 'asomatic', in which the subject, at his new point of view, does not appear to be associated with a body at all – in other words, he feels he is just a disembodied consciousness or 'a pin-point of presence', as one subject puts it. On the other hand, the subject may describe himself as 'looking at himself from nothing'.

The circumstances under which out-of-the-body experiences may occur are extremely various. Some subjects, such as the one first quoted, may be walking at the time of the experience, or carrying out such everyday activities as gardening or housework.

Many of the cases collected occurred when the subject was involved in an accident or suffering from physical illness of some kind, but some seem to have occurred when the subject was simply in an 'everyday' frame of mind, or even feeling particularly happy or relaxed.

If the subject is engaged in some kind of physical activity at the time of his experience his body may continue to function in an apparently normal way while he appears merely to observe it from outside. In one case reported to the Institute, a dentist extracted a tooth while 'standing some three feet behind myself and to the left'. Other subjects describe watching themselves from above as they drove cars or motorcycles, or hearing their own singing performances or lecture from the back of the hall.

More Real than Reality

Cases such as this clearly raise the question: how can someone continue functioning in an apparently normal way while his 'consciousness' is concerned only in watching his movements from an external point? In some cases the subject may be performing an action which is so habitual that it is completely 'automatic' anyway, but in others some degree of conscious skill appears involved. Skill does not seem to be impaired while the subject 'watches' himself – though one woman who was 'settled firmly on the roof' of the car watched herself 'making every sort of fool of herself' in a driving test.

The emotions felt by the subject during an out-of-the-body experience are nearly always positive ones. Subjects appear to feel completely normal or natural in the out-of-the-body state and may comment on how 'solid' or 'real' they felt, despite the fact that they were apparently disembodied. Some even describing the out-of-the-body state as feeling more real than the normal state.

Leaving the Body At Will

Although many out-of-the-body experiences occur involuntarily and, more often than not, only once in a lifetime, there are people who claim to be able to induce the out-of-the-body state more or less at will. Three methods of inducing or encouraging these states are predominant among those mentioned by people who have made a practice of doing so. These are firstly, physical relaxation exercises, secondly, various kinds of concentration and meditation, and thirdly, the cultivation of lucid dreams, in which the subject is certainly quite conscious that he is dreaming.

Once out of his body the subject may attempt various kinds of experiment. For example, he may move about or 'travel' to a distant place to 'see' what is going on there. Sometimes he appears to obtain information in this way that he could not have obtained in the normal state.

Out-of-the-body experiences raise important questions for philosophers and psychologists. When someone perceives his surroundings in an apparently normal way but from a position which is different from that of his physical body, what part do his visual and other sense organs play in producing the experience? Indeed what part do his sense organs play in his normal mode of perception if he can apparently do without them in the out-of-the-body state? We must remember that in about one third of the cases the subject's physical body is unconscious at the time of the experience, so that his eyes are shut throughout, and cannot therefore be helping him to construct a picture of the world as it would look from the new point of view. Nevertheless, some subjects have described what was going on around them while unconscious, and those present have subsequently confirmed their accounts.

The experience of getting out of one's body has naturally interested occultists: 'The World', a Tarot card often interpreted as a symbol of release from the everyday physical plane and entry into the astral: Italian, early 19th century

IL MONDO

ASTRAL BODY

For centuries it has been a common idea that man is made of two components – a soul or spirit which comes from God, and a material body of flesh and blood. But some philosophers and occult theorists have suggested that each man has a third component, an astral body, meaning literally 'starry body' and sometimes they may be referred to as 'the body of light'.

This astral body is an exact copy of the flesh and blood body but is made of a finer material and has a shining and luminous appearance. It is supposed to be capable of separating itself from the physical body and travelling about, passing through walls, ceilings and other solid obstructions. It is also said to survive death, when it leaves the physical body. It exists in what is called the astral plane, which includes the normal everyday world but extends beyond it.

Among the magicians of the West Indies the projection of the astral body is achieved by singing special charm songs. They speak of this accomplishment as 'hagging', and those of either sex who are feared as possessors of this power are 'hags'.

The most experienced of modern astral travellers, the American author Sylvan Muldoon, attaches importance first to the building into the subconscious of a strong desire to be conscious in the astral body, then to the practice of concentrating on one's own image in a mirror. Next, attention is to be centred on the rhythm of the heart-beats, and the attempt made to be conscious of the heart beating at any point in the body. Then by repeated mental suggestion the heart should be slowed down. Needless to say, no one with heart weakness or irregularity should use this method.

Apparitions

The evidence points to the possibility that some apparitions, or immaterial appearances of persons living or dead, are due to the presence of an astral body. There is the phenomenon of an observed apparition where more than one person, differently situated, sees the figure from an angle appropriate to his position. An example is the case of Lady B. and her daughter, who in about 1892 claimed they had seen the ghostly figure of a woman looking at herself in a mirror in their bedroom. Hornell Hart writes of the occurrence in *The Enigma of Survival*. 'Lady B. saw the face in quarter profile, the head intercepting its own reflection in the mirror. Miss B. saw the back of the figure with its long dark hair; the face was not directly visible to her, but she saw it clearly reflected in the mirror.' The record

The astral body departing after death, as seen in a clairvoyant vision. It is also said to be capable of leaving the physical body during life, and travelling independently through walls and ceilings. This illustration is from The Projection of the Astral Body *by S. Muldoon and H. C. Carrington (Rider, 1929)*

shows that the aspects seen by the two ladies were just as if a physical person had stood there.

The notion of the astral body has a continuous history in the West from classical times on. Dante's *Purgatorio* (canto 25), written in the 14th century, says that after death the soul 'around it beams its own creative power, like to its living form in shape and size . . . the circumambient air adopts the shape the soul imposes on it'. In the 16th century, Agrippa von Nettesheim seems to be referring to astral travel when he talks of 'vacation of the body, when the spirit is enabled to transcend its bounds, and as a light escaped from a lantern to spread over space'.

The Etheric Double

The terms 'astral body' and 'double' are used to cover several different types of phenomena. One of them is what is called the 'etheric double', identical with the Egyptian *Ka*, the vital force which gave the body life and which was represented in art as an exact replica of the physical body. The Hindus called it the *linga sharira* or 'vital form' which was, so to speak, the body's 'wiring system'.

REINCARNATION

Belief in reincarnation is very old, and is found in widely scattered primitive and preliterate communities. Its postulates are basic to Hinduism and most schools of Buddhism. Roman writers said it was prevalent among the Gauls and Druids. Several Greek schools of thought, notably the Orphics and Pythagoreans, subscribed to it, and Plato mentions it in the concluding part of his *Republic*. In later times the doctrine was adopted by the Essenes, Pharisees, Karaites and other Jewish and semi-Jewish religious groups. The Neoplatonists and Gnostics also held the theory, and it formed part of the cabalistic theology of medieval Jewry.

St Jerome (340–420) said that reincarnation in a special sense was taught among the early Christians and was given an esoteric interpretation that was communicated to a select few. Origen (186–253) thought that only in the light of reincarnation could certain scriptural passages be explained. But it was condemned by the Second Council of Constantinople, convened by the Emperor Justinian in 553, and became for a time a heretical doctrine. 'If anyone assert the fabulous pre-existence of souls,' decreed the Council, 'and shall submit to the monstrous doctrine that follows from it, let him be anathema.' Some scholars nonetheless believe that they can detect traces of the teaching in the writings of St Augustine, St Gregory and even St Francis of Assisi. Among its modern exponents are Theosophists, Anthroposophists and certain Spiritualists.

The Law of Destiny

Many people feel that the theory of reincarnation is in keeping with the idea of evolution and human progress and perfectibility. If man has shown a progressive advance from the lower animal forms to his present state of intellectual and moral development, it is clear that further progress is part of the plan for his future. The physical universe provides the environment for this advance to perfection, and it is here that he must work out his own destiny.

If the ultimate reasonableness of the cosmic purpose is accepted, a theory that can so logically account for the birth of congenital idiots, for those who die in childhood, and for others who have been given no chance to live out their lives, should clearly be given serious consideration.

According to reincarnationists, the still-born baby, the mongol, the child who dies in infancy, are all merely adjusting the balance sheet of their own previous lives by these temporary shifts and accommodations. Some are receiving their reward, some their punishment, for what they have done before. It will all work out equitably in the end.

In what form does the soul return to earth? Some schools of belief, particularly in Hinduism, hold that a man does not necessarily assume a human form in his next incarnation. Certain Hindu sects teach that the soul may be reborn as a plant, or an animal.

Someone who has lived a life of vice or crime may be re-embodied as a cactus, a poison ivy, a lizard or a toad. According to the early Hindu law-giver Manu, the slayer of a Brahmin enters the womb of a sow or she-ass; a drunkard will be reborn as a bird that lives on dung; and other sinners and reprobates will become hyenas, rodents, insects and creatures of low and repulsive estate. Those who have done well will return to earth as men and women once more.

Plant and animal transmigrations are not as a rule accepted by Western reincarnationists, who believe that once a soul has reached the human stage in its evolution it never returns to animal form. Human beings can only be reborn as men and women, and have the status and grade commensurate with their deserts, earned in their previous lives. On this basis it is possible to be born a prince, a blind man or a leper.

The number of chances each person has is said to range from three (once as a man, once as a woman, and once in the sex in which the soul fared better) to many thousands, some of which started at the beginning of Creation and may continue to the end of time. But it is generally believed that the cycle of birth-death-rebirth can be terminated by one or more of the various disciplines prescribed in the religious texts. Among them are renunciation, asceticism, good works, prayer, ritual and faith.

Modern exponents of the doctrine of the

transmigration of souls claim to remember their past lives, some going back to Rome, Greece, ancient Egypt or prehistory. The Theosophist Annie Besant believed that she had lived as the female Neoplatonist martyr Hypatia (d. 415 AD), and as the philosopher and martyr Giordano Bruno (d. 1600). Her colleague Colonel Olcott had been a prince in Atlantis, and then Odysseus, as well as other eminent people.

There is at present at least one researcher doing practical work on the subject of reincarnation. He is Professor Hemendra Banerjee, director of the Department of Parapsychology in Rajasthan University, India, who has devoted over 12 years to the subject. He has investigated the claims made on behalf of rebirth, and tested girls and boys as they led him or members of his team to former homes where they recognized relatives and identified their belongings.

In Europe practical work has been conducted in what is called age-regression which, according to some reincarnationists, has provided further reinforcement of their claims. Experiments involve putting a subject under hypnosis and making him go back, by suggestion, to his childhood and even his infancy, to re-live his early years. In certain cases this regression can ostensibly be carried back into what is claimed to have been a previous existence. Early in this century a French investigator, Colonel Eugène Rochas (d. 1914), allegedly took hypnotized subjects back to their past lives.

Lamas, the priests of Tibet, were regarded by Tibetans as being reincarnations of saintly predecessors: 17th century painting

G. Tomsich/Spectrum

PSYCHIC RESEARCH

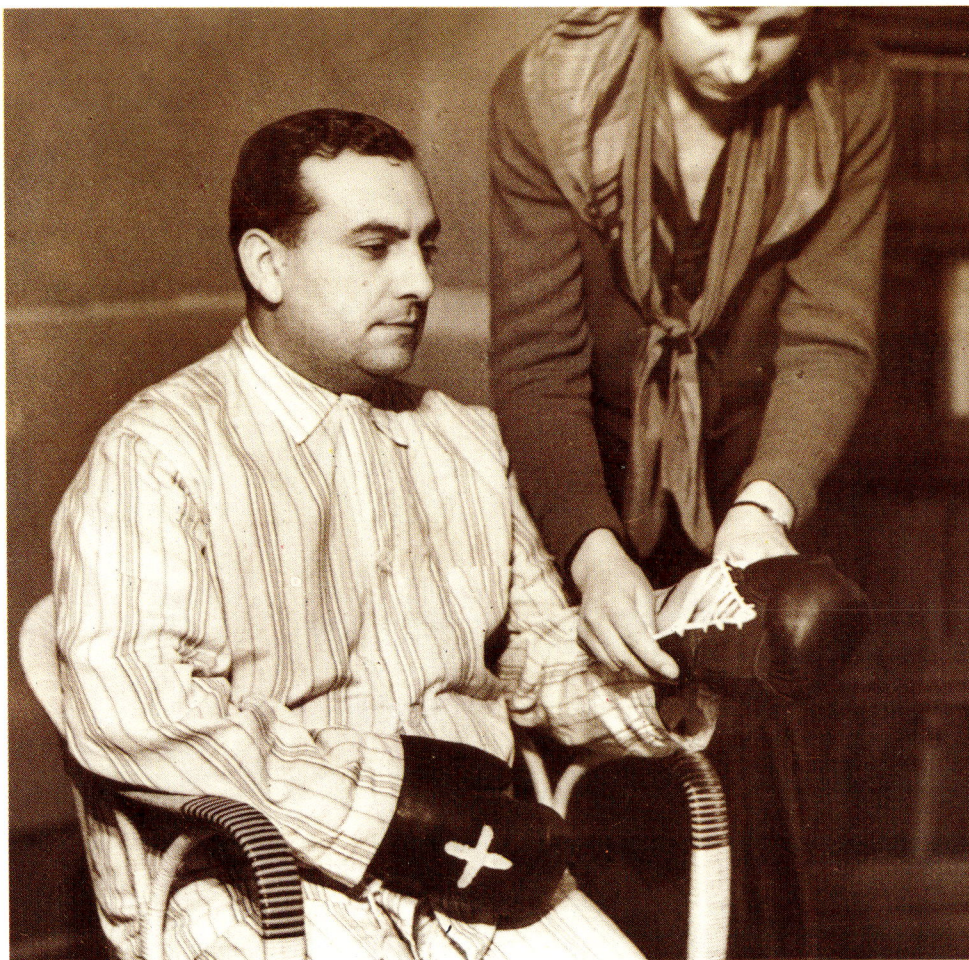

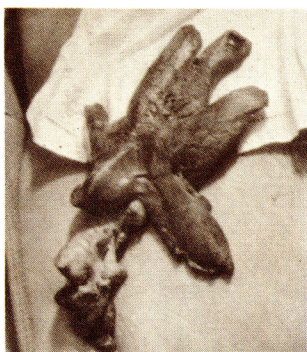

Top *A flashlight photograph taken during a seance reveals a dark mass of ectoplasm behind the test tubes. After analysis by Massachusetts Institute of Technology and a medical school, its composition was reported as being 'sodium, potassium, water, chlorine, albumen, epithelial cells and fresh red blood corpuscles'* Above *Before a seance Pasquale Erto, an Italian medium, is fitted with boxing gloves as a control* Left *Ectoplasmic 'hand' produced during a seance by Mrs Margery Crandon, an American medium active in the 1920s*

If you ask the average citizen what psychical research is about, he is likely to say that it is 'about the supernatural' or 'about the occult'. Pressed for a more precise answer he will perhaps tell you that it is 'about ghosts' or 'about mediums'.

None of these descriptions is at all complete or accurate. It is true that many of the phenomena which the psychical researcher studies have been attributed in the past to the agency of supernatural beings, gods or devils; but whatever his personal religious beliefs, as a psychical researcher he is concerned, like any other scientist, only with the natural order of things. Nor must he be confused with the occultist. They have a common subject-matter in those unexplained happenings which are nowadays called 'parapsychological', or more briefly 'psi'. But they approach this common ground with different aims and by different methods. The occultist is a kind of intellectual anarchist, a rebel against the accepted order: he is fascinated by whatever seems to conflict with that order; he would like, if he could, to undermine the whole arrogant structure of modern science.

The aims of the psychical researcher are less ambitious. He too is attracted by the unexplained, but only because he believes that it can and should be explained. His long-term objective is not to glorify the 'occult' but to abolish it by fitting it into its place in a coherent world picture. Far from wishing to destroy the edifice of science, his highest hope is to construct a modest annexe which will serve, at least provisionally, to house his new facts with the minimum of disturbance to the original plan of the building. If he explores, as he often must, the waste lands of superstition, he does so not as a fugitive from scientific law but in the hope of reclaiming them for science.

In this pioneering task of reclamation the initiative came from the group of Cambridge scholars, philosophers and scientists who in 1882 founded the Society for Psychical Research. Its aim, they said, 'will be to approach these various problems without prejudice or prepossession of any kind, and in the same spirit of unimpassioned and exact inquiry which has enabled science to solve so many problems, once not less obscure nor less hotly debated'. To this aim the Society has remained faithful: it holds no collective views and engages in no propaganda, but promotes research through discussion, publication and the resources of its unique library.

How far, then, has the work of reclamation got? To this question experienced researchers would still give widely differing answers. One thing, however, would be generally agreed: the evidence for the reality of certain phenomena – notably telepathy and clairvoyance, which are now very often grouped together under the heading 'extrasensory perception' (ESP) – has been greatly strengthened by the development of quantitative tests which enable us to measure the exact degree by which the results obtained exceed the level to be expected on the basis of pure chance. At the same time many of the traditional 'occult' phenomena have been subjected to a continuing process of re-interpretation in the light of modern

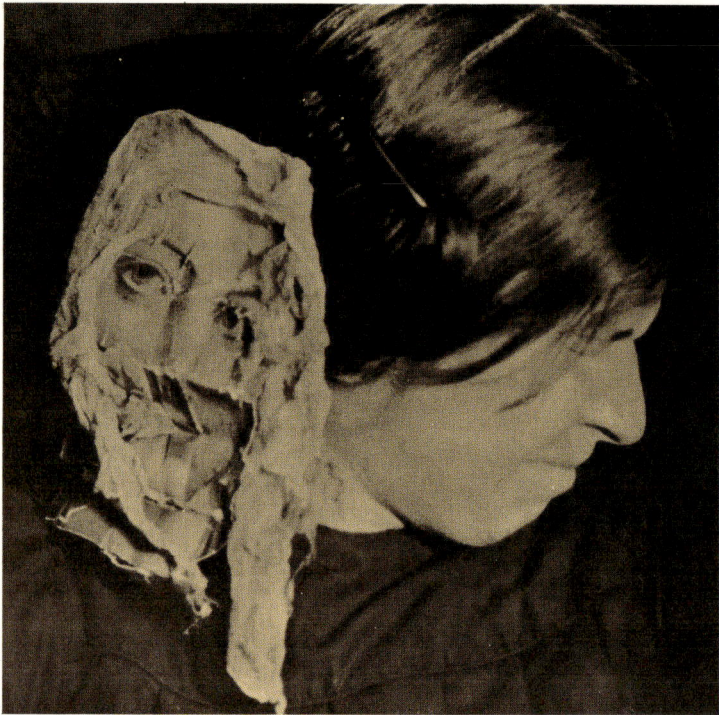

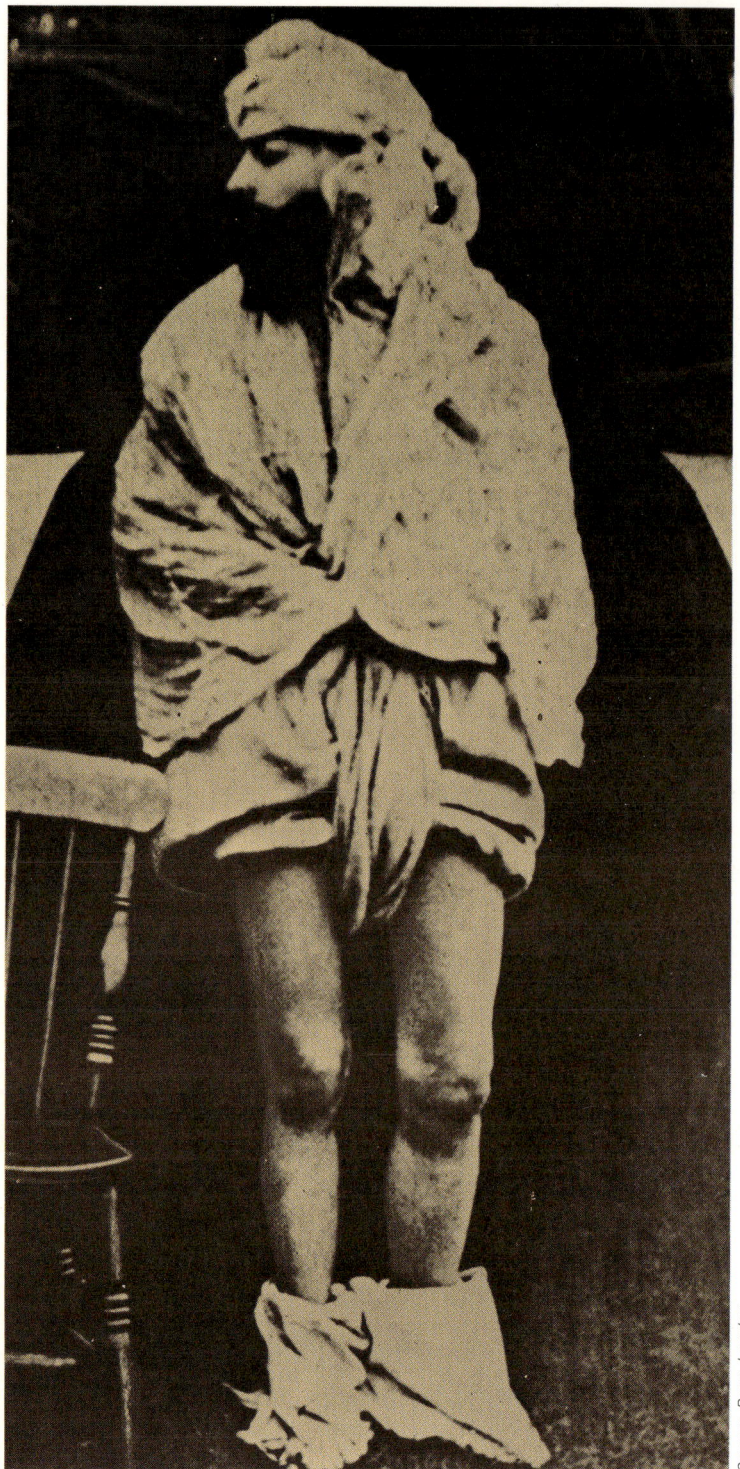

psychology. We may take as examples the two topics which perhaps still bulk largest in the popular view of psychical research, 'ghosts' and 'mediumship'.

Apparitions Observed

'Ghost' is a question-begging term which the psychical researcher prefers to avoid; he speaks instead of 'apparitions' or 'phantasms'. He can be said to 'believe in ghosts' in the sense of believing that phantasms, whether of the dead or of the living, are not infrequently seen by sane persons in waking life, just as they are seen by all of us in dreams. But he does not assume that the phantasm is physically present; in the ordinary case he regards it, for good reasons, as a self-induced hallucination. The cases which interest him are the exceptional ones which on various grounds appear not to be purely self-induced. These include 'crisis-apparitions', where the vision coincides with the death or endangerment of the person whose figure is seen; 'collective apparitions', where the same figure is seen simultaneously at the same point in space by two or more observers; and lastly, 'haunts', where the same figure is seen in or near the same place by a succession of *independent* witnesses (the requirement of independence is vital). The first of these types is well attested; it is usually, and no doubt rightly, explained as the externalization of an unconsciously received telepathic impression. Collective cases (which are rather rare) have also been explained by assuming telepathic infection.

'Haunting' over a long period presents much more difficult problems, but water-tight examples are hard to come by.

'Mediumship' is another question-begging term to which modern psychology has given a new meaning. The spiritualists who coined the word saw the medium as a channel of communication between the living and the dead; we see him as a member of a much wiser class, a person capable of falling more or less at will into a state of temporary dissociation in which secondary personalities can develop. Such people have always existed, and have generally been credited with super-normal powers; the nature of the 'voices' has depended on the current religious belief.

A growing emphasis on statistical methods and laboratory techniques in psychical re-

Camera Press London

'Physical' mediums have been responsible for a variety of phenomena, including levitation and materializations of spirit bodies, though many practitioners have proved to be charlatans Above Canon Pierce Higgins of Southwark Cathedral works with a medium to exorcise a spirit from an old house in Nottingham Right Accordion belonging to D. D. Home, which floated in the air at one of his seances, playing exquisite music Far left (above) On close examination, 'ectoplasm' often turns out to be cheese cloth: a 'spirit face' produced by Eva C, a famous medium at the turn of the century. The death mask of Daniel Dunglas Home (below), the Victorian physical medium who was never proved to be an imposter Left 'Georgie', a medium's accomplice of the 1890s who had the misfortune of being caught with his ectoplasm trousers down

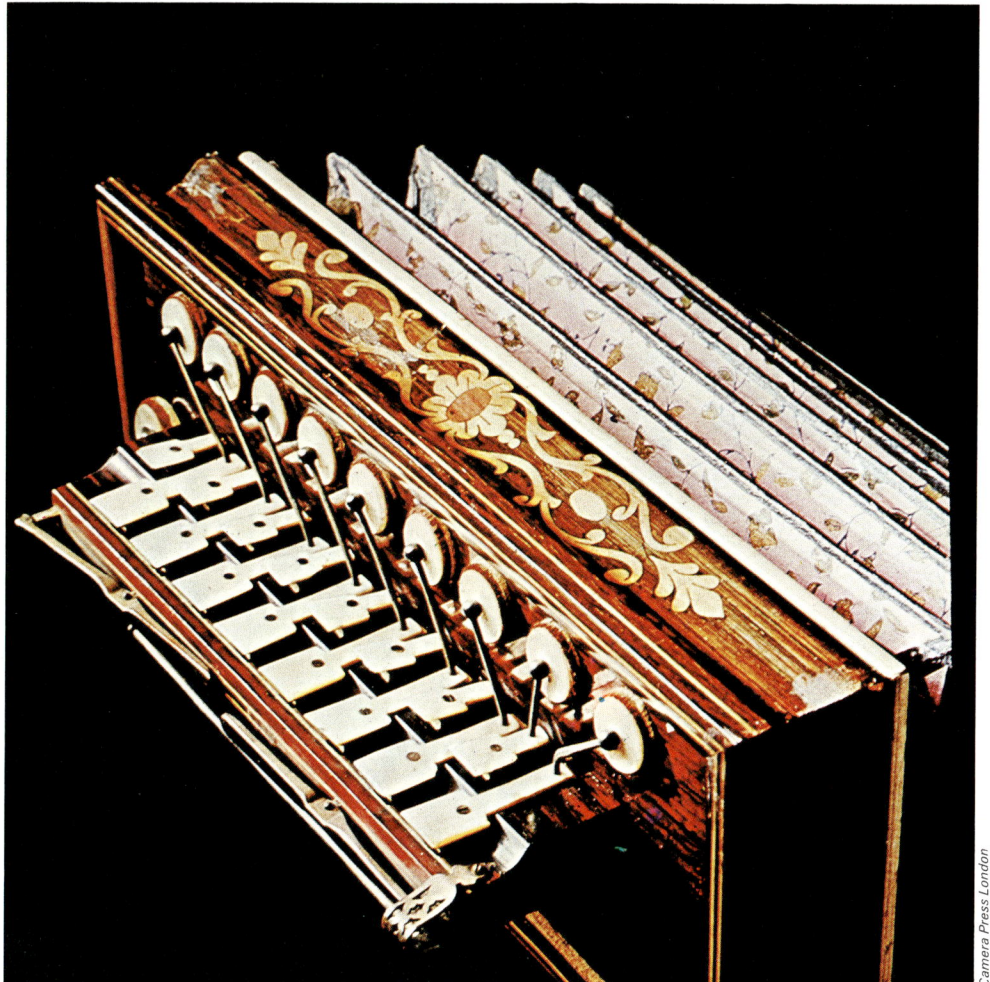

Camera Press London

search between the wars may be regarded as a reaction to the fact that academic psychology had become steadily more behaviouristic and more 'scientific', and correspondingly more hostile to the kind of psychical research which had been predominant during the first quarter of the century. Orthodox psychologists showed themselves if anything less tolerant of psychical researchers than scientists from other fields; no doubt they found it hard enough to win recognition of the scientific status of their own subject, without its being joined to so dubious a yoke-fellow.

In the last two decades the centre of activity in psychical research has shifted away from Great Britain and Europe to the United States of America. By far the greatest percentage of practical work now being done is carried out in America, and two new and important parapsychological organizations have been established there, the Parapsychology Foundation of New York (1951) and the Foundation for Research on the Nature of Man (1964), successor to the Duke University laboratories. Recently a Division of Parapsychology has been set up at the University of Virginia, and other institutions in the United States have provided facilities for research.

The hope that they may reveal some short cut to repeatable significant scoring in ESP and PK tests has helped to produce a renewed interest in spontaneous cases – apparitions, poltergeists and 'out-of-the-body' experiences – and in mediumistic and related phenomena.

Of particular note here have been Dr Louisa Rhine's analyses of spontaneous cases in the files at Duke University, Miss Celia Green's studies of out-of-the-body experiences, and Professor I. Stevenson's unique *Twenty Cases Suggestive of Reincarnation* (*Proceedings* of the American S.P.R. 1966).

Although it would not be true to say that the occurrence of ESP and of other paranormal phenomena is now widely accepted by scientists and by the general public, there is no doubt that general attitudes to the subject are much more tolerant than they once were. Should the elusive 'repeatable experiment' be hit upon within the next decade or so, psychical research might well win rapid and widespread recognition by scientists and others, and take a place as a

legitimate part of orthodox psychology. If, on the other hand, experimental findings continue indefinitely in their present somewhat unsatisfactory state, psychical research will not disappear, but it may well pass more and more into the hands of cranks as its present relatively respectable supporters drop away.

Opposite In all societies and from the earliest times men have feared the return of the dead. The spirits of the ancestors might be reverenced in Japan, but hostile ghosts were still feared: A lean spectre peers over a victim's shoulder Below Photographs of a spirit named Silver Belle, allegedly materializing at a seance held in the United States

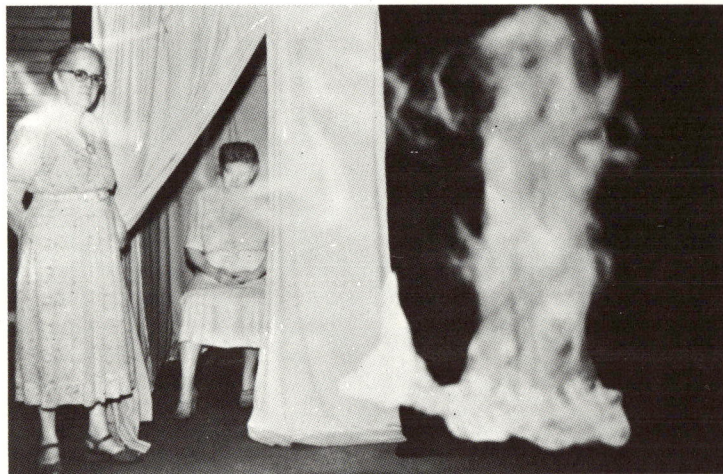

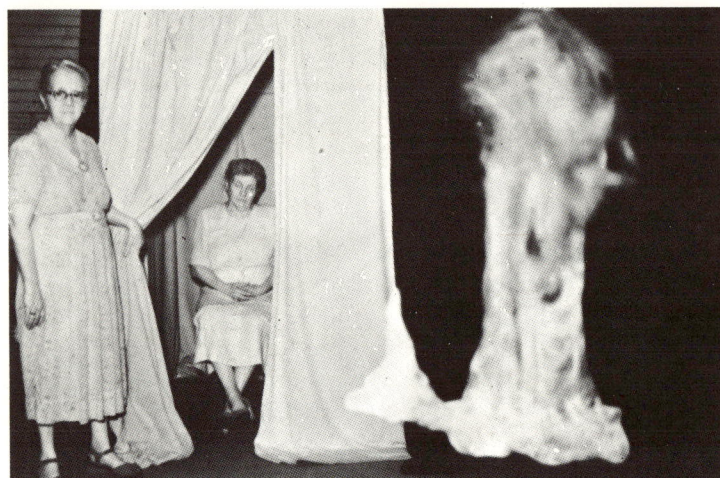

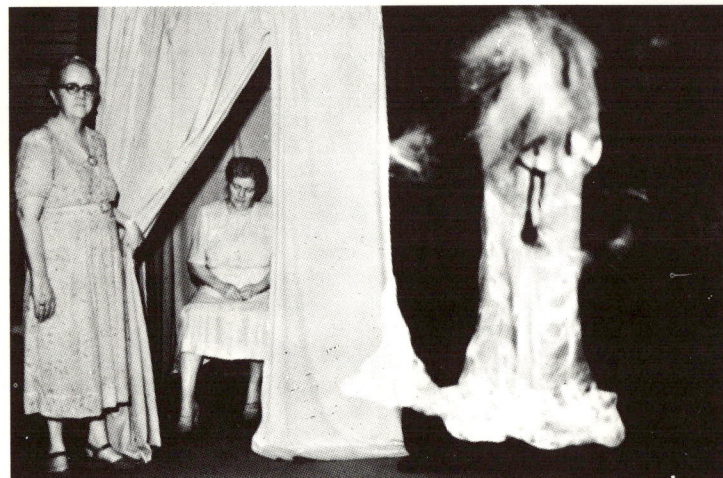

Psychic News

漢
準
源氏
源頼光
薄雲

一勇齋國芳画

79

Ghosts

UNIVERSAL HUMAN NEED

Belief in ghosts means to many people an unequivocal acceptance of the souls of the dead in sheets and chains, squeaking and gibbering in Gothic ruins. This caricature has grown from second-rate horror stories, films and comic strips, and it remains current in spite of the impressive number of people who go on seeing much less melodramatic spectres.

For instance, a British family were rehoused by their local authority in 1966 because of the effect on their health of strange happenings in their two-year-old council house. The father saw a man's shadow on the stairs where no man was standing; the daughter saw weird lights moving in her room. Police, clergymen and others investigated and found nothing, but no one seemed to scoff; the council produced another house, the priest exorcized the first one, and the *Guardian* reported it all without any of the contempt that newspapers once reserved for such stories.

It may be that belief in ghosts grows out of, and is a response to, some basic and universal human need. The need, of course, is for some assurance of survival after death. In history and prehistory, ghosts were an integral part of religious belief. Religion carried the promise of immortality, which meant that the spirits of the dead had to be taken into consideration.

The Ancestral Spirits

Naturally the ghosts of a community's forebears would be the most prevalent. So ancestor worship can be said to be one of the first, perhaps the first, form of religious

awareness that developed in man. Even the cave dwellers of the early Stone Age buried their dead with some ceremony, which suggests belief in an afterlife and also some kind of worship of the dead.

Where ancestors are worshipped, they have taken on the role of gods, gaining supernatural power as they enter the supernatural world. Often they are only minor gods, perhaps divine only to their own families. But equally often the forebears can be the major gods of the community. They then become the principal overseers of the tribe's ethical and spiritual welfare.

The ancestors are viewed as protectors, interposing their power between the living and various supernatural evils. More important is the negative view that if the goodwill of the ghosts is not maintained – if the offerings, praises and so on slacken off – the ghosts punish such laxity with calamities like disease, crop failure, accidents and death. If such disasters occur a whole system of appeasement, or *propitiation*, is sparked off and goes into action.

The need to propitiate ghosts is just as important in those primitive societies which do not directly worship their forebears. It is as if the fact of death makes the spirit automatically hostile to the living, whatever its personality while alive. Sometimes the object is not appeasement so much as warding

Opposite John Dee employed the services of a man named Edward Kelley as his 'scryer', or crystal-gazer, because he did not possess the necessary talents himself. Kelley would sit before the crystal and describe whatever spirits he saw and what they said to him. With a friend named Waring, Kelley was alleged to have dug up a corpse in a churchyard at Walton Le Dale in Lancashire, and by magic incantations forced it to speak: imaginative picture of the scene, from The Astrologer of the 19th Century *Right* The death of the Duke of Buckingham was foretold by an armour-clad apparition of his father, which appeared several times to one of the Duke's servants. Ghosts are often harbingers of death

off the spirit: magic spells are set up in a house after a death in the family, to keep the ghost at a distance; or the body is buried in such a way that the ghost cannot find its way back. Ghosts are often believed to have a poor sense of direction: in fairly recent times the bodies of hanged criminals, executed witches and so on were buried at cross-roads to confuse the ghosts.

Doomed to Walk the Earth

The more complex primitive societies and most civilizations developed the idea of a distinct spirit world – the happy hunting ground, Elysian Fields, Valhalla and the like. They saw ghosts as yearning for these places but being somehow balked. Thus arises the concept of the wandering ghost who infests this world while craving access to the next world and his eternal rest. Ghosts of murder victims remain to harass the living, like Hamlet's father, until vengeance is done. Ghosts remain also when their bodies have been improperly buried, or not buried at all, as with Odysseus's friend Elpenor. This idea remains strong today: Britain's famous ghost hunter, Harry Price, felt in the 1930s that the main 'haunt' of Borley Rectory would depart once Christian burial had been given to some old bones he found under the Rectory.

The association of ghosts with improper burial reveals another long-lived assumption: that there is a mystical connection after death between the corpse and the spirit. Many of the propitiations aimed at ghosts by primitives are in fact performed upon the corpse or the grave. Offerings are placed at the graveside, and all over the world the dead have been buried with food, ornaments, amulets and weapons for the spirit to have with him after death. Of course desecration of the grave or disturbance of the bones brought instant retaliation from the ghost.

In spite of the various links between corpse and spirit, the notion of a land of the dead became of vital importance, and the corollary idea began to arise that for a ghost to be operating in this world was a clear punishment. Shades of evil-doers remained among the living because they had earned no right to eternal rest. Others, not evil in life, were trapped here if they had been murdered or inadequately buried, or if they had left something important undone. No wonder so many ghosts are supposed to be malevolent; no wonder that moans and howls and shrieks are associated with them, as they bewail to the world their inability to rest.

Many of the foregoing primitive attitudes to ghosts and the dead remain in folklore and legend. But the old beliefs about what ghosts look like, and their nature generally, have been added to a little. Primitive ghosts are often indistinguishable from devils, and so may appear as horned giants breathing fire or as unusually large and vicious animals. Such visions do indeed still figure in old wives' tales; but a great many ghosts seen by modern man apparently take remarkably human form. This tendency has been confirmed by various societies of psychical research, which try very hard to take a scientific, clear-eyed view of ghosts. They are at pains to show that most of the more reliable and straightforward accounts of apparitions describe the figures seen as quite ordinary-looking people – three-dimensional, solid and wholly human.

Apparitions of the Living

Many of these accounts are of apparitions of the living, which usually appear at some crisis in the life of the person who is seen. A well-known case illustrates the point: a young Englishwoman living in India in 1917 was startled to see her brother, a Royal Flying Corps pilot, standing in her living room one day. She thought he had come on a surprise visit; only when the brother disappeared did she realize she had seen an apparition. She later learned that it had materialized at the moment when her brother's aeroplane was being shot down over France. Apparitions of the dead (which are often of loved ones or close relatives) share this apparent realness; so do the many other apparitions that have been seen at the point of death of the person who appears.

Sometimes, indeed, the reality and solidity of the apparition is more than visual – as in the case of a bewhiskered ghost in a 19th century Bristol vicarage, who had a nasty habit of entering bedrooms and waking people up by shaking the bed. Or the affectionate 'haunt' of a British stately home, about 1885, who awoke a maiden lady sleeping in the haunted room by bestowing a ghostly kiss. But many other apparitions lack any other aspect of a physical presence

than their appearance, and so are all the more frightening. Many accounts mention that the apparition seems to 'glide' soundlessly; few apparitions have left footprints where a flesh and blood person would have done; many have seemed to float well above the ground. Odd clothing is often abnormality enough: strange figures roaming the night become all the more eerie when they are wearing authentic 18th century dress. And terror would mount if they were also seen to walk through a wall or give the appearance of being transparent.

One compiler of modern ghost stories tells of a company director driving through the British countryside at night, who saw what appeared to be an encampment of Roman soldiers in some woods. He assumed it was a film company on location, until he realized that he could see the trunks of trees through the soldiers' bodies. Nor was he the only person to have seen that ghostly camp. In another case, a tall clergyman was seen regularly to visit a London church to pray: quite unremarkable, thought the vicar of the church, until one day he accidentally bumped into the praying figure and walked right through it.

Apparitions often reveal their non-corporeal nature by suddenly disappearing for no obvious reason. They may also disappear if the living interfere with them. Ghosts may sometimes like to touch people or kiss them or shake their beds, but they seem to object when the living take the initiative. Try to grasp an apparition, to set traps for it, like hidden cameras or powder for possible footprints, and it will vanish. In fact, though there are hundreds of alleged photographs of apparitions, the creatures are notoriously camera-shy.

Some mention must be made of the ghostly occupants of 'haunted houses'. 'Haunts' are above all, recurrent, walking regularly as clockwork – the same night, the same time, over the same distance. They often take little or no notice of the living (less, anyway, than most of the apparitions which appear only once), but they, too, will promptly disappear if the perceivers try to interfere with them. Haunts generally seem less likelike than other apparitions; some authorities have described them as 'somnambulistic', even mindless. Patrolling the same area, performing the same actions, they are frequently considered to resemble a visual record which has become stuck in one groove.

The Sheeted Dead

For every lifelike apparition in psychical research files or in folktale – lifelike even when the illusion slips a little, as when the ghost floats or is transparent – there are

Opposite *A Japanese realization of the notion of a hostile otherworldly being. Some primitive peoples, like many South American jungle tribes, see all spirits as vindictive and dangerous* Right *Though ghosts are reckoned to be very difficult to photograph, there are hundreds of alleged photographs of apparitions in existence, usually conforming to accepted ideas of what a ghost should look like: 'Yolande', photographed in 1890, wears a veil and drifting shroudlike garments, giving a transparent impression*

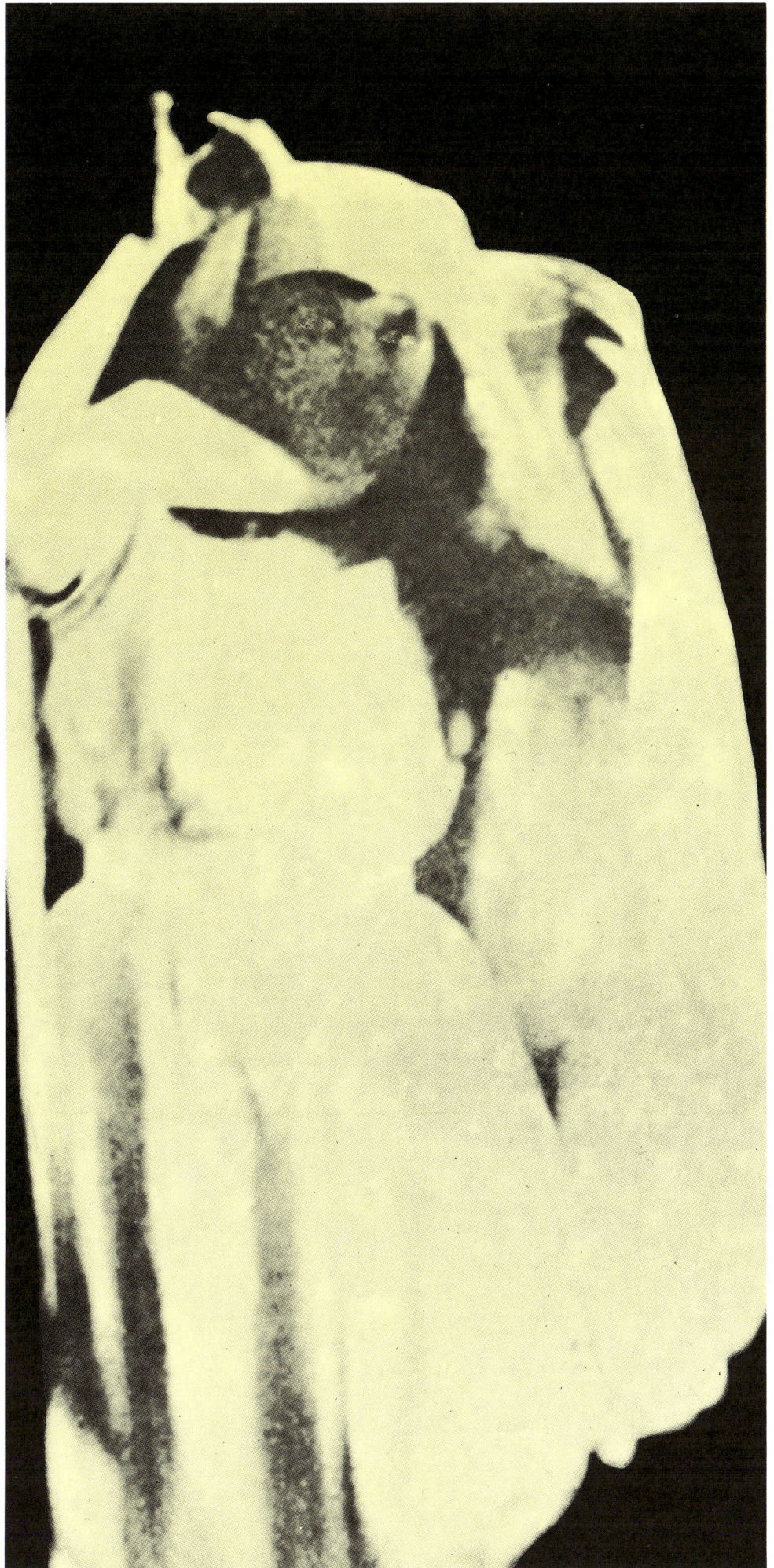

Popperfoto

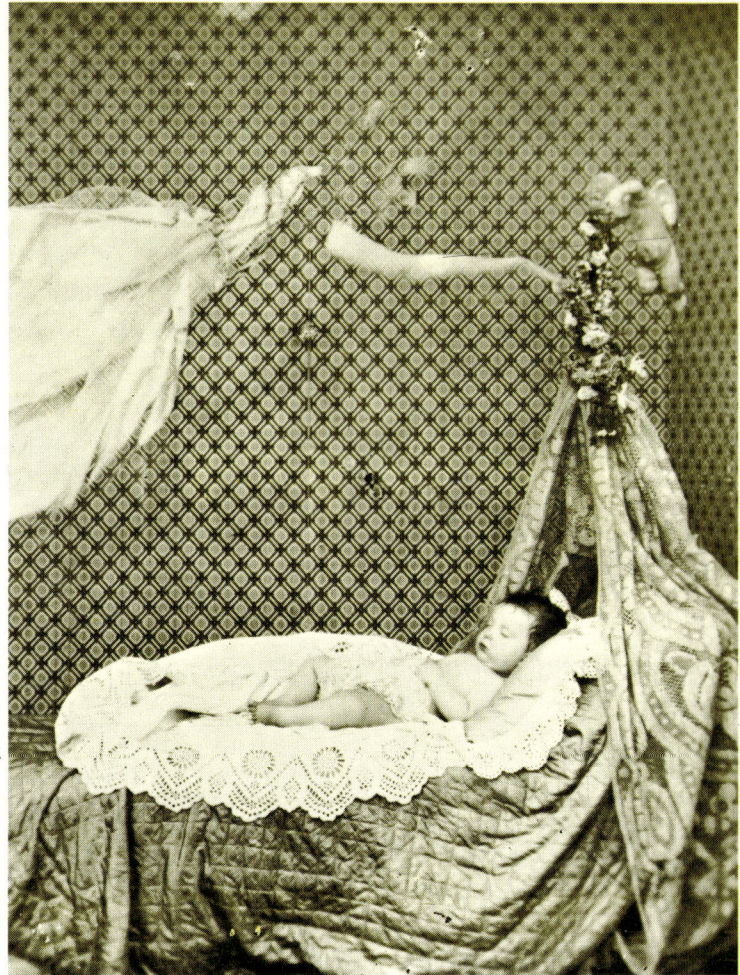

Radio Times Hulton Picture Library

Radio Times Hulton Picture Library

at least an equal number of stories of visitations that resemble rather the inventions of horror fiction. These include the female ghost in a Norfolk manor who had empty, fathomless hollows instead of eyes; the faceless woman who haunted a churchyard in Canewdon, Essex; and the bodiless head which in 1953 drove a series of residents from a house in Hamburg, in spite of a cruel housing shortage. Other outlandish horrors carry with them the signs of how they met their deaths, like the victim of drowning who was said to haunt a New Orleans bridge, and who was always seen dripping with spectral seaweed. Numerous cases exist of apparitions in the form of mouldering corpses, even skeletons; these are related to the appearances of ghosts in sheets (in other words the shroud or winding sheet from the grave), which provide further instances of the age-old connection of corpse with spirit.

Nor do all apparitions manifest themselves in human or even partly human form. Spectral animals are widely common, with Britain predictably leading the field; dogs figure most frequently in these tales. In many cases the animal ghosts are friendly, but more often they are semi-demonic, like the Manthe Dog that traditionally haunted a castle on the Isle of Man and the ghostly pack of hounds that made Cornwall's moors horrible with their baying. Horses occur in many ghost legends, often with a rider, just as often as not; they also are seen pulling phantom coaches. So it seems legends allow inanimate objects a ghostly existence.

Prominent among such objects are various means of transport. Many are phantom ships, including the famous *Flying Dutchman* and the French ship *La Belle Rosalie*. Ghost trains also reappear to rumble through the night on their old runs, whether the railway lines still exist or not. One famous legend concerns the funeral train carrying the coffin of Abraham Lincoln, which is said to roll along a stretch of track in New York State every April, and to have on board a phantom military band playing busily, though its music cannot be heard by the ears of humans alive today.

Apparitions may take much less substantial and well-defined forms than the ones considered so far. For instance, a revenant (one who comes back from the dead) created by some violent death in the past may be not a full-scale haunt but instead take the form of a mere bloodstain. A 19th century tavern keeper in Massachusetts murdered and robbed a traveller one night, but from then on was plagued by bloodstains in the victim's room which could not be removed. Several cases exist of ghostly manifestations in the form of clouds of mist; sometimes, though, the mist will form itself into a recognizable human shape, as happened in France in 1951 when a film writer believed he saw such a mist cloud take the form of the ghost of the actress Maria Montez.

An Eerie Moving Light

Ghostly lights frequently occur when other forms of apparition are absent, and often contribute to haunted-house legends, as with the flickering lights repeatedly seen round

Above *Two early montages show spirits in* (left) *hostile and* (right) *more benevolent aspects* Opposite above left *Eleonore Zugrun, a Rumanian medium, whose face was scratched by a 'spirit' which attacked her;* right *The Curé of Ars, a victim of a poltergeist phenomenon. The word 'poltergeist' was originally a German folklore term compounded from* polter *(a noise or racket) and* geist *(a spirit)* Opposite *Scribblings by a poltergeist on a wall at Borley Rectory; the questions were written by Marianne Foyster who lived there in the 1930s. At the same time pencil scrawls asking for prayers also appeared*

the notorious Borley Rectory during its several uninhabited periods. It is obvious that an empty house could easily have temporary tenants, such as tramps, exploring children or vandals, who might light their way with flickering candles or matches. Yet the legends go on, related to the notion that spirits sometimes glow in the dark. So, in America, the ghost of a North Carolina railway conductor haunts a particular trestle bridge in the form of an eerie moving light: he had been decapitated near that spot, and the light is said to be his head on an eternal and forlorn search for its body.

With phantoms formed of mist and light must be reckoned the phantoms associated with smoke. Even the smell of smoke can apparently breed ghost legends, as in the story of the 17th century American girl who was burned to death for no good reason, and whose ghostly presence is recognizable by its accompanying pungent odour of

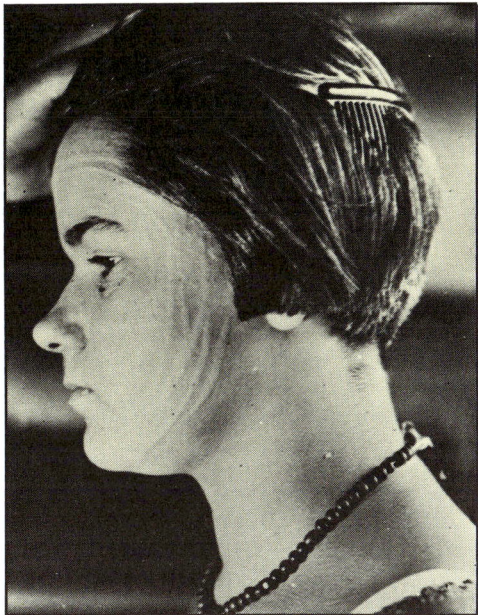

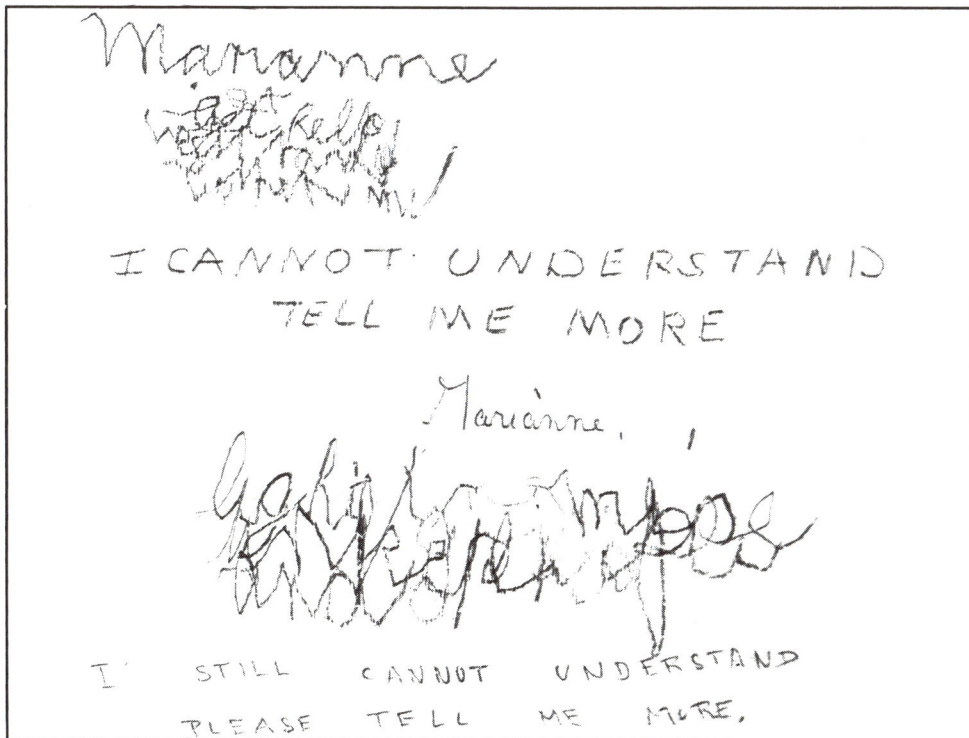

smoke. Visible smoke led to another ghost tale being added to the lore of the Tower of London. In 1954 a sentry left his post in pursuit of a smoke cloud that moved as if of its own volition, changed its shape, but did not seem to diffuse or drift like ordinary smoke – until it disappeared with alarming suddenness.

Lying Beside a Ghost

Setting aside apparitions, of whatever shape or form, there is an immense variety of non-visual ghostly happenings. Many of these must be ascribed to the poltergeist, seemingly the most widely occurring form of haunting in the present day. Poltergeists are those ghosts which tend to toss objects around, whatever their weight or danger to bystanders, and also (as the name implies, meaning 'noisy spirit') to produce various kinds of noises. Spiritualism first began by investigating the kind of poltergeist that

announces itself by knocking, and much of its continued research is based on the kind of poltergeist that moves tables. Associated with poltergeists are all those uncanny occurrences of church bells ringing themselves, pianos or organs being played by invisible fingers, weird laughter or screams or footsteps echoing through empty corridors.

Less overtly poltergeist ghosts would include those invisible manifestations that lay their cold hands on people or touch them in other ways, like the kissing ghost mentioned earlier. In Sheffield in 1956 an invisible phantom made itself known to an elderly lady by lying down on the bed beside her, making the mattress sink and the springs creak. Somewhat closer to the traditional poltergeist, perhaps, is the invisible ghost of a former Bank of England cashier who now tends playfully to disarm the guards; and the Bavarian ghost first heard of in 1949 who gained the name 'Gus the Nazi' when he

persecuted women who fraternized with Allied Occupation troops. He was said to have cropped the hair of one girl, with scissors held by his invisible hand, in full view of her parents.

A Sense of Evil

Last of all the categories of ghosts are the totally intangible phenomena which can loosely be described as 'eerie feelings'. In a large majority of cases of clearly seen or heard ghosts, those who have experienced such phenomena have reported a definite sensation of cold, a feature that occurs as often in well-attested psychical research files as in the annals of folklore. But sometimes this chill that has no physical cause can occur entirely on its own, or can occur before the apparition is seen, usually giving the percipient an almost instinctive feeling that something evil or fearful is present. Animals, particularly dogs, are believed by occultists to be specially attuned to supernatural manifestations; many sensible people have told psychical investigators of their pets' unexplained fear of something that apparently only the animal could see. Dogs, for instance, were often frightened round Borley Rectory, even in broad daylight; and Dennis Bardens relates the story of a modern visitor to Compton Castle near Torquay, whose pet greyhound was riveted to the spot in utter terror of something only it could perceive.

Sometimes such presences make themselves felt without the aid of chills or whatever special senses dogs may have. A 'creepy feeling' – a non-physical awareness of some presence – occurs to a great many people in quite ordinary circumstances. It often happens that someone enters unfamiliar but quite ordinary surroundings (like an empty house or flat visited during a house-hunting excursion) and has a definite feeling of oppression, depression or similar 'atmospheric' reaction from the place. Nor need this reaction be due to any perceptible physical factors, such as poor lighting, dank overshadowing trees, rising damp, atrocious wallpaper or bad smells. Many people have admitted their personal experience of this unpleasant sensation in an apparently ideal dwelling, as if there were some sort of 'psychic emanation' from the very walls of the place, which is reminiscent of terrible horrors that had taken place there in the past.

The forms and habits of ghosts may be incredibly varied, but their reasons for returning, the basic purposes behind their presence among us, tend according to folklore to be fairly limited. Many of the reasons for ghosts returning suggested by past and primitive societies can still be found in modern legend. So ghosts can return apparently out of sheer malevolence. Vampires, a special kind of revenant, return solely for evil purposes as, in many tales, do the ghosts of executed witches.

Return for a Purpose

Haunting ghosts seem to return to re-enact some crisis scene from their former lives – usually their death scene. Ghosts in modern lore, as in the past, have been said to return to seek vengeance on their slayers, to punish the living for crimes against them or against their descendants, to seek proper burial, to complete some task left undone or merely to continue one. The ghost of an American farmer returned for the specific purpose of informing his heirs where he had hidden his will; another American ghost returned to claim what it felt to be rightfully its own. This was the deceased wife of a thrifty New England farmer, whose husband had removed her rings before the funeral, eventually to pass them on to his next wife. But the second wife awoke in terror one night to find the apparition of her predecessor angrily pulling the rings off her fingers.

Quite a number of ghosts have appeared to announce their own deaths, in the 'point of death' form of apparition met so often in psychical research. But others are said to appear as harbingers of someone else's imminent death. The spirit of a deceased loved one might appear to a person, perhaps beckoning; Josephine's ghost apparently came to Napoleon in this way, some days before he died. Or some ancestral figure might appear to the title-holder of a noble family, heralding his death, as a spectral Black Friar was supposed to visit members of Lord Byron's family.

Tricks of the Senses?

The foregoing must of course be taken as only a broad sample of what people have believed regarding ghosts, their nature and habits. To make some sense of it, we must now look at some of the answers that experts have given to the question of the reasons that may lie behind this universal belief.

The short answer that is often given is, obviously, that people who see ghosts experience nothing except a temporary derangement of their senses. It is true that our senses do often play tricks on us, when we are in an excitable or suggestible state, or when we are drunk, ill or half-asleep. Certainly quite a few accounts of ghosts can be dismissed on this account. The 'creepy feeling' mentioned before in connection with specific houses might be ascribable to a collection of possibly unconscious impressions – signs of decay or odours and the like, not consciously perceived but nonetheless affecting our reactions. At the very least, no occultist has yet come up with a convincing explanation of why certain tragedies in certain houses should breed these ghostly emanations while others do not.

Many psychologists tend instantly to dismiss accounts of ghost sightings as the 'product of a disturbed mind'. But for a few men in this field the easy answer does not satisfy. Freud searched for explanations among the repressed relics from our primitive past, the ancient ghost fears of primeval man now hidden within the unconscious mind, but sometimes slithering into conscious awareness. Jung looked for answers in his theory of the collective unconscious, the contents of which can in his view take on almost an autonomous life of their own, being projected or manifested as seemingly outer occurrences.

Both Freud and Jung made it clear that these views should not be taken as complete answers, but more as avenues of approach for psychoanalytic researchers. Other theorists depart from these standpoints, but still share with the two great psychological pioneers the idea that phenomena like ghosts are at least worth the time and effort of study. As the American psychologist William James put it, 'it is bad method to ignore them'. James himself produced one of the more interesting theories concerning apparitions, based on the idea of spontaneously produced hallucinations. Like other psychical researchers after him, he turned to extra-sensory perception – telepathy, clairvoyance and so on – as the possible cause of these hallucinations.

Opposite: Above A photograph taken by the vicar of Newby Church in Yorkshire reveals a cowled figure standing to the right of the altar. Photographic laboratories have confirmed that the film has not been interfered with in any way Opposite below left Ghosts have always been thought of as malevolent: this ghost from an early German film appears as a tall, threatening figure Below right Spirits are sometimes said to glow in the dark, and a ghostly manifestation may take the form of a light which has no natural cause. Photograph of a 'ghost light', taken in 1907 at Basle Zoological Gardens in Switzerland Below An early 19th century engraving by George Cruikshank depicts an enraged ghost rising from the earth, a thighbone in each hand, to ward off a graverobber

HAUNTED HOUSES

Most people, when they think of ghosts, think first of haunted houses. This is not, of course, because apparitions are generally supposed to appear, or strange happenings to occur, only in family dwellings. On the contrary, if it were possible to compile a detailed map of all the places which are now, or once were, said to be haunted, a great diversity of open-air sites would have to be marked upon it, as well as many buildings other than homes. Ghostly manifestations have been recorded in the vicinity of prehistoric barrows and ancient burial-grounds, in fields where medieval deserted villages once stood, on battlefields known to history and sometimes in places where tradition preserves the memory of some battle or local skirmish about which history has nothing to say.

Nevertheless, a host of stories, some very well attested, support the popular belief that many houses of all ages and sizes, from castles to cottages, are or have been haunted by those who lived or died in them, and some-times by entities more difficult to account for than simply the returning dead. Sights and sounds outside normal experience have un-doubtedly been seen and heard in such houses, and have been vouched for by a great number of reliable and serious witnesses. Various theories have been put forward in an attempt to explain these happenings, ranging from acceptance of the oldest and most usual belief that they are straight-forward visitations from beyond the grave, or possibly instances of telepathy between the living and the dead, down to the view that every such experience is purely subjective and due to hallucination on the part of the percipient.

Ghostly manifestations are of many differ-ent kinds. Some apparitions are no more than

Chris Barker

fleeting and elusive forms, suddenly perceived and quickly gone. Often they are quite unknown to those who see them, no legend accounts for them, and they seem to be unaware of, or uninterested in, the living occupants of the house. Yet they cannot be dismissed as mere illusion, because they appear again and again, and have been seen at different times by a variety of witnesses. Others are distinct and recognizable figures, and some are so normal in appearance that they are mistaken for living people, at least at first. Or that which haunts the house may not be seen at all. Noises are heard, though nothing visible makes them, sometimes loud and terrifying, sometimes slight yet clearly audible, like the faint murmur of voices, or the sound of crying, or footsteps passing along a corridor or down the stairs. There are houses which contain rooms that are 'restless'. They are not haunted in the sense that anything ghostly has been seen or heard in them, yet it is impossible to sit in peace in them, or concentrate upon any work, for more than a very short period. Others have rooms or passages which from time to time are filled with a brooding atmosphere of sadness or fear. A curious phenomenon frequently recorded by ghost-hunters as a preliminary to certain forms of psychical activity is a sudden and distinct fall in room-temperature, and in one haunted farmhouse at Yarnton in Oxfordshire, the inmates are warned that the ghost is about to 'walk' by the slow spread through the house of a peculiarly sweet scent.

To the difficult question of what causes some houses to be persistently haunted, sometimes by more than one ghost, there can be no certain answer in the present state of our knowledge. These ghosts may perhaps be bound to their old homes by emotional ties so strong that even death cannot sever them. The popular belief is that these ties are nearly always the result of some past state

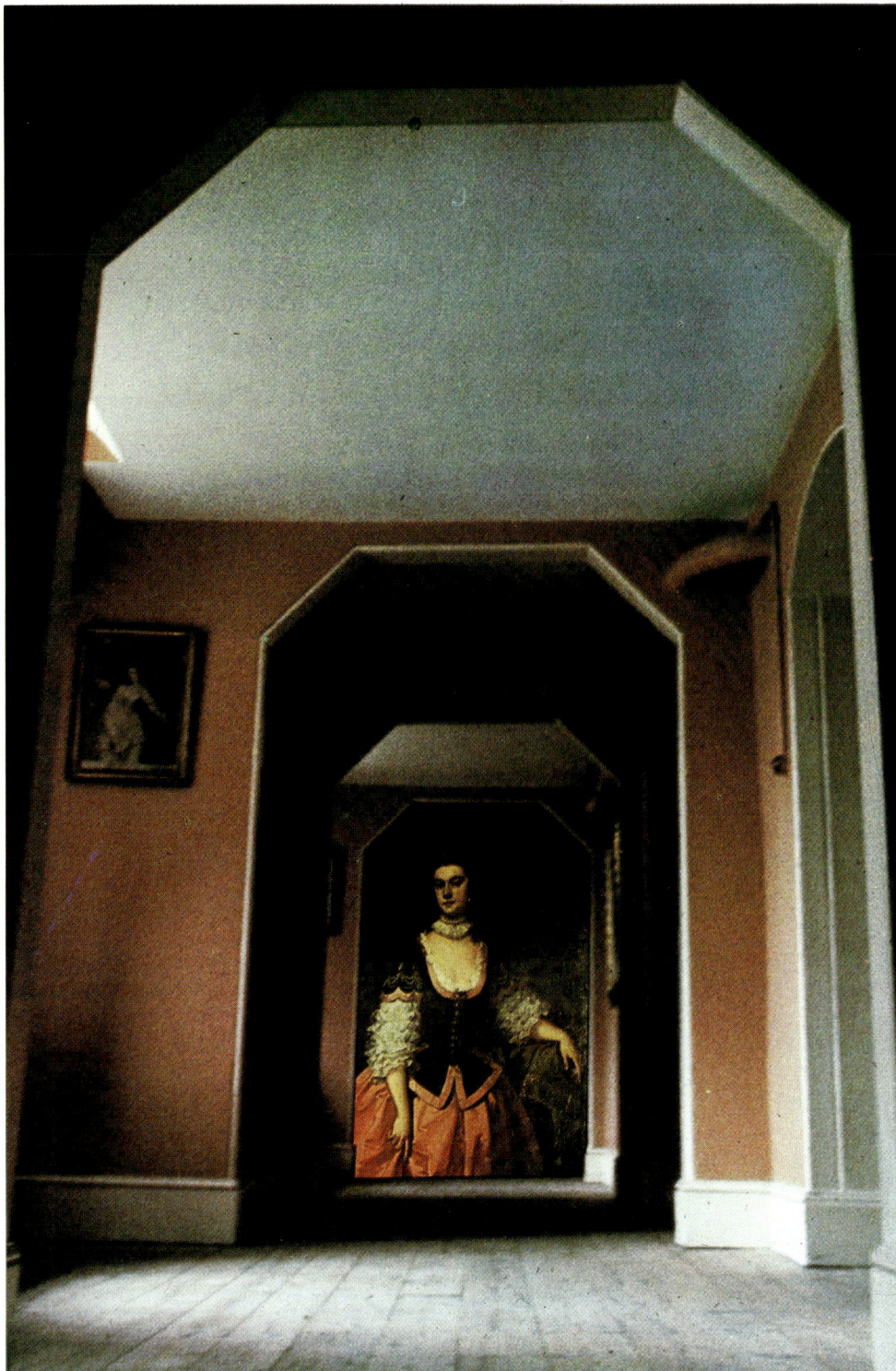

Clive Barda

Opposite Lady Lisgar, who in 1881 married Sir Francis Fortescue-Turvile of Bosworth Hall, a Roman Catholic stronghold since 1630, refused to allow a priest to give supreme unction to a dying maidservant; as a result she was condemned to haunt the house, and her ghostly figure has been seen in her bedroom and at the end of corridors. 'Some people have experienced such intolerable sensations of misery and fear in that corridor that they have found it impossible to remain in it': *there are so many well-attested cases of hauntings that it is hard to write the whole phenomenon off as an illusion Above The name 'Jane' was allegedly carved into the wall of Beauchamp Tower in the Tower of London by the husband of Lady Jane Grey; one of the many ghosts that haunt the Tower, she was imprisoned there after her short reign of only nine days Left One of the two ghosts that have been seen at Longleat, home of the Marquess of Bath, is that of a woman, said to be the wife of the second Viscount Weymouth, who appears in a passage at the top of the house in an agony of terror and grief; according to tradition she was present when her husband killed her lover in a duel and then buried the body. Some years ago when central heating was being installed in the house, the remains of a young man wearing 18th century clothing were found in the cellar*

of bitter unhappiness, or violent terror, or the guilt of an unexpiated sin, and in many recorded cases, family tradition runs along the same lines. There are, however, other tales which suggest that the dead sometimes return for no other reason than that they loved, and were happy in, the places that they now haunt.

The *Athenaeum* of January 1880 contains an account of what must surely have been a ghost of this unharassed type, written by Dr Augustus Jessop, the antiquary. He relates how, on 10 October 1879, he went to stay with Lord Orford at Mannington Hall in Norfolk. His purpose was to consult certain rare books in the library, and that night, at his own request, he was left alone to work in an adjoining room after the rest of the household had gone to bed. At about one o'clock in the morning, while he was quietly writing, he suddenly perceived, first, a hand within a foot of his own elbow, and then, when he turned his head, a figure which he described as 'a somewhat large man, with his back to the fire, bending slightly over the table and apparently examining the pile of books that I had been at work upon.' The apparition was seated, with his face turned away from the observer, so that only part of it was visible; he had closely cut reddish-brown hair and wore 'a kind of ecclesiastical habit of thick corded silk, or some such material', with a close-fitting upstanding collar. Dr Jessop realized instantly that the figure was not of this world but he felt no fear, only curiosity and keen interest. 'There he sat,' he writes, 'and I was fascinated: afraid, not of his staying, but lest he should go.' He did go, a moment later, when the antiquary stretched out his hand to move one of the books. Then, his work being done, he carried the books back to the library; but on second thought, he kept one of them 'and laid it upon the table where I had been writing when the phantom did me the honour to appear to me.' He went to bed and slept very soundly, and we shall never know now whether his visitor returned or not to read the book that had been left out for him.

In his *Early Reminiscences* (1923), Sabine Baring-Gould describes the haunting of his

house at Lew Trenchard in Devon, by the ghost of an ancestress, known in her day as Madam Gould. Her son dissipated a good part of the estate by his extravagances, and when he died, she set herself to restore the property. This she did by sheer hard work and business ability. She died in 1795, sitting upright in her chair because she refused to allow illness to drive her to bed, and thereafter she haunted the house.

Footsteps believed to be hers were heard on more than one occasion, passing down the Long Gallery. Once, when a member of the family was very ill, the night-nurse was roused from sleep by a loud knock on the door and a woman's voice saying, 'It is time for her to have her medicine.' No one was visible when the door was opened, and no one was afterwards traced as the speaker. In 1918, when two of Baring-Gould's grandchildren were staying at Lew Trenchard, their two nurses gave notice because they had both seen a ghostly figure bending over the children as they slept. A guest going alone into the drawing-room saw an elderly lady in a satin dress and an old white-haired man sitting, as though in conversation, on opposite sides of the fireplace. No such people were staying in the house but from the description, it seemed likely that they were Madam Gould and her friend Parson Elford, who often used to sit together there when they were alive. A variety of other stories were remembered by the local people.

Corridor of Agony

Longleat in Wiltshire, now famous as the home of lions, has at least two ghosts. One of them is a friendly and unalarming figure, an old man wearing a long black robe reminiscent of the garments favoured by

Glamis Castle, the home of the Earl and Countess of Strathmore: somewhere in its thick walls lies the Secret of Glamis, a chamber where a previous Earl is supposed to have hidden his son who was half man and half beast; Malcolm II of Scotland was murdered in the castle in 1033, and for years there was a bloodstain on the floor of a room known as 'Malcolm's Room'

elderly Elizabethan gentlemen, who haunts the Red Library. The identity of this phantom is not altogether certain but the most probable theory is that he is Sir John Thynne, the builder of the house, who died in 1580. If he now returns occasionally to the immense and lovely house which was his greatest achievement, it is perhaps not entirely surprising.

The second haunting is of a quite different character. In a passage at the top of the house, the ghost of a woman appears, walking up and down in an agony of grief and terror. Even when she is not visible, some people have experienced such intolerable sensations of misery and fear in that corridor that they have found it impossible to remain in it. The ghost is believed to be that of Lady Louisa Carteret, whose portrait may be seen in the Lower Dining-Room. She died in 1736, and a grim family legend accounts for her continued presence in the house.

She was the daughter of the Earl of Granville and the wife of the second Viscount Weymouth. The latter seems to have been a man of somewhat difficult temperament, and the marriage was not happy. Tradition says that she had a lover, though who he was is not now remembered, and that her husband, returning unexpectedly to Longleat after an absence, found the young man and his wife together. The two men fought a duel then and there, up and down the passage, without seconds or any witnesses except the horrified girl. The lover was killed; and since his death in this furtive and unwitnessed fight was legally murder, his body was hastily and

'Hauntings have been scientifically investigated for many years': Benson Herbert, who has studied the subject with unusual thoroughness, has constructed machines designed to detect ghosts, in his paraphysical laboratory

secretly buried in the cellar.

This story is legend, not history, but there is some evidence to support it. Soon after the time when the duel is supposed to have taken place, Lord Weymouth appears to have taken a strong dislike to Longleat. He left it and went to live at Horningsham, returning to his home only on rare occasions. From then on, he neglected the place entirely, and when his son (afterwards the first Marquess of Bath) inherited it in 1751, he found the house in a state of disrepair, and the once elaborate formal gardens an overgrown wilderness. We do not know what reasons Lord Weymouth had for acting in this way but if he had in fact murdered a man and buried his corpse there, that might be a sufficient explanation. Some years ago, a curious discovery was made, which looks very much like a confirmation of the legend. When central heating was being put into the house, the cellar flagstones had to be lifted. Under them the remains of a young man wearing jackboots and clothes of the early 18th century were found. It cannot be proved that these bones were those of the unhappy lover but it seems very probable that they were, especially as no other known incident in the history of the house can account for them.

We cannot tell why, of the three persons involved in this tale of hatred, jealousy and crime, it should be Lady Louisa alone who haunts the house, and not either the murderer or his victim. As yet, we do not understand the laws that govern these matters; nor do we know what it is that causes some ghostly manifestations to persist for years, even centuries, and then cease for no obvious reason, either abruptly, or by a gradual process of fading. Genuine ghost-tales are rarely neatly rounded off, as are their fictional counterparts, though there

are, of course, cases where the haunting has, apparently, been ended by some human action, such as resort to exorcism, or the burial in consecrated ground of hitherto unhallowed remains, or occasionally the destruction of the house involved. This last is not always as effective as might be expected; sometimes the psychic power is transferred to a new building on the same site, which may account for curious happenings recorded in council houses.

In a Black Cloak

Sudden death, and especially death of violence, has often been cited as a reason for known hauntings. So has suicide, which was once widely regarded as an unforgivable sin, and which in any case presupposes extreme unhappiness, amounting to despair, in the person concerned. A house at Clifton Hampden in Oxfordshire was haunted for many years by the ghost of Sarah Fletcher, who hanged herself from the curtain-rod in her bedroom in 1799, when she was only 29 years old. She is traditionally said to have been driven to suicide by the news that her husband, a naval officer then away from home, was planning a bigamous marriage with another woman. No mention is made of this in the report of the inquest printed in *Jackson's Oxford Journal* for 15 June 1799, but we are told that 'the derangement of her mind appearing very evident, as well as from many other circumstances, the jury, without hesitation, found a verdict – Lunacy.' It was thus made possible for her to be buried in Dorchester Abbey, where her tombstone can still be seen. Nevertheless, from then on her house at Clifton Hampden was haunted by her restless ghost.

In the mid-19th century it became a boys' school, but the disturbances continued until the school moved elsewhere.

BORLEY RECTORY

Harry Price was unquestionably Britain's most widely known ghost-hunter and his investigations of Borley Rectory, termed by him 'the most haunted house in England', have caused violent controversy among modern psychical researchers.

The Rectory was an unattractive Victorian brick building of many rambling rooms, damp, dark and uninviting, in the parish of Borley on the Essex-Suffolk border. It had been built in 1863 by the Rev. Henry Bull, whose son Harry succeeded him as rector and remained there until his death in 1927. By that time the ghost stories had begun to rise like ivy around the Rectory – partly, it is thought, because of the Spiritualist leanings of Harry Bull.

Local tales concerned a mysterious coach and horses which galloped along the roads; visions of headless men; a girl in white; sounds of dragging footsteps and other weird noises in the house. Above all, there was the apparition of a nun who occasionally walked the house and grounds. In 1929, when the Rev. G. E. Smith and his wife had taken the house, these tales came to the ears of Harry Price.

Harry Price Investigates

Harry Price had by then made a name for himself by exposing fraudulent mediums, investigating haunted houses and founding the National Laboratory for Psychical Research. At Borley, Price interviewed people, pursued local legends tirelessly, and began to piece together a romantic tale of illicit love and murder in the 14th century, in which the victim was a nun.

Meanwhile there were reports of further outbreaks of ghostly activity, involving a poltergeist. Bells rang inexplicably; stones and other objects flew through the air; things went bump in the night. Price assiduously took notes on all this, continued his interviews, and held a seance – in which communication was obtained with the spirit of the Rev. Harry Bull.

It is a typical and very puzzling feature of poltergeist outbreaks that they do not continue indefinitely. They last only a few days or weeks. It is difficult therefore to get conclusive evidence; by the time an outbreak becomes known outside the immediate vicinity, it is likely to be over or on the decline. When the investigator arrives on the scene things may be quiet again and he has to depend on the testimony of others. Very often the witnesses are persons of intelligence and integrity but the investigator may hesitate to accept what they say at its face value if they are members of the disturbed household, because he may feel that they are inclined to 'back one another up' or are trying to shield a member of the family whom they suspect of trickery.

Shortly afterwards the Smiths moved out, mainly because of the impossible living conditions of the decaying old house and were succeeded by an elderly rector named Foyster, with his pretty young wife Marianne. The activity of the following months made all previous happenings seem very trivial.

By all accounts the poltergeist caused objects to fly through the air, overturned furniture, scattered clothing and even produced objects from nowhere. Doors locked themselves, bells rang and knockings came from the walls. Much of this fury centred on Marianne: she was struck, dumped out of bed, locked in her room. Curious writings began to appear on the walls – pencil scrawls that often seemed to ask for prayers and Masses (as if to pacify a 'lost soul'), always addressed to Marianne.

Price makes clear in his first book on Borley, *The Most Haunted House in England* (1940), that he suspected Marianne of being responsible for many of these happenings. Most people since have agreed. And Price shows that almost all of the phenomena during the Foysters' occupation happened

Harry Price, the famous ghost-hunter, who called Borley Rectory 'the most haunted house in England', though whether there were really any ghosts there has been heatedly disputed. Price died in 1948, after writing two books about Borley

while Marianne was out of sight, or happened to her while she was alone, or could have been contrived by her in front of others.

But Marianne denied the accusation and Price went on noting phenomena and building up 'the most haunted house' story. And this in spite of the fact that the ghosts were no longer in action. They remained absent, except for a few wild tales by sightseers, after the Foysters left Borley in 1935.

Ghosts at Empty Windows

In 1937 Price himself rented the house and he brought with him a team of observers, all experienced but supposedly level-headed, to keep a regular watch on subsequent events. But very little happened. The ghosts had gone away long since. Now the poltergeist, with the Foysters gone, also became quiet. Price paid great attention to new pencil marks appearing on the walls – but no words were formed and the markings were so small as to be easily missed.

By 1938, when Price moved out, the house had become a tourist attraction and was frequently visited by Spiritualists and ghost-mongers. Some of these claimed they had seen the ghosts but none of the reports is reliable. Then, shortly after a Captain Gregson had bought the Rectory, it was gutted by an accidental fire.

The blaze gave new life to the legends. A police constable was among those who claimed to have seen weird figures moving through the flames. Other stories told of apparitions at the empty windows of the burnt-out shell. Price's second book *The End of Borley Rectory* written in 1945, years after the fire, retails most of these stories.

In this book Price amplified the legend about the nun and alluded to the fact that digging had revealed human remains in the Rectory cellar.

Harry Price died in 1948, and his obituaries brought the Borley story to the boil again. In 1956 the Society for Psychical Research published (disclaiming editorial responsibility) an assessment by three of its members, E. J. Dingwall, K. M. Goldney and Trevor Hall entitled *The Haunting of Borley Rectory*.

The three authors build up a damning case against Harry Price, scything away at the details and incidents that fill his two books. They point scornfully at the amateurishness of Price's team of observers, and at the way in which Price prepared their minds to see things. They indicate the often incompetent nature of these observations and suggest, for example, that the best way to ensure the newness of the later pencil marks would have been to put fresh whitewash on the walls. Worst of all, they cast doubt on Price's own integrity, making it clear that Price could have caused some of the poltergeist phenomena that sprang up when he arrived at Borley – and adding that some people definitely thought that he did.

Price did not lack defenders and the case of Borley Rectory has caused bitter dissension.

In *New Light on Old Ghosts* (1965) Trevor Hall discusses Borley with reference to some new evidence – including an alleged confession from Marianne Foyster. A reviewer of this book, writing in the Society for Psychical Research's *Journal,* was not impressed. 'Neither the "confession" nor Mr Hall's own researches into this lady's affairs seem to be available for study; if this is so, it must diminish the evidential value of Mr Hall's abbreviated paraphrase of Mrs Foyster's alleged remarks to an unnamed interviewer.'

A few facts can still be discerned among all the arguments. First, Borley Rectory had a long history of hauntings but not a single ghost appeared to Price or to any other potentially reliable witness – only to laymen and suggestible sightseers, and mostly under dubious circumstances. Secondly, no accounts of poltergeist activity came from Borley until Price and later Marianne Foyster went there. Yet from then on the bulk of ghostly happenings involved a poltergeist.

If there are genuine poltergeist cases in which these strange movements of objects occur, it raises challenging problems. At the least we have proof that there are physical forces at present unknown to science. Even if these forces should prove to be operated by 'spirits' or 'elementals', nonetheless they are physical forces as defined by the engineer, because to lift even a weight of only an ounce requires a force of one ounce weight. The 'poltergeist force', if not generated 'supernaturally', may have a purely physiological origin. On the other hand psychological factors may play a part in the genesis of this mysterious force.

Thirdly, no one piece of evidence presented by Price is in any way conclusive or convincing *in itself* – certainly not by the exacting standards of the Society for Psychical Research. Borley becomes impressive only for the *quantity* of its phenomena. Fourthly, Price's three antagonists make a great many unarguable points against him, especially in terms of his suppression or distortion of facts.

A new, open-minded and scholarly assessment of the Borley case has been prepared for the *Proceedings* of the Society for Psychical Research by Mr R. J. Hastings. His thorough and cogent judgement seems rather more like a magistrate's summing-up than like the 'prosecutor's case' of Dingwall, Hall and Goldney. Out of his detailed weighing of the evidence comes an important conclusion: that while Price's hunger for publicity may have created some confusion, and his journalistic style and outright carelessness may have produced some lapses and contradictions, there is no proof of fraud.

Mr Hastings's monograph only underlines the mournful wish that the Society had been able to launch one of its own full-scale, expert and reliable investigations while the Rectory was standing and Price still alive. Without doubt, Borley Rectory continues to be one of the world's most complex and controversial haunted houses.

Exterior of Borley Rectory, the scene of violent poltergeist phenomena in the 1930s: legends of a murdered nun and visions of headless men and a ghostly coach and horses were also associated with it. After the house burned down, there were stories of weird figures among the flames and apparitions at the empty windows of the gutted shell

Peter Underwood

VISIONS

The word vision is used in the religious sphere to mean what elsewhere is called an apparition. The percipient of an apparition has the experience of 'seeing' (in some sense or other) something which is not present in the same way as ordinary physical objects are. Sir Francis Galton (1822–1911), in his researches into human faculties, encountered a perfect example of an apparition. A lady novelist assured him that she once saw the principal character of one of her novels come through the door and glide towards her. As the character was fictional there was no possibility that the apparition corresponded to any external cause. The experience thus appears quite clearly to have originated within the lady's mind and can be described as *endogenic* (caused from within).

Apparitions are sometimes loosely called hallucinations (from Latin *hallucinatio* – I dream) bearing the implication that they are endogenic. This is because apparitions commonly result from drugs, fever, exhaustion or mental illness. The present writer prefers to reserve the term hallucination for endogenic hallucinations, and to use the word apparition or vision for an appearance whose cause may, in fact, be either internal or external.

About 1899 the Society for Psychical Research carried out a census of apparitions and obtained 17,000 replies to their questionnaire. It appeared that about one person in 16 sees an apparition about once in the course of a lifetime. About a third of all apparitions are of animals, lights, indefinite or inanimate objects, but the remaining two-thirds are of realistically human figures. More than half of these human apparitions are of persons living or dead and known to the percipient. It was found also that about one in 30 of all apparitions are of a religious, exalted or highly poetic nature. In mentally normal persons only a very small proportion of apparitions are grotesque or horrible. Even if an apparition is not frightening in itself it may puzzle the percipient who often fears that his reason is failing, but this alarm is unnecessary, because the statistics quoted refer mainly to people in normal physical and mental health.

Modern brain surgery has given some insight into the causes of some hallucinations (though less than is sometimes claimed). If the normal functioning of a part of the brain concerned in ocular perception is prevented, the person may have *compensatory hallucinations*. Thus a patient with a tumour in the right temporal lobe had consequently no normal vision of things on the left. But while in darkness he 'saw' a non-existent man to his left sitting at a non-existent

The Vision of Father Simon by Francesca Ribalta: Simon was a 16th century Italian aesthete who walked the streets at night meditating on the Road to Calvary; one night he believed that he heard trumpets and saw Christ, carrying the cross, turn to look at him

National Gallery

fireside. Visions of this sort consist of re-activated memories; men blind from birth have no visual hallucinations, although they can have auditory ones. Occasionally, sane and intelligent persons have spontaneous electrical discharges in the brain which, besides producing involuntary movements of the limbs, engender remarkably vivid hallucinations often identifiable as revived memories. When in the course of remedial brain surgery certain areas of the cerebral cortex are stimulated mildly with an electrode, *sensory hallucinations* result – effects of dispersed light or shade, coloured lights, stars, wheels. Stimulation of the temporal lobe and the posterior parietal cortex produce more elaborate hallucinations. Some neurologists tend therefore to refer all apparitions to random electrical flickers in the brain.

A Wavering Rose

Many hallucinations are extremely vivid and lifelike so that, as with some crisis apparitions, the percipient may think he is actually seeing in the ordinary way. But with many visions, particularly in the religious sphere, it is hard to decide from the visionary's words exactly in what sense the vision was 'seen'. Roman Catholic theorists such as St Thomas Aquinas (1226–74) recognized three types of vision: the intellectual vision, the imaginative vision and the corporeal vision. The theory of the corporeal vision was akin to the modern astral body explanation of crisis apparitions. If one had a vision of Jesus, it *might* be a corporeal vision; one

was actually seeing either the resurrected body of the Christ or alternatively a kind of wraith fashioned by the angels, the handymen of heaven. On the other hand, it might be that the percipient received only an imaginative vision – a purely mental image, though a vivid one and induced by the action of God. St Thomas, of course, like all reputable theologians, reserved the possibility of a vision being an endogenic hallucination not divinely caused.

Galton came across a few visionaries who said that they received their visions in two entirely distinct ways. Thus one informant could experience eidetic images at conscious command but these were vague and shadowy in comparison with his spontaneous visions, which occurred unexpectedly and quite outside his mental control. These visions were of landscapes more strange and beautiful than any he had ever seen in the ordinary way. Such visions which arise, as it were, of their own motion can be called autonomous, but they are not necessarily exogenic. Not all autonomous visions are idyllic or romantic. A visionary who bought a Dutch cheese at a shop in Tottenham Court Road, London, saw the shopkeeper roll it on the counter. He told Galton that chancing to close his eyes the next day, he saw a bodiless head rolling on a white surface. Its face was that of the cheesemonger. Such visions resemble the more trivial type of dream which is a patchwork of recent experiences and jumbled recollections, but the visions of people with a poetic or literary bent, like their dreams, have an intellectual and idyllic content. In

1944 Jung, who was recovering after a heart attack, would awake at midnight and would spend an hour or so in 'an utterly transformed state' as if 'in ecstasy'. He saw unfolding before him various mythical occurrences such as the wedding of the cabalistic beings Malkhuth and Tifereth in the 'garden of pomegranates' or the sacred marriage of Zeus and Hera in a classical amphitheatre.

Ecstasy is a peculiar state which is sometimes entered spontaneously or in the course of prayer or meditation on sublime themes. During it the ecstatic person consciously experiences any or all of a variety of thoughts and feelings. Visions are common but there can be also a sense of bliss or of union with the deity or a benign cosmic power.

The greatest of the mystical doctors of the Church, St Francis of Sales and St John of the Cross, were profoundly suspicious of the accuracy of visions. St John used to quote with some relish the posthumous appearance of St Teresa of Avila to a Carmelite nun. The great foundress and mystic warned the visionary that most visions were untrustworthy. Whether the saint actually returned from paradise is uncertain, but her advice was in character. In his old age Loyola doubted the validity of his own youthful visions.

The Angels of Mons were the creation of an English journalist, but many British soldiers came to believe that they had actually seen the heavenly warriors hold back the might of the German army at Mons in 1914: French painting of the event, 1920

GOLEM

A golem is a creature, especially a human being, created artificially by magic. In the late Jewish form of the legend, as told by Jakob Grimm in his *Journal of Hermits* (1808), the golem is the figure of a man, made of clay or mud, and brought to life when the miraculous name of God is pronounced over it. The golem is dumb (though other versions of the legend do credit it with the power of speech) but it can understand orders and is used as a servant to do the housework. It must never be allowed to leave the house. On its forehead is written the word *emeth* (truth). With every day that goes by, the golem gains weight and it gradually becomes bigger and stronger than anyone in the house, until they become afraid of it. They then rub out the first letter of the word on its forehead, altering it to *meth* (he is dead). The golem immediately collapses and turns back into its earlier clay form once again.

One man's golem, according to Grimm, grew so tall that its forehead was too high to reach. Its owner ordered the golem to take off its boots, so that when it bent down he would be able to reach its forehead. The golem did as it was told, and the owner succeeded in erasing the first letter but the mass of dead clay fell on top of him and crushed him.

The Hebrew word *golem* occurs once in the Old Testament (Psalm 139. 16), where it means a human being which is not yet fully formed, an embryo. In the Talmud (the oldest extant code of Jewish law) the word is used once for Adam's body during the first hours of its existence but before it was fully endowed with life and consciousness. Elsewhere in the Talmud the word is used to denote an uncultured, boorish man. In medieval Hebrew the word was used as a technical philosophical term equivalent to the Greek *hyle*, that is, hylic matter, matter without form. Only at a much later stage was the word golem associated with magical traditions about the possibility of creating human and other beings by means of formulae, divine names, and permutations and combinations of Hebrew letters.

Act of Creation

The idea that it is possible to create living beings or to endow lifeless images or statues with life by magical means is widespread. In classical antiquity it was frequently associated with the alleged imparting of the power of speech to idols and statues. The Talmud too contains evidence that legends about such magical feats were current among Jews. One rabbi is said to have 'created a man' and sent him to a colleague. When the latter spoke to the messenger but received no reply, he recognized his true character and commanded him, 'Return to your dust'. Two other rabbis are reported to 'have made a calf for themselves' on the eve of every Sabbath and to have eaten it. They produced this calf by busying themselves with the book *Yetsirah*.

The reference to the *Sefer Yetsirah* (the Book of Creation) indicates the range of ideas and concepts underlying the theory of the magical creation of living beings. These ideas go back in part to Talmudic notions concerning the creative power of the letters of the name of God or of the Hebrew letters in general.

In the circle of Jewish mystics of the 12th–13th centuries known as the 'Hasidim of Germany' these conceptions gave rise to a mystical rite of creating a golem. There is little doubt that this ritual, in spite of its magical character, did not serve any materialist purpose (such as creating a robot servant) but was essentially a spiritual experience fraught with symbolic meaning.

Rebellious Servant

What was essentially a mystic-symbolic ritual in the circles of the German Hasidim soon became a subject for popular folklore and legend. Concurrently the golem too became an actual creature serving his master and fulfilling menial and other tasks laid upon him. Legends of this kind were fairly widespread among German Jews after the 15th century and came also to be known among non-Jews; Goethe's *Sorcerer's Apprentice* is indebted to the golem legend.

Head of the golem, from a famous film, The Golem. *The story of the artificially created human being which turns on its master became associated with Rabbi Judah Loew, of Prague in the 16th century, but without historical foundation*

EXORCISM

The expulsion of an evil spirit by a command, ritual or prayer is called exorcism and supposes some theory of the inhabitation or infestation of a human soul or a place by evil spirits. Until quite recently much modern thinking on the subject was dominated by the view of E. B. Tylor (*Primitive Culture*, 1871), who propounded a theory of animism, saying that primitive man, when once he has built up a concept of his own soul out of dreams and other psychic experiences, extrapolates this same soul, finding its semblance in beasts and even in lifeless objects. Professor Evans-Pritchard, however, in his work on the Azande, a tribe in Central Africa, refuted the theory of animism in this connection.

The Azande have the idea that the powers of witchcraft reside within a witch's body, and think that by cutting out a gland or pouch in the region of the witch's liver they can be removed. They hold that a wizard can have wizard sons but no witch daughters, and a witch likewise has witch daughters but no wizard sons. The Azande say that when a man has been bewitched 'the soul of the wizard's magic has eaten the soul of the flesh of that man'. Below the grade of wizard they recognize what they call 'gall-bladder men', who are thought to be less dangerous. All this is very physical. In a modern primitive tribe one does not necessarily see the same process of thought as can be projected back into the earliest stages of humanity, yet this example is helpful because it suggests one way in which the idea of possession by evil spirits may have developed.

At the root of exorcism lies belief in the power to transfer a spiritual being from place to place by ritual acts and words. Such a belief seems to have been at work in the minds of the early Romans when they carried out their *evocatio*, which may be looked upon as an exorcism of a community rather than of an individual. In war, before the final assault on a hostile town, the Romans conducted a solemn ritual of calling out the gods of the enemy. This happened, for instance, in the campaign against the city of Veii. The gods were invited to join Rome, with promises of worship and good treatment if they did. Correct use of the name of the god or goddess was an essential part of the ritual, and fear lest an enemy should try to evoke Roman gods led to the concealment of the true name of the *genius* or guardian spirit of Rome; the Roman writers Servius and Pliny say that it was not known whether this original tutelary deity was male or female.

The Romans must have begun by regarding the gods of the enemy as themselves hostile, for otherwise the ritual of propitiation would have been pointless. This belief can be traced with some probability to the Hittites of Asia Minor; one of their tablets speaks of an offering of beer being set out for three gods of an enemy town, along with coloured ribbons to mark the way to the beer. The colours used are red, white and blue.

Below and right The man kneeling before the altar, a postman, believes that he is possessed by an evil spirit which is trying to kill him; he has come for help to a London vicar who regularly performs exorcisms. The vicar lays his hands on the man's head, becomes tense with concentration and begins the exorcism: 'I rebuke thee! I rebuke thee! I rebuke thee! I abjure thee and summon thee forth from this man . . .' Opposite Detail from Botticelli's painting, Three Miracles of St Zenobius: *the saint has successfully exorcized two young men of evil spirits, which issue from their mouths in the form of black imps. It was believed for many years that such evil spirits would enter and depart from the body through the natural orifices*

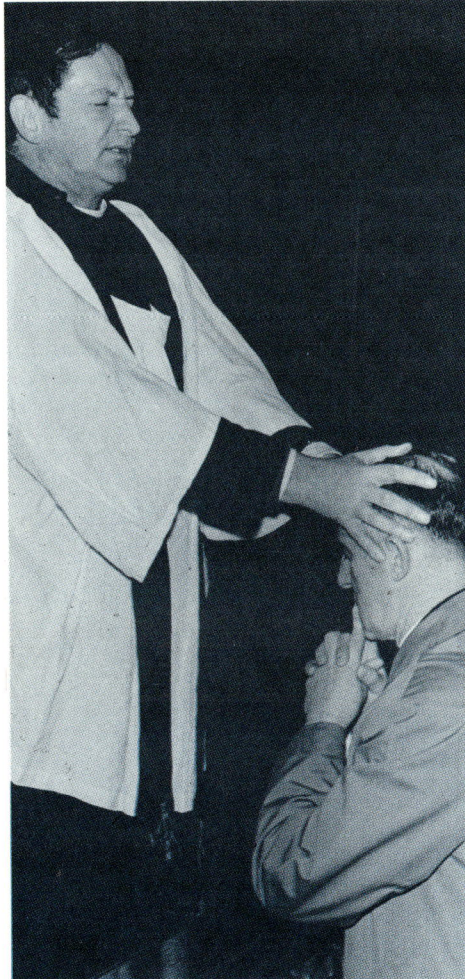

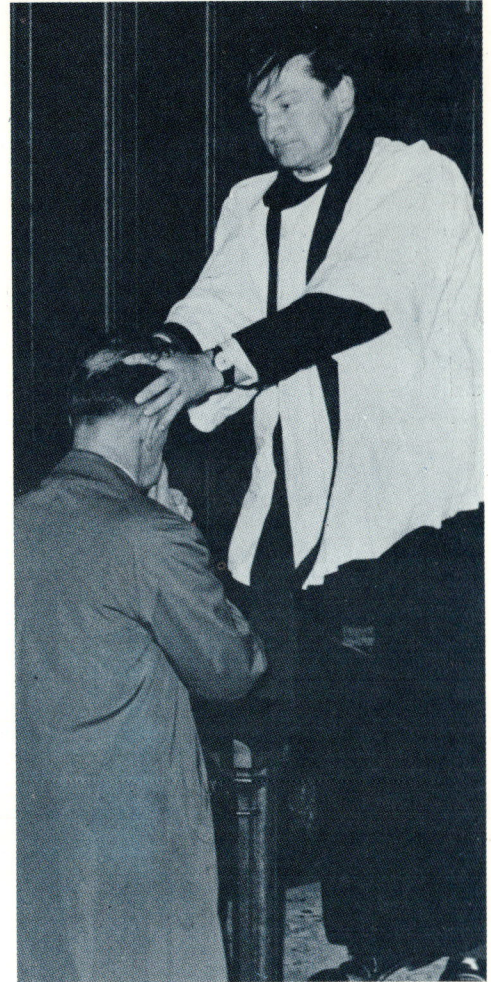

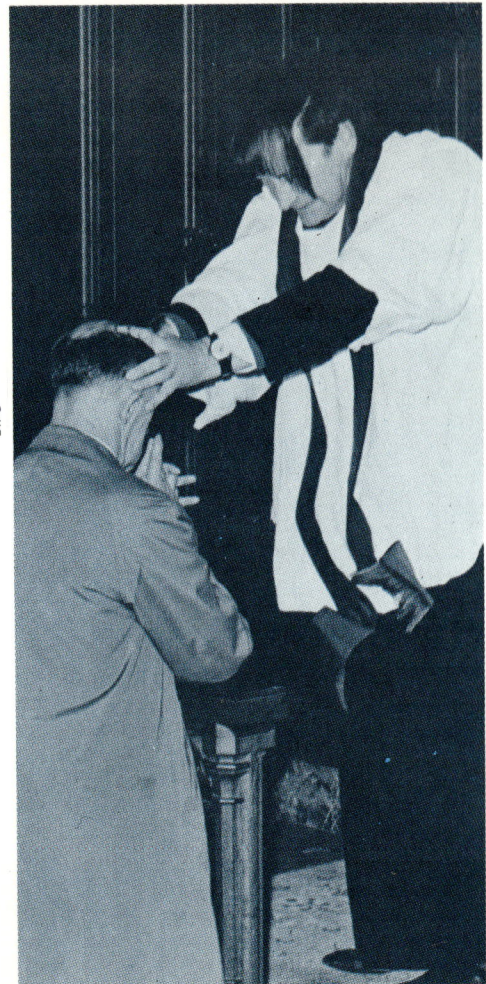

The Forgiveness of Sins

The Jews of the Old Testament were quite different in their outlook; the Baals – gods of enemy Canaanite towns – were not propitiated but looked upon as captives and slaves when victory had been won. In the Old Testament there are no stories of exorcism save for the episode of Tobias and Sarah in the Apocrypha (Tobit, chapters 6–8). Sarah was not in fact possessed by a demon but guarded by one, much as in later stories the princess is guarded by a dragon. Later Jewish writings have plenty of exorcism stories and the Qumran documents have shown (in the so-called Prayer of Nabonidus) that a Jewish exorcist could be credited with the forgiveness of sins and consequent healing. Josephus made the claim that

Solomon had been taught by God the art of exorcism and that he passed this on in his writings, but the Scripture has no trace of this. Certainly by the time of Christ exorcism was well established among the Jews; apocryphal writings such as the *Testaments of the Twelve Patriarchs* bear witness to it, and in the Gospels (Matthew 12.27 and Luke 11.19) Christ refers to it as a well-known fact.

Christian exorcism was not originally confused with healing, for the Gospels differentiate between the two in their accounts of the work of Christ (Matthew 4.24 and 8.16; Luke 6.17). Sometimes disease and diabolical infestation are regarded as combined: for instance, the woman bent double is said by Christ to have been bound by Satan (Luke 13.16). Some take this as a concession to the contemporary Jewish way of thinking, but

more reasonably one may argue that psychosomatic maladies (whose roots are in mind, body and soul) are sometimes more and sometimes less spiritual in their origins. Human suggestion, by hypnosis or even by telepathy, can go to work upon a bodily flaw or weakness; superhuman intellects, if such can be thought to exist, would clearly be more powerful still.

Exorcizing the Water

Waterless places are spoken of in the Gospel (Matthew 12.43) as an unsatisfactory abode for evil spirits when they have been driven out of a man. It was generally thought that water was their element, and the Christian Church began quite early – about 150 AD – to have a blessing or exorcism of the water that was to be used for baptism.

The practice grew of treating all mental defectives and epileptics as if they were troubled by the Devil. A part of the church was set aside for those who came within this broad category and exorcists were appointed to stay with these sufferers during the service and keep them quiet. In Rome in 251 Pope Cornelius had a total of 52 men as exorcists, readers and doorkeepers. The regions into which Rome was traditionally divided were 14, and it is probable that the exorcists were one to each region. The over-riding idea seems to have been that the afflicted should as far as possible be treated as a part of the Christian community, since this would help their rehabilitation. These official exorcists were more like male nurses and differed wholly from those rare individuals who were considered to have a gift from God to deliver

99

men from evil spirits. St Paul drove a spirit out of a girl who foretold the future (Acts chapter 16) and he had unsuccessful imitators (Acts chapter 19). Even Christ had such imitators (Mark 9.38 and Luke 9.49–50). The magical papyri that have come to light in recent times advise exorcism in the name of 'Jesus, god of the Hebrews'; spectacular success in exorcism naturally bred imitation.

Baptism was preceded by exorcism from the earliest Christian times. The theory was that the candidate for baptism had been engaged in worshipping pagan gods who were no better than a cover for demons; in fact, the whole world was considered to be in the power of the Devil until it was redeemed by Christ. A voluntary renunciation of the Devil was required of the candidate, because the human will was a vital factor in the problem of possession; no one could be manoeuvred by the Devil unless he had given his consent. When infants were baptized, the renunciation was undertaken by sponsors on their behalf. An apocryphal work of the 2nd century, *The Gospel of Truth,* compares the baptized to jars which have been filled and then sealed; before filling with the Spirit of God they would have to be emptied of all previous contents.

A Willing Surrender

St Thomas Aquinas (c 1225–74) argued that intellect and will, the finer points of the human soul, are opaque to devilish scrutiny. Devils can infer from the play of imagination and stirring of sense-appetite what a man is thinking about or choosing, but they cannot be sure. Possession, when it occurs, must be due to a willing surrender on the part of the man or woman. An exorcism formula going back to Anglo-Saxon times prays that God will turn the thoughts and heart of the possessed man, that he may confess all his sins. It continues: 'Wherefore, accursed demon, recognize thy doom; give honour to God; depart from this his servant, so that, when grace comes to him, he may serve God with a pure mind.'

Such views excluded the possibility that men could be bewitched against their will. None the less, the influence of Arabic medicine and the beginnings of what may be called the experimental science of the Middle Ages (a confused welter of ideas about the properties of gems, herbs and rare or fabulous animals) led those familiar with the Neoplatonist teaching about demonic bodies of air to a ready belief that bewitchment and exorcism might both come about without reference to a man's own choice.

The period of the witch-craze runs approximately from 1484 to 1648, Lorraine, the Rhineland, Scotland, East Anglia and Switzerland being the areas most affected.

Exorcism was a more merciful proceeding in those times than witch trial, when at the trial search was made for the witch's mark, or the victim was condemned on the hearsay evidence of scared or hysterical citizens.

Onlookers beat their drums feverishly in an attempt to expel the evil spirits which have possessed the bodies of these two Zambian girls. Psychiatrists might attribute the girls' behaviour to depression

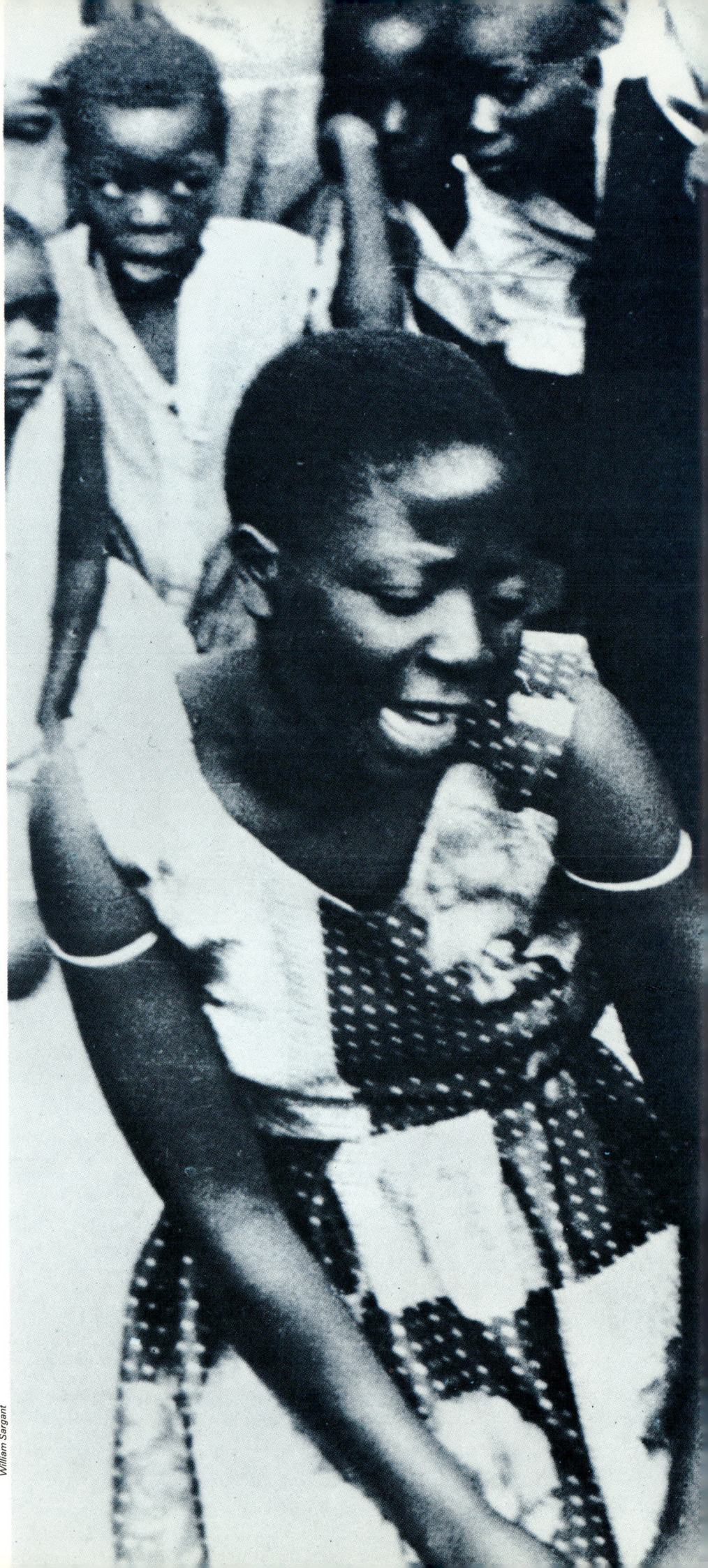

William Sargant

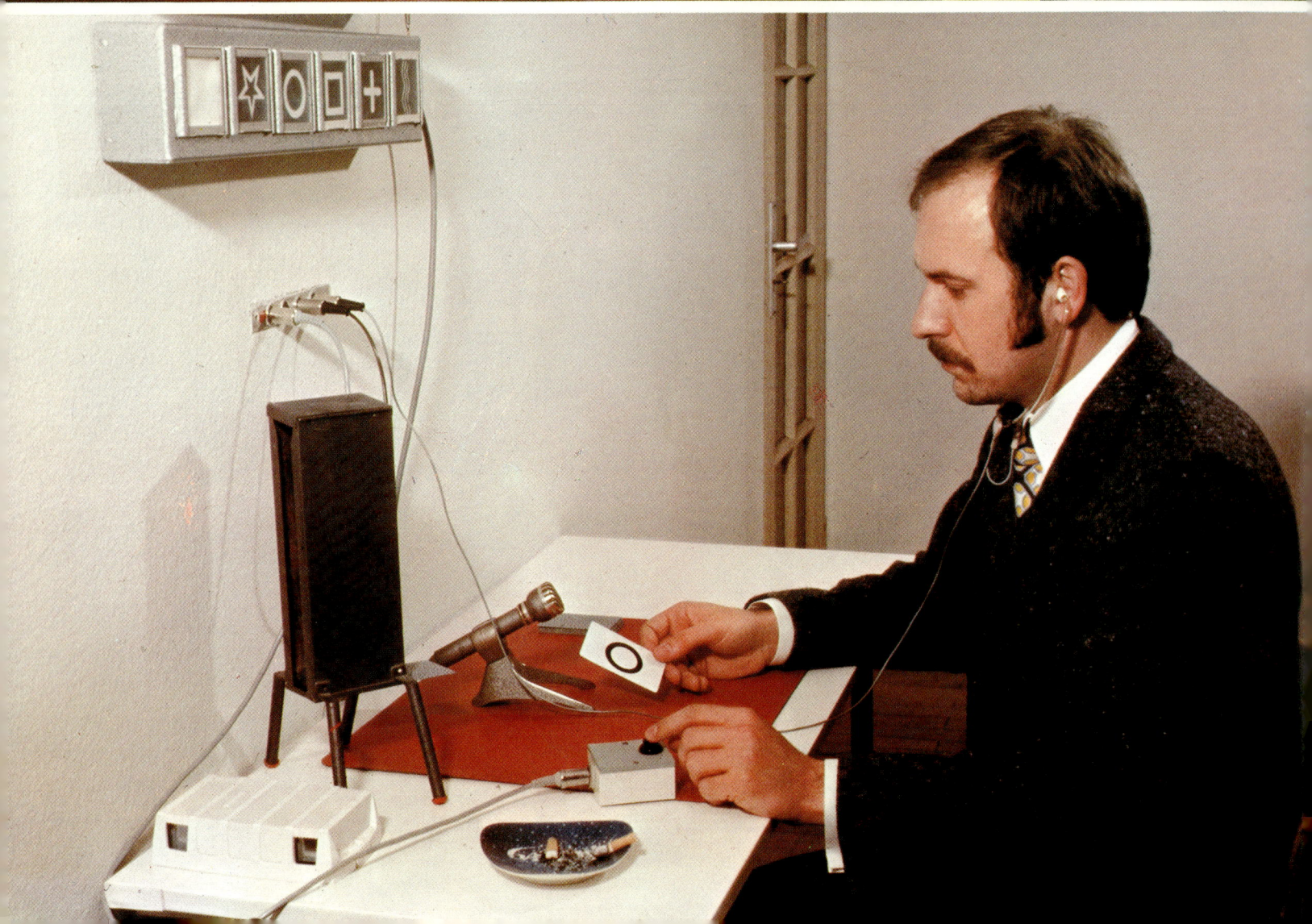

The Unexplained

EXTRA-SENSORY PERCEPTION

The reception of information by a person through other means than the senses is known as extra-sensory perception or ESP. It is thus one aspect of a two-way exchange with the environment that is not mediated by the senses and muscles. This more inclusive 'extra-sensorimotor' interaction is the area of study of the branch of science known as *parapsychology* (or psychical research), and it now conveniently identified in common practice by the use of the Greek letter *psi*. Extra-sensory perception is therefore one kind of psi communication, the other or 'extra-motor' part of the exchange being called *psychokinesis* (the manipulating of matter by mind alone) or PK.

Three types of ESP have so far been recognized. They were known long before the term extra-sensory perception was first used in 1934. Clairvoyance is the ESP of objects or events, precognition that of future

events, and telepathy the direct experience of another person's mental state.

This is obviously an odd way to divide up the sources from which knowledge might be gained by ESP – that is into objective events, future events and the thoughts of other people. Other claims have been made, as, for example, that of *retrocognition*, the ESP of past events, but it has no basis for acceptance in parapsychology.

The types of human experience represented by these three ESP classifications are not only very old but broadly distributed through the cultures of mankind. One recognizes the similarity of examples throughout this very wide distribution. For example premonitory dreams of personal tragedies, which are among the most commonly reported psi experiences in our own time, can be found among the records of ancient times. The dream credited to King Croesus, in which he foresaw the murder of his son, differed from the general type today chiefly in the point that it was the guard the King appointed as a consequence of his dream who turned out to be the murderer. This circular feature, which rarely appears in modern premonitory dreams, could well have been invented by a clever storyteller, as indeed the whole story itself may have been.

Abraham Lincoln's dream too, in which he is said to have seen himself in the coffin in which he lay some days later, also has to be viewed against the background of literary licence. But the point is that this type of ESP, precognition, in which information of a future event is seemingly acquired in the dreaming state, is typical of a really vast amount of reported human experience. The dream is one of the vehicles of extra-

sensory communication; future events definitely appear to be conveyed in some way, even against the stream of time; and all this has been going on a long, long time all around the world. Just how many of the dreams people have are ESP dreams it is futile to guess. Not all ESP dreams are precognitive either; they can also be clairvoyant or telepathic.

The Person 'Just Knows'

In the waking state, however, while ESP can be carried along in the daydreams that sometimes intrude, the device that most often gets ESP to the conscious experience of the individual is intuition, a form of knowledge that hides the means by which it is accomplished. The person 'just knows', and while he may know of something yet to happen or may intuitively know the thought of a distant friend or loved one, somewhat more commonly he knows of an objective event. But in most of these cases of ESP in everyday life there is no sharp boundary and no one can tell for certain that a case is pure clairvoyance or half telepathy. The woman who knew there was something wrong at home and who insisted on being driven home by her host in the midst of a dinner party seemed to have only a dim half-awareness of the tragic situation; but this and the house afire, and her invalid husband asleep, at least suggest clairvoyance.

But the mother who in the midst of a bridge game telephoned her home to ask what was the matter with the baby may have been telepathically experiencing the baby's painful predicament at the moment rather than 'seeing' the objective picture by clairvoyance. What emerges is the strong

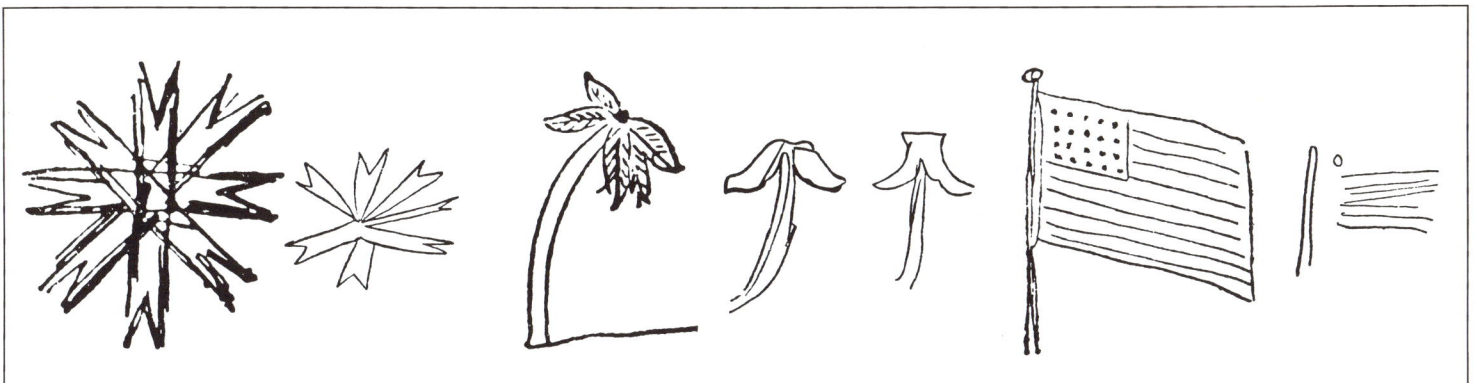

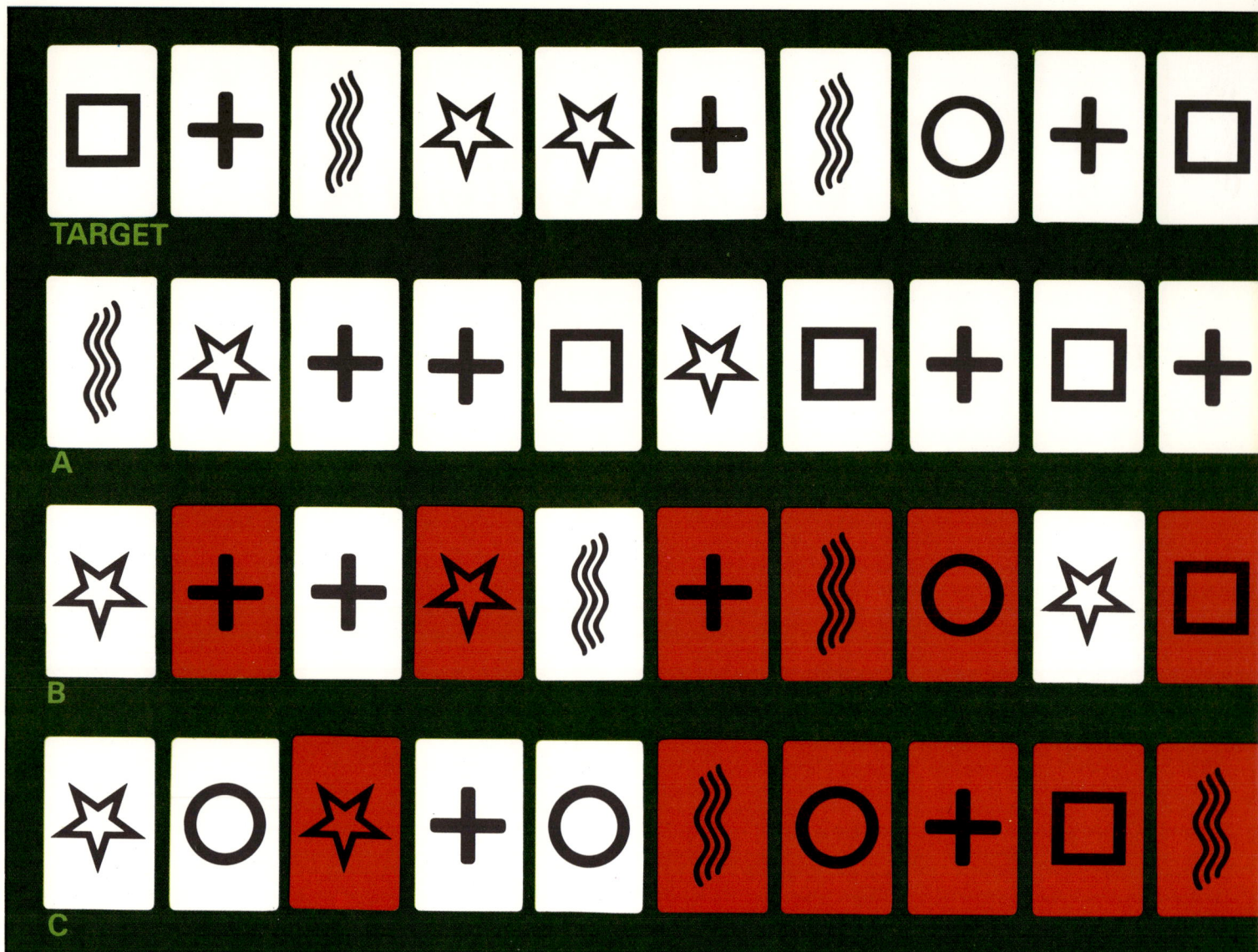

TARGET

A

B

C

probability that in a few rare cases it is thought alone that is conveyed. In other cases it seems as clearly to be the objective situation that is conveyed. Such experiences have provoked the scientist to ask the question: 'Is it possible for one mind to convey a message directly to another without using sensory channels? It is possible for an objective crisis to be picked up in some way by a person far beyond sensory range?' The experiences as they accumulated and fell into types threaded themselves on a common hypothesis long before any experiments were undertaken to verify it.

In the waking state there are other ways of getting information to a person's mind by ESP besides intuitions. One of these is hallucination, which is a comparatively rare experience, but among those that do occur telepathy is a common ingredient. The recipient usually sees or hears the person from whom he seems to be getting a message. Voices are more common than visual apparitions. A person experiencing the mental state of his 'sender' may undergo the specific state and even the suffering actually felt by the sender. This may involve going through the birth pains of the other, or the agonies of a heart attack, or even falling to the ground as the other had done in his crisis.

There will be no doubt in anyone's mind about the importance of these puzzling human experiences if they are what they seem. It was the fact, however, that it was impossible to be sure about them that so long delayed the investigation of the questions they raised. They were also not as easy to investigate as were the phenomena of the more objective and seemingly straight forward physical and biological sciences.

These case reports of mysterious happenings represent a class by themselves. If reported, as most of them are, by sane and respectable people, they cannot be lumped with the pathological and they definitely do not fit in easily with any other branch of the sciences. If then they have any sound basis of fact it would have to be something new for the scientific world – something different, radically different.

Because of this sharp difference the tendency developed among the easier and earlier sciences to regard these claims as not amenable to serious scientific treatment. They were looked down on as something that could not be explained, as most scientific findings could, by the known and familiar principles of Nature. This meant they would have to be classified as supernatural, which amounted to putting them on the shelf so

far as scientific investigation went, and of course it greatly delayed their investigation.

ESP in Religion

It can be said with unreserved confidence that man's belief in ESP (and the related ability, psychokinesis) has had a long and a powerful impact on his life and his institutions. Quite probably no other single belief has exerted so large an influence on mankind. But this is much harder to see now that over much of the world belief in ESP is at a low ebb in comparison with ancient times. Consider first what such belief did for the individual who could impress his fellow men with his superior powers of knowing of events to come, of distant happenings, of matters on all sides which the senses could not reach. Such a man, other things being equal, would assume leadership and power. Governing systems long clung to the counsel of the 'wise men', the prophets, the soothsayers, the oracles. Most of the magic which was such an important part of all cultures the farther back from modern technology we go, depended heavily upon belief in extra-sensorial cognitive powers. Even such magic as lingers in our Western cultures still usually carries an element of belief in ESP, obscured as a rule

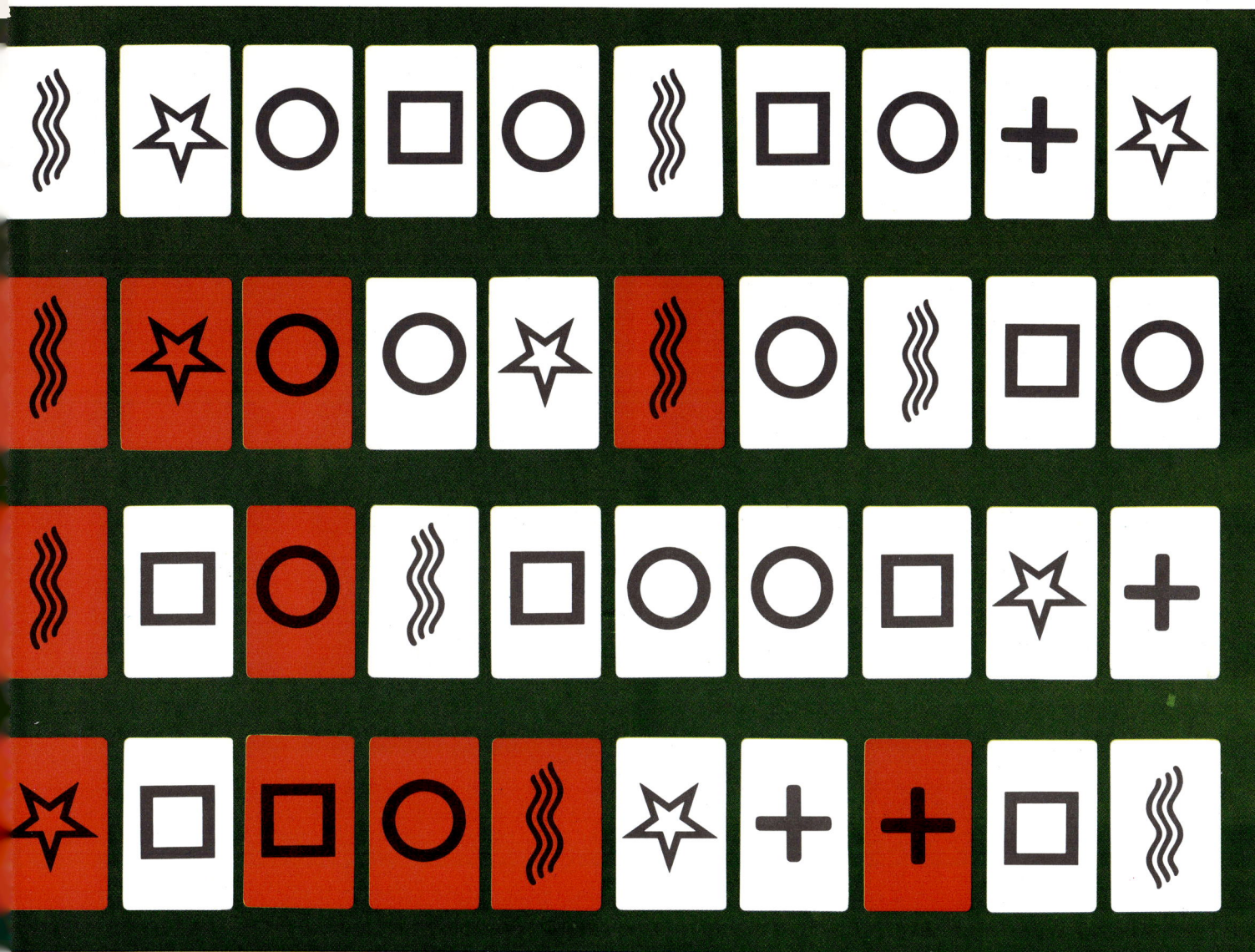

under other formulations. The dowser may have his theory of terrestrial magnetism, while essentially assuming an ability more properly recognizable as clairvoyance.

Even the popular concept of luck in games of chance comes close to qualifying as magic; and the casino games themselves so far approximate to loose tests of psi ability as to provide important elements for testing techniques for ESP and PK.

It is in religion, however, that psi has played by far its greatest role in human life, and here it is important to stress that it is belief in psi that is under discussion. How much genuine capacity has underlain this belief would be difficult to estimate. But it can be said that it is the belief in the powers of psi that has given the religions of mankind their main principles of communication between man and the divine. There is of course a great deal more to religion than the mere basis of exchange, the modes of interaction. But what has come to be called the supernatural (the miraculous and the transcendent) in religion is much the same as the types of capacity that are now the subject of study in parapsychology.

The parallel is rather impressive. All the types of psi are present in the theological system: precognition as prophecy, clairvoy-ance as revelation, telepathy in prayer, and the answer to prayer through physical miracles as psychokinesis. It would be hard to conceive of religion without psi principles of communication. In a word, the religious follower is bound to believe in psi. This is obvious regardless of the validity of either psi or religious doctrine.

The change from thinking of divine agency as the reason behind such puzzling phenomena as psi, to thinking of psi as a natural principle of communication, called for some explanatory idea that made sense. The mere thought of a natural principle of that kind had to wait until men were at the cultural stage when they began to grasp at general laws that could explain natural phenomena. By the 18th century, however, the emergence of the science of physics had brought forth theories of universal fluids and interplanetary forces. Franz Mesmer's theory of a universal animal magnetism encouraged rational thinking as to how people could influence each other without sensory contact and how communication with the spirit world might occur. Emanuel Swedenborg was believed by his followers to have demonstrated that it actually did so. The 19th century concept of a universal ether and of wavelike communication in this

medium favoured the search for a natural explanation for what had been hitherto regarded as completely miraculous. It brought within the bounds of the more venturesome speculation of the day the claim of survival after death of spiritual or ethereal bodies, as well as possible communication with the dead on telepathic lines.

The Spiritualist movement based on communication with the dead through mediums was a natural result of these and other favouring systems of thought. The somnambulism that developed from later mesmeric practices contributed an important device for the practice of mediumship. By the 1880s enough evidence from mediumship had accumulated to impress a number of scholarly people and to bring the methods of science to bear on the claims made. The

105

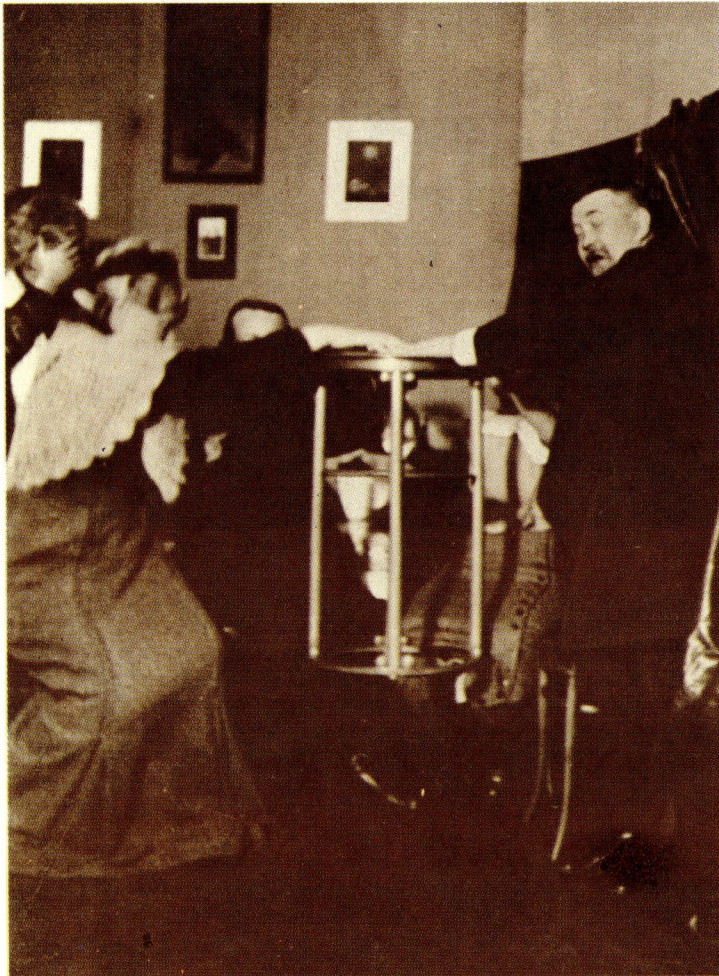
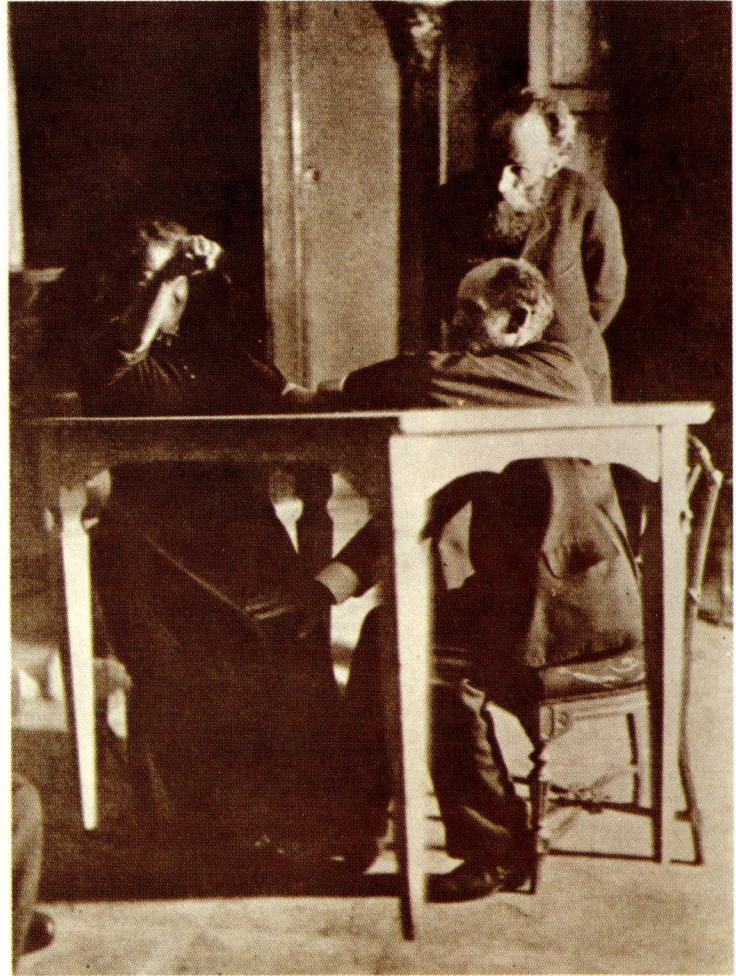

Serious investigation of parapsychology, with testing under controlled conditions, grew out of the intense interest in Spiritualism and mediums of the 19th century, when controls were at first rudimentary Above *The famous medium Eusapia Palladino levitating a table (if genuine, a case of psychokinesis)* Right *An observer holds Eusapia's arm and leg to prevent trickery*

Society for Psychical Research, founded in 1882 in England to investigate 'mesmeric, psychical and spiritualistic claims', set an example that was followed by similar societies in a number of other countries in succeeding years. This movement was capably led, especially in Britain, and made considerable progress in drawing the problems connected with mediumship into better focus, but it did not succeed in bringing the major issue, that of spirit communication, to a scientific conclusion. Rather there was a growing realization over the next 40 years that the problem was much more difficult than the Spiritualist demonstrations had suggested.

Nevertheless the attack on the problem of survival after death did direct attention to the claim of thought transference. It was obvious from the start that a medium would have to be gifted with telepathy to intermediate between two worlds; but at the same time, if she were gifted with telepathy she might in this way be able to get the information for her messages from living sources rather than non-material. Telepathy became almost as important an issue as the survival issue itself. It led to experimental work not

only under the sponsorship of the Society for Psychical Research but also, during the first quarter of this century, within university departments of psychology, particularly in America. The American universities of Harvard and Stanford and the University of Groningen in Holland, stand out especially. The experiments at these three universities, judged by the standards of the day, fully justified continuance but in no case did this happen. Telepathy turned out to be much more difficult to work with than most of the other mental abilities being tested in those days, and ease of demonstration had much to do with the eligibility of a subject for a university programme. Psychology itself was still on trial. Psychical research could add nothing to its respectability, and it could not offer young scientists a successful career. The effort was premature.

But something was established that was important. First, a number of psychologists had obtained significant results in telepathy tests; beginnings had been made. Second, in some of these tests the subjects were unselected volunteers, not especially gifted individuals. The way had certainly been made easier for the work undertaken at Duke University in North Carolina in 1927.

With the sponsoring interest of the Professor of Psychology, William McDougall, and a new and liberal university administration, a more favourable setting was provided for psychical research at Duke University in 1927 than had existed anywhere before. In addition, the two biologists, J. B. and Louisa E. Rhine, who went to Duke to work

under McDougall, had undertaken the exploration after some years of independent and critical study of the claims and the evidence for ESP.

Clairvoyance Testing

The major problem, however, which brought the Rhines to Duke was not the problem of telepathy. It was the question of survival after death, as based upon the analysis of mediumistic communication. The telepathy problem was recognized as important, and research was to be carried out on that and related problems too. But the first issue which concerned them was survival, so long as it could be scientifically handled.

That, however, was the question. Eight years later a tentative conclusion was reached that the mediumistic approach to the problem of survival could not bring a solution. The medium tested in the Duke Laboratory did obtain reliable information pertinent to the appropriate sitter in the adjoining room; and the evaluation of the results was done under what are called 'double-blind' conditions. But the question as to where the medium obtained her information could not be answered. Because it need not have been from non-material sources, the method could not be considered conclusive, and there the matter still stands.

Telepathy of course was part of the alternative explanation of the medium's success. Accordingly, as the survival question had lost ground, ESP had received more attention and by 1933 and 1934 was clearly in the ascendancy. In 1934 the Duke

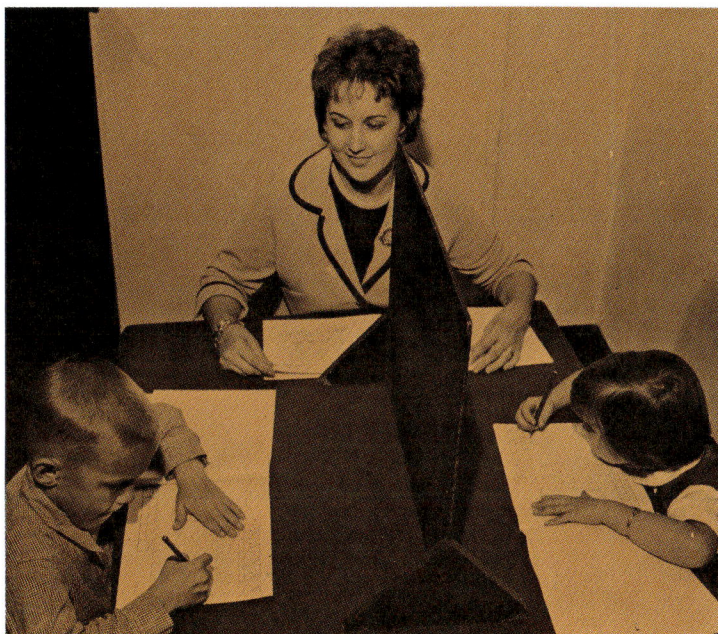

Researchers now class the types of parapsychical ability (clairvoyance, precognition, telepathy and psychokinesis) as effects of a single ability, called 'psi'. Evidence for one of these effects, precognition, or the ability to forecast future events, has been found through tests which raise difficult questions about the nature of time Left One of the Schmidt Psi-Test machines with which significantly successful results have recently been obtained. The girl presses one of four buttons to indicate which of four coloured lights will come on next. The machine selects the order of lights by a method that starts with electrons emitted from a radioactive substance Above Children, who frequently do better in the tests than adults, try to guess which one of the pictures they are shown will fit the story being told

Laboratory issued its first report, a monograph entitled *Extra-sensory Perception*.

But telepathy testing too hit a snag almost at the outset. It was found, on making a survey of all the past telepathy experiments, that none had ever been carried out properly – that is, in such a way that the subject (the person trying to establish extra-sensory perception) could not have got his information by clairvoyance as well as by telepathy. The sender of the message had always looked at a card or other object. There had never been a pure telepathy test controlled to exclude clairvoyance.

By December 1933 the clairvoyant type of ESP seemed well enough established to justify taking the next step.

The actual testing techniques for precognition were so simple a modification of those of clairvoyance, that they seemed almost too casual and trivial for so great an issue. In the last month of 1933 a subject who had done very well in the distance tests of clairvoyance was asked to predict the order of cards in a pack as it would be after the cards had been put through a certain shuffling routine. For comparison he was also asked to call down through a pack of 25 cards as it lay in its box until the end of the guessing. In these two series, the one testing precognition and the other merely calling down through the pack as it was, the subject obtained approximately the same (significant) rate of scoring. A few months after the precognition experiments had begun, the experimenters in the Duke Department of Psychology were precipitated,

ahead of schedule, into an exploration of the claim popularly known as 'mind over matter'. The group had undertaken to test the claim that rolling dice could be directly influenced by mental concentration to fall as they were willed, with a designated face or combination of faces uppermost. This work had progressed to the point where the PK hypothesis, as it came to be called, was being taken seriously as probably another 'parapsychical phenomenon', one that was to be considered along with clairvoyance, telepathy and precognition.

Telepathy on the Cards

As soon as enthusiasm cooled a little with regard to precognition and PK, as had happened by the mid-40s when finally the results of both developments had got into publication, the psi research group at the Duke parapsychology laboratory turned its attention to the long-shelved problems of telepathy.

The results were quite significant and the experiment was so well supervised that it seemed to make a good case as far as this design can be considered a test of telepathy. Later a comparable and similar successful demonstration of pure telepathy was carried out by S. G. Soal in England. These two experiments are the only two cases on record in support of the telepathy hypothesis.

But as the English researchers R. H. Thouless and B. P. Wiesner pointed out, there are a number of ways of getting round the necessity of direct mental exchange even under the carefully guarded conditions of

these experiments. Conceivably some contact with the receiver's or the sender's brain might intermediate and still leave no detectable indication.

The Unity of Psi

Another important development was the growing tendency to think of the different types of psi as only surface effects of a basically unified ability. With the suggestion of Thouless and Wiesner of a common inclusive term, the Greek letter *psi*, this became easier to adopt and there has been little discussion in recent years of any one of the types as an independent function in itself. Rather, as knowledge grows about these different psi phenomena, their common properties and similarities are so striking as to leave little doubt that a single psi process is involved, but one that can both bring information extra-sensorially and effect an extra-motor influence in PK. However, the integrated problem area loses none of its complexity in this working hypothesis of unity and each type still raises its own particular set of questions.

A few biologists will admit even to considering an extra-physical factor in the living organism. This means that biology has been largely physicalistic and has resisted the idea of a peculiar life energy, a specific vital principle. One sees no escape, however, even for the biologist now, since parapsychology has given psi the status of fact. At least the human organism no longer completely fits the mechanistic theory that has long dominated the life sciences.

PSYCHOKINESIS

Psychokinesis or PK is what the layman calls 'mind over matter'. It is the ability to influence the objective environment without the use of the motor system of the body (the muscles and glands). PK is the counterpart of extra-sensory perception or ESP, which is the acquisition of knowledge without sensory aid.

Reports of PK happenings appear in the records of the past as far back as records go. Today of course it is impossible to check on the reliability of such older reports as are available, but at least men believed they were witnessing miraculous physical events that seemed to have their origin in superhuman agency.

Whether the production of these mysterious physical effects was associated with the prevailing religious doctrine or attributed to one of the many systems of magic, the indi-

Belief in 'mind over matter' is very old, and there are many reports of the human mind influencing its physical environment in ways which were thought supernatural and miraculous. They include accounts of magical healing, rain-making and other types of weather control, and such peculiar powers as the ability to levitate: The disciples saw Jesus walking on the water, and St Peter tried to emulate him but began to sink

vidual who was believed to exercise control over them was likely to become an influential member of the community, whether priest or magician. He might be the tribal rainmaker or healer or the practitioner of some strange power to save or destroy. Belief in this ability to control the physical environment may still be found even today, and not only in less sophisticated cultures. There are actually many unorthodox practices of healing that suggest PK still going on within sight of some of the modern medical centres. For example, warts are reported to be removed from men and animals, at least without known physical intermediation. Other 'magical' therapies are practised as well, such as the control of bleeding or the counteraction of injury from burns. Most of these healings are not expressly in the name of religion, although the practitioner may personally believe that it is the work of God that he is carrying out.

How valid these claims are no one can safely say. Certainly no practically dependable application of the alleged powers has emerged and persisted over the centuries as evidence of a reliable principle. Belief in supernatural physical effects has steadily declined with the advancement of the natural sciences, but this does not in itself prove that no PK function ever operated

to produce the effects men believed were unexplainable by physics. At most it indicates that the evidence for the PK interpretation has not been good enough for the educated modern intellect.

The Nature of PK

Enough is already known about PK, however, to allow some illuminating generalizations about its nature. Of these, first consideration should be given to the relation of PK to the physical world. Almost immediately in the early testing at Duke, it was noticed that none of the physical properties of the dice seemed to be important in relation to the scoring rate – that is unless they led to psychological preferences. For example, the subjects found that they could achieve a better scoring rate (a better rate per die) while throwing two dice at a time instead of one. Yet two dice certainly made the task more difficult from a purely physical viewpoint. Again, when two dice per throw were compared with six, the larger number gave the better rate of success per dice. But the subjects recognized in all these comparisons that they *liked* to throw two dice better than one and preferred six to two. The larger number made a faster moving and more efficient procedure than the smaller.

Essentially the same type of effect was observed with respect to two different sizes of dice used in the test. Very small dice did not do well and exceptionally large ones were not as high in yield as medium sizes (from $\frac{5}{8}$ to $\frac{3}{4}$ of an inch). Again the rate of success seemed to be largely a matter of the size

Leif Geiges

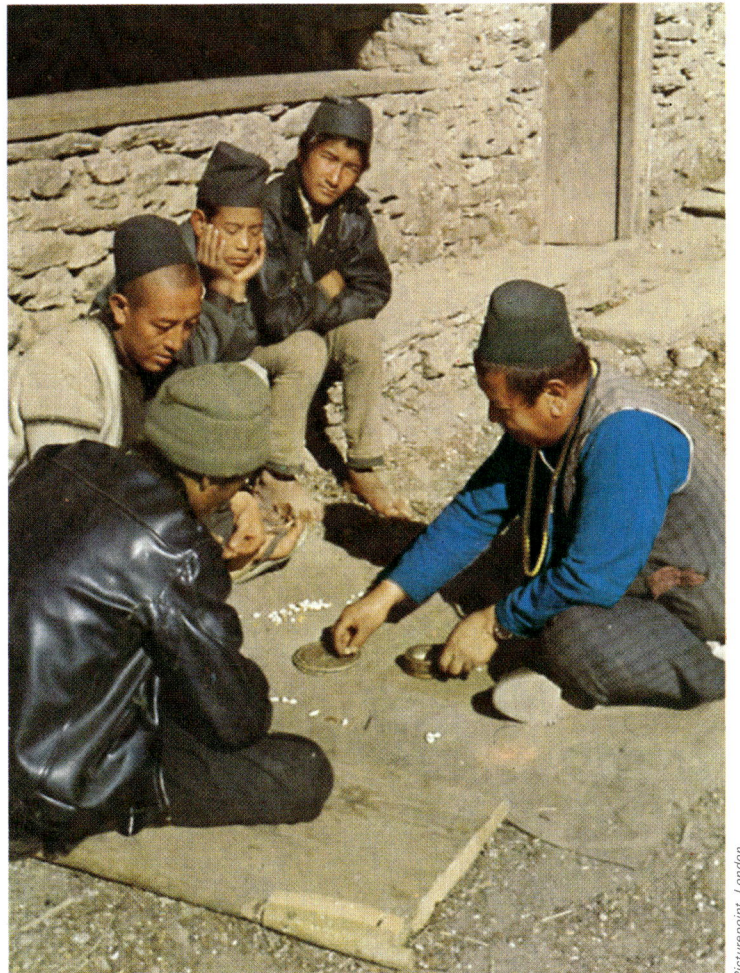

Top illustrations *Psychokinesis (PK) became an important competing hypothesis to ESP, for it was suggested that significant scoring of hits in card-guessing tests might be due, not to precognition, but to the ability to influence the shuffle, so as to make the fall of cards match the 'predictions' made by the subject. It is now considered that ESP and PK are not separated or competing abilities but effects of a single ability, which parapsychologists call 'psi'. PK required ESP for any intelligent hypothesis of its operation and in most experiments the subject could not give intelligent guidance to PK without using ESP at the same time, for example to know where, how and when to apply the effort*

Above *Much of the evidence for PK has come from experiments with dice throwing, testing a subject's ability to will the dice to fall with specified faces showing. PK may account for what the gambler calls a winning, or losing, streak of luck, which may in fact be the product of psi ability* Right *Sherpas playing dice in a village in Nepal: the belief that in certain states of mind one can psychologically control the fall of the dice is a concept which is familiar to gamblers the world over*

Picturepoint, London

that could most easily be picked up.

At this point, of course, the concept of a psi energy is not much more than a working hypothesis. It is true that mental energy has from time to time been suggested by psychologists, but until the work in experimental parapsychology began they had no way of testing the hypothesis of an energy that is different from the recognized physical systems. PK research experiments with dice, conducted by Haakon Forwald, were found to produce effects that were measurable in terms of standard units of energy; yet under the test conditions no known physical energy could conceivably have been responsible for these effects. It is true that the only measurement possible was the physical differences in the results produced. These were the mean distances between dice released from the same point and allowed to roll by gravity, with one side of the table the designated target in one set of trials and the opposite side in another. Thus the cubes of known weight were caused by PK to roll to the side intended to a measurable average distance.

Forwald, of course, was not directly measuring the energy which influenced the dice but rather the resultant lateral displacement. However, at this point it is a question as to whether concepts such as quantity (associated primarily with the physical order) are indeed applicable to this psi function or for that matter to any process that is distinctly mental.

Targets in PK Tests

What kinds and states of matter can PK influence? First approaches have usually to be made at the easiest point of attack. Clairvoyance was the simplest starting point for assault on the ESP side. In PK it had to be something with moving targets (PK-MT) since matter in motion offers advantages; almost all the PK work done since the beginning of 1934 has been with targets in motion, mostly dice.

A certain amount of testing of PK with moving targets has involved the use of electrical equipment, such as electric clocks and pendulum devices adapted to the tests. The attempt has been made also to use the flow of liquids or sand as target matter. Tests have likewise been made on micro-physical targets, as in the emanation of electrons from radioactive substances.

On the whole, nothing in the PK testing has thus far consistently exceeded the rate of success with the dice throwing methods. It still remains to be seen how the new work with electronic targets will compare with dice tests. So far there is no indication of a new level of magnitude of PK performance to correspond to the microscopic size of the targets.

As stated, all these materials have been inanimate objects in motion. What about PK on living targets, or PK-LT? The idea has long prevailed in popular folklore that some individuals have the power to influence plant growth and others to affect animals, including man, physically in various ways. The plant specialists are said to possess what is known as a 'green thumb', and others are believed to be able to induce healing of the sick by unknown powers that suggest

PK. In recent years efforts have been made to test these healing and growth-promoting powers in the laboratory. The PK tests most often tried were based on the attempt to influence the growth rate of seedlings and the best known of these efforts is the work of Dr Bernard Grad of McGill University Medical School. But there have been a few efforts to influence animal healing and other effects on the animal organism. It would be fair to say that altogether a good beginning has been made on PK tests with living targets; but a hard and fast valuation need not be forced at this stage. The research continues, but it should not be confused with fantastic and prematurely popularized claims of emotional reactions of plants and so-called plant perception.

OBJECT READING

The use of an article, called an 'inductor', as a means of receiving extra-sensory impressions is known as object reading, or psychoscopy; the term more usually employed in this country is psychometry. Extra-sensory perception (paragnosis) is a broad term covering various concepts, of which the most important are telepathy and clairvoyance. Clairvoyance, the ability to see objects not actually present, may be in time – seeing into the past, present or future – or in space (telaesthesia), in which case it should be considered as synonymous with clairvoyance in the present.

When we observe psychometrists during experiments and ask them about their ways of working, it appears that they usually get their impressions in the form of images coming to them or being 'forced' upon them: this is how the various thoughts connected with the object handed to them are experienced. These 'enforced' thoughts may be regarded as the forerunners of the 'veridical hallucinations' (hallucinations bearing a correspondence with reality, with actual fact) which occur to sensitives.

The self-observations of our subjects show us that their 'hallucinations', just like eidetic images, can sometimes be exceptionally sharp and detailed. The veridical hallucinations of sensitives seem not only to be limited to sight, and the same is true for the hallucinations of people with eidetic abilities.

Seeing Bits and Pieces

When we try to remember a name heard in the past, or an event which happened a long time ago, it can happen that this name or event suddenly 'stands before our eyes'. But it also can happen that such a name or event will return to us in bits and pieces. Every event is built up of a number of various elements. The same difficulty in getting a complete 'picture' can be observed in psychometrists. Often they will get only a few letters of a first or last name 'thrust onto' them in a paranormal way, or they very often 'see' only a few elements of the totality of events occurring in the past of people with whom they are in telepathic rapport. In one psi experiment the subject, on being introduced to a lady unknown to him, suddenly 'saw' the image of a pair of long white gloves and long ear-rings. The sensitive told the lady that both images went together and had something to do with her, but he did not know what the connection was. She then explained that as a member of a theatrical group she had recently played a

part in which she had to wear long white gloves and long ear-rings. For the second act she had to change costumes, and one evening one of the gloves got caught in an ear-ring. This agitated her a great deal especially since she had so little time before she was obliged to return to the stage again

A Lowered Consciousness

A lowered state of consciousness, that causes the person to be less inhibited, is evidently favourable to psychometry. In observing psychometrists, their level of consciousness during the experiments is seen to be lowered totally or in part. In most cases this lower level is so slight that it can only be detected with special instruments. With a few subjects this lowering of the level of consciousness goes so far, however, that one may speak of trance and auto-hypnosis. The state of lessening of inhibition resulting from the auto-hypnosis enhances the flow of telepathically received impressions.

Experiments with psychometrists have shown that not only are they not affected in their functioning by distance between experimenter and subject but that they can also break through the time barrier. Some of their experiences show that they are able to get impressions from persons they will meet – by chance – in the future.

Extensive experiments in the Parapsychological Institute of the State University of Utrecht have proved that some sensitives are able under certain circumstances to furnish data about lost persons, thefts and murders; the Institute has now initiated extensive research into this subject.

Reasons for Blind Spots

The man in the street tends to think, incorrectly, that sensitives are able to see anything and everything. Nothing is further from the truth. Continual research has taught us that in nearly all such persons we find a more or less specialized interest determined in part by their own experiences. A psychoanalytical approach should, then, provide a knowledge of the urges which motivate them towards their interest.

In contradistinction to the urge to see certain things, there exists also the urge *not* to see certain things. It is self-evident that this negative urge ought to interest the researcher just as much as the positive one. The following case is a starting point. In October 1958, a Mrs A.B., who has often given evidence of psi abilities, was visited by a woman. In the course of the visit, Mrs A.B.

spontaneously asked her visitor whether her father was possibly interested in the play *Gijsbrecht van Amstel,* as she got the impression that in some way or other he had something to do with this Dutch tragedy. On receiving a negative answer, Mrs A.B. did not pursue the matter further.

On 17 January 1960 the visitor's father died. The family inserted the announcement of his death in the newspaper *Tubantia* the following day and Mrs A.B.'s visitor also signed the announcement. Under this insertion, at a distance of about 6 inches, there was an advertisement of the traditional January performance of *Gijsbrecht van Amstel.* Because both announcements were coincidentally associated in space as well as in time, and both were read by the visitor, we may accept that we have here a case of a so-called 'displacement' or substitution based on 'defence' mechanism which certainly originated in a repression.

Some years ago a 23-year-old student was contacted who was gifted with psi abilities to some degree. A series of psychometric experiments followed which on the whole produced satisfying results. One day, when handed a cap to be used as an inductor, the subject said that this object gave him a very unpleasant feeling. The cap, which had been made available by the police, belonged to a man sought in connection with the murder of the new-born child of his unmarried daughter. The student told me that he felt terrified. Suddenly he threw the inductor away, stating that he did not get any impressions.

Some days later, the test subject asked me whether it had something to do with the murder of a new-born child. When asked why he put this question, he said that he had had a dream about a man who had put a new-born child under a heap of pillows. Afterwards a conversation followed about 'displacements' in time as observed by Whately Carington, S. G. Soal and others. Suddenly the subject exclaimed: 'Now I know why I did not get any impressions a few days ago.' He began to talk in detail about an event in his childhood. His mother gave birth to a second child and gave so much care and attention to the new baby that it aroused feelings of hate and repugnance in him. One day, an aunt who happened to visit them saw him deliberately throwing bricks into the cradle: his aunt gave him a good spanking.

When asked if he could find any connection between this experience of his youth and his not being able to tell anything about the inductor (that is, the cap) given to him a few days previously, the subject answered: 'It's quite clear. Unwittingly I identified myself with the murderer of the child. Something within me told me: "You might have done the same thing: you are capable of doing something like that." Therefore I did not want to see it.' When he was asked if he could account for his anxiety when he took the inductor in his hand, the subject answered without hesitation that this anxiety must have resulted from a deep repression. 'Evidently, I knew at once when you handed me the inductor that this had to do with the murderer of a child. Because I identified myself with the murderer, however, I must immediately have repressed these impressions, which caused anxiety. During my

sleep, when censorship was weakened, the story loomed up in me.'

In the dreams and hallucinations of sensitives the phenomenon of condensation or compression has also frequently been noticed. The following is an interesting case of such condensation. It concerns a sensitive, W. Tholen, who, like Gerard Croiset, has succeeded innumerable times in supplying details by telephone about missing persons, animals and objects. In August 1964 he was consulted on the telephone by a doctor, unknown to him, whose wife had mislaid three trinkets. Mr Tholen gave a description of an antique cupboard which was supposedly in the consultant's home. He 'saw' the missing objects in this cupboard. Since the doctor did not possess such a cupboard he paid no further attention to the sensitive's words. One day he did find the three trinkets, but in three different cupboards. He then realized that the sensitive had amalgamated parts of these three cupboards into a new piece of furniture.

Many descriptions by sensitives have been recorded in which situations both from the past and the future blend with situations from the present into a new and at first unrecognizable whole. Croiset, for instance, when asked to indicate where a missing person might be found, described a stretch of river where ships were moored. The ships were at that time no longer there but had been moored there some days previously. It was the place where the missing person had drowned, and Croiset had wanted to indicate where to look.

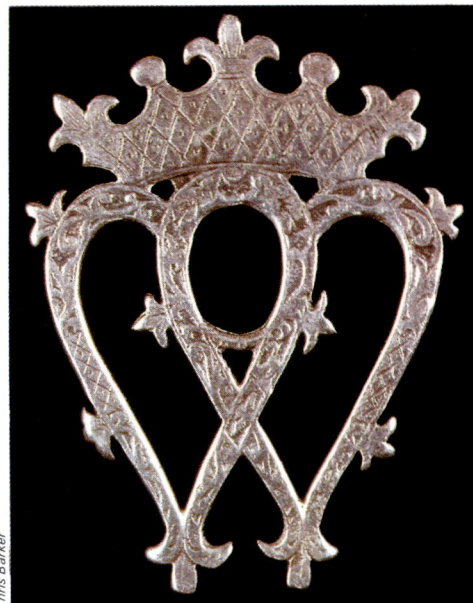

Chris Barker

Above *This brooch is said to have belonged to the ill-fated Mary Queen of Scots. A 'sensitive' may provide accurate information about the owner of an object (an 'inductor') and experiments suggest that in some cases the explanation is telepathy from the mind of an investigator who knows the object's history*
Below *The famous Dutch 'sensitive' Gerard Croiset holds a ring during an object reading session. He has often helped to trace missing objects and persons, and has assisted police with their investigations of thefts and murders*

Leif Geiges

SPONTANEOUS PSI EXPERIENCES

Spontaneous psychic experiences include widely diversified kinds of unusual occurrences. They range over unaccountable 'awarenesses', true dreams, seemingly uncaused movements of physical objects, and unexplainable sights and sounds sometimes taken to be caused by the dead. The common element in all of them, however, is that by them the persons involved secure information not revealed by their senses, or produce effects not mediated by their muscles. This is the characteristic that divides these experiences from sensorimotor ones on the one hand, and instances of fantasy, imagination or delusion on the other.

Historically, psychic experiences had no rational explanation, since the phenomena were not caused by the senses or muscles, and therefore seemed mysterious, even supernatural. Research in parapsychology, however, has thrown light on their nature and origin. They turn out to be the result of normal but obscure mental processes, that

Visual and other hallucinations sometimes carry a powerful and terrifying sense of impending danger, which may prove to have been justified: King Belshazzar sees a hand writing on the wall of his palace during a drunken feast; detail taken from a painting by Rembrandt

do not operate like the sensorimotor ones but have their own laws and regularities. These processes constitute what is known as psi ability, the subject of parapsychological research.

The experimental work, besides showing that psi ability exists, has also led to a degree of understanding of it, so that the experiences can now be taken as the probable spontaneous natural operation of a known human capacity. At the present stage their range offers a wider perspective on psi ability than the experimental researches have as yet verified. Therefore they can be the source of further suggestions about the still unknown aspects of it, suggestions that will inevitably be supported or discarded later according to the outcome of both current and future experimental testing.

It is easy to see now why psychic manifestations have been baffling and mysterious, because it is now recognized that the psi process is an unconscious one. The person does not know when it operates or that he himself was involved in the operation. It was largely because of this unconscious origin that psi was long unsuspected and its effects generally misunderstood and often misinterpreted. For because the person is unaware of his own role in the production of a psi effect the tendency has been to assume it to be

something imposed upon or communicated to him from the outside. This has been particularly true when a dying or deceased person seemed to play an active role in the phenomena or when it was possible to suppose that such an influence was involved at some time or other.

Besides the mystery raised by the unconscious operation of psi, the manifestations themselves took many different forms and no unifying underlying principle was obvious. Only after decades of controlled research has it been established that the phenomena are the result of an underlying mental process (the psi process) that it is possible to express in various ways according to the different situations.

The concept of the psi process can be simplified by considering it as consisting of two stages. Stage 1 is that in which an item of information somehow becomes 'accessible', at an unconscious level. How this can occur is the true unknown of the psychic process. Also unknown are the factors or influences that permit one specific item to be 'chosen', picked out from all others, as the topic of a given experience. Stage 2 is a psychological rather than a parapsychological one, for in it the selected item is transferred to consciousness in a psychological form or as a physical effect. Nearly all of the facts about the psi

112

National Gallery/Brompton Studio

process that have now been established concern this psychological stage.

Certain psi experiences are just like the intuitions of ordinary life except that their subject matter was apparently received (in Stage 1) by ESP. The characteristic of intuitive experience, both when ESP is involved and when it is not, is the sudden 'awareness' of the given item of information without any recognizable reason for knowing it and without mental imagery, as in the case reported by a woman in Michigan. During the Second World War, when she was in hospital after the birth of her child, a letter came saying that her husband in France had died of a heart attack. But she said, 'It wasn't a heart attack. He was poisoned.'

'I honestly did not know I was going to say it,' she said. 'It was as if someone else had said it for me. I insisted that they check with Washington. They did and I was right. He had been poisoned. I never knew why they first said it was a heart attack.'

Hallucinations are pseudo-perceptual impressions; they occur when no external objective stimulus is present to cause them. Usually they do not involve ESP, but when they do the experience brings information about a real situation. In these any sense modality may be involved but the auditory is reported most frequently. The human voice is perhaps the sound that is reported as most frequently 'heard'.

Probably better known, even if actually reported more rarely than the auditory, are visual hallucinations. Many of them coincide with the death of the individual 'seen', the experience thus seeming to serve as a communication to report it. A typical case comes from a woman in Kansas, who said: 'At an early hour one morning my father sat up suddenly in bed. My mother asked, "What is the matter, Bob?" He replied, "Mother

Dreams carry their meanings by imagery, not the imagery of pseudo-sense experiences as in hallucinations but a dramatization of memories of sense experience. In the Romance of the Rose *the hero dreams of his quest for love – the Rose: he finds the Rose in a beautiful garden but is driven away by Danger, Scandal and Shame; French* MS, *15th century, in the British Museum*

is dead." She tried to convince him it was a nightmare, but he said, "No, I was never wider awake. Mother was standing by the bed just looking at me. She was pale, her hair was down, she was dressed in a white gown. There was a large red spot on the right side of her neck. I know she's dead." Word came that she died from an aneurism at about the same time on the same date.'

Not quite all of the ESP experiences that feature imagery occur in sleep. Occasionally a person while awake may have an experience involving imagery (day-dream) which also brings information by ESP. Since the form is the same as that of a dream such experiences, whether realistic or unrealistic, can be classed as dreams even though the person was not sleeping.

All ESP experiences come in one or other of these forms – intuitive, hallucinatory, or realistic or unrealistic dreams, and bring items of information in varying degrees of completeness. The forms usually are fairly distinct from each other, although in occasional instances a tendency to change from one to another in the same dream has been known to occur.

The PK form never produces a complete item of information, and is also the form least frequently reported. This may mean that relatively few personalities can produce cases of spontaneous PK. It also may be partly because this is the most difficult form of all to identify with a degree of certainty. For not only must the effect be timed with the crisis but the absence of ordinary causes, too, must be established. These points often are difficult to make, for usually it is only some time afterwards that the details are noted. Consequently they are often unconvincing.

Who Chooses the Message?

Even though psi experiences may bring information about a practically unlimited range of topics, the message in any particular case concerns only one specific topic. Obviously it is selected from all other thoughts, things or future events that might have concerned the person. But is it a topic that impresses itself upon the person from the outside, something like a telegram bringing an item of news? Or does he himself 'reach out' and pick this particular item from all the others, because of his interest in it? Indirectly, if not directly, it is possible now to get something of an answer to this question, both logically and by studying the range of topics involved in a large number of experiences.

Logically, the choice between the two alternatives is different now than in the past. Before the occurrence of precognition had been recognized, it seemed more likely that the person was the receiver of a message impressed upon or communicated to him from the outside, for all experiences under consideration then were contemporaneous with the time of the event. But now no such necessary temporal connection exists. Presumably an experience involving a future event could occur at any time beforehand, and besides that it would be difficult to think of a future event as being 'sent' to a person.

Earlier, another impression was also current, which was that psychic experiences nearly always concern crises of great importance to the person, and that they frequently involve communications from the dead. Both ideas implied that the psi message was at least urgent, if not that it actually induced a sensitive person to have an experience about it.

Psi and the Dead

Psi experiences in which someone dead appears to play an active part are infrequent in comparison to those in which no such personality is involved. They occur, but once all types of spontaneous ESP, and especially the precognitive, are now recognized, those that involve the deceased have been found to make up a very small part of the total number.

Reported cases that seem to involve the deceased are of two general kinds which are different superficially, though not in the basic psi process. One of these is the simple related kind, like those mentioned above; the other is more complicated and the phenomena tend to recur in such the same way for an indefinite time. The second category includes haunting and poltergeist phenomena.

Unrepeated experiences in which deceased persons appear to be involved take some of the same forms discussed in earlier sections. One of these is the dream. Dreams involving the deceased are usually realistic in details, but the appearance of someone dead in an active role in a dream of course cannot be considered to be realistic. Such dreams are therefore classified as unrealistic in form. An example was reported by a woman in Detroit. She said that after her mother died, her father said she should have her mother's jewels; they lived in the same apartment and he kept them in his possession. Later he moved to another city and she supposed he took the jewels with him. After his death there, she did not find them among his belongings and she began to worry about them. One night in a dream her father appeared and told her she had worried enough, and she would find the jewels in the dresser in his old room. She should pull out a certain drawer and at the back she would find a small box built into the dresser, so that it could not be seen unless one knew where to look. She did as he said and found the jewels hidden as he had described.

Even better known than dreams of the deceased are hallucinatory experiences involving them. (Hallucinatory, it should be recalled, is a term to denote that the person thought a sense, or senses, was involved when no objective reason was present.) A visual hallucinatory experience was reported by a woman in Connecticut. Her father had died some years before. She was awakened very early one morning. She heard nothing but saw her father standing at the foot of her bed. Somehow, though he did not speak, she got the command to go to her mother's home at once. She felt it was so urgent that she got up and within the hour had started on the trip home, a distance of over four hundred miles. She found her mother very ill and alone, and almost certainly she would have died without the help of her daughter.

Even more frequent than visual hallucina-tions are auditory ones involving someone deceased. An example comes from a woman in South Dakota. Her father, on whom she had depended a great deal, had recently died, and she felt very much alone and helpless in the midst of many troubles. Her husband had long been ill and the family was badly in debt. They were behind in their car payments, and a man came one day to repossess the car. As she reports, 'While I was talking to the man at the front door, just as clear as my own voice, I heard my father say, "Tell him to wait till Friday." Without hesitation I told him to wait till Friday and I would pay him. He agreed and went on. Then I began to wonder how I could raise the $280 due. Thursday afternoon my father's lawyer called me and told me to come to his office and pick up a check for $117. The court had collected an old account owed to my father.'

PK effects that seem to relate to the deceased also occur. Such an experience was reported by a woman in New York. The occasion was a dinner party that she gave for five couples, all of whom had known a man who had suddenly died of a heart attack two days before, while on a trip to South America. When the wine was passed, the closest friend of the deceased rose and proposed the toast. She was holding her glass by the bowl, the stem broke off and fell to the floor. Her glass had not touched anything – she was just holding it. They all felt that their deceased friend was present.

The imagery of dreams carries information secured by psi to levels of consciousness where memory of the dream can take over, and it is clear that the imagery itself is unconsciously constructed to fit the case. The hallucinatory forms and PK are also vehicles for the expression of information below the conscious level, and are forms in which information may be expressed when no deceased person is involved. Presumably, therefore, when a spirit agent appears as a character in the drama he could be another imaginary creation. The *forms* of the experiences in themselves can thus have no definitive significance for survival.

If spirit personalities exist after death and are in any way actually involved in these experiences, then detection of the fact would have to depend on evidence other than that the dead person *appeared* to play an active role in the drama of a psi experience. It would have to distinguish between influences ascribable to the deceased and those that might be exerted by the living person.

Possibly such evidence might be found in differences between the reasons or motives for communicating which the two persons, the living and the dead, might be presumed to have had. If the motive of the dead person in making the specific communication was much stronger than that of the living, then the bearing of the case would at least favour the idea that the deceased had influenced or caused the experience.

It can be observed, however, that experiences in which the dead seem to play an active role, if considered as unconscious dramatizations, do involve more complicated happenings than other unrealistic psi dreams usually do. In these not only do the deceased appear as self-activated characters, but they also deliver the message. This may mean that these appearances of the deceased are not purely dramatizations, but actual influences; or on the other hand, it may mean that the unconscious dramatizing ability of very few dreamers is of sufficient force to be able to produce this level of fantasy.

The situation regarding these experiences, therefore, is that they cannot be finally interpreted now that psi is known to be an ability that living persons possess. But at the same time that psi prevents an interpretation for or against the survival hypothesis, it does permit the question to be raised. If survival does occur, psi would be the necessary form by which communications from the deceased to the living would take place. But if it does occur, the methods of research by which the fact could be established have not yet been developed.

Above *Florentine mosaic of Pharaoh's prophetic dream of plenty and hunger* Above right *Collective hallucination has been suggested as a possible explanation of some strange cases reported in the past: from a broadsheet of 1681, describing a battle between two phantom armies in the sky* Right *A night phantom, traditionally believed in Normandy to lure men to their deaths in marshes*

Catalogue of Occultists

ANNIE BESANT (1847–1933)

This remarkable woman gave unstintingly of her restless gifts in her successive devotions to Anglo-Catholicism, atheism, women's emancipation, Theosophy and Indian nationalism. Her interest in the occult was a devouring passion.

Of all Annie Besant's manifold activities, it is her work in helping to arouse Indian national sentiment that is most likely to be remembered by posterity, although her labours in the cause of women's emancipation in late 19th century England were scarcely less important. Her sincerity few would question; her judgement was another matter altogether. She was proud, and although she had a sense of fun, most who knew her suspected that she had no sense of humour, and little genuine capacity for self-criticism. This may go some way toward explaining her errors of judgement, but it can never explain away a fascinating and incredibly many-sided personality, a lover of mankind and a woman whose need for commerce with the unseen world can be described as a devouring passion.

MME BLAVATSKY (1831–1891)

Towards the end of the 19th century the eccentric and extraordinary Helena Petrovna Blavatsky, founder of the Theosophical Society, dominated the occult scene in a career which moved from Spiritualism to an attempt to unite the eastern and western magical traditions, and from the performance of apparent miracles to violent accusations of fraud.

The Frenchman, Eliphas Levi, in his attempts to resuscitate western ceremonial magic with its roots in the Cabala, had entered the field before her, but it was Mme Blavatsky's peculiar merit to have made the bridge between the western and eastern magical systems and found the source of occult wisdom in the eastern Wisdom tradition.

Mme Blavatsky's mystic brooch, with her initials in a hexagram (spirit and matter interlocked) topped by a swastika (the ceaseless coming into being of life) enclosed in a snake swallowing its own tail (immortality), surmounted by the crown of perfection

John Symonds

ANTONIO CONSELHEIRO (1835–1897)

This holy man, who predicted that the world would end in 1900, aroused the hostility of both the government and the Church in Brazil but his followers regarded him with reverence and fought to the last man for his beliefs.

The most spectacular of the various leaders of millennial movements that have arisen in Brazil, Antonio Vicente Mendes Maciel, called Conselheiro, 'the Counsellor', was born in 1835. He was the child of a family of impoverished landowners in north-east Brazil. As a wandering preacher, he quickly gained the respect of the superstitious peasants, and acquired the name of 'Counsellor' because of a reputation he gained for wisdom and as an arbitrator in local disputes.

After the establishment of the Republic of Brazil in 1889, Conselheiro's prophetic utterances came to have a clear anti-republican character.

He led his following north into the arid backlands and settled in the village of Canudos, remote from civilization.

Eventually, a force of over 5000 was dispatched by an alarmed government which feared a major insurrection. A long campaign ensued. Only when a regular supply line was established, and larger cannon brought into the difficult positions around Canudos, was there a prospect of victory for the government. The cannon destroyed the towers of the new church and soon afterwards, in 1897, Conselheiro became ill, apparently suffering from dysentery, and died.

WILLIAM CROOKES (1832–1919)

Eminent among a group of distinguished Victorian scientists who interested themselves in Spiritualist phenomena, Sir William Crookes was a meticulous and penetrating experimentalist. He was elected to the Royal Society at the early age of 31, following his discovery of a new element, thallium. He was President of a number of learned societies, ranging from the Chemical Society to the Society for Psychical Research, and was President of the Royal Society itself from 1913 to 1915. His great versatility was reflected in the stream of papers reporting his work published between 1851 and 1918.

Almost all of Crookes's records of his psychical experiments seem to have fallen into irresponsible hands and been destroyed after his death, so his work must be judged almost entirely from his published reports and the accounts of a few eyewitnesses. His contemporary papers were collected and published in book form: *Researches in the Phenomena of Spiritualism* (1874).

Most present-day parapsychologists are sceptical of at least the more extreme phenomena accepted by Crookes and would consider him deluded. In the words of his friend Sir Oliver Lodge: 'It is almost as difficult to resist the testimony as it is to accept the things testified.'

ALEISTER CROWLEY (1875–1947)

An air of unsavoury mystery still surrounds the life and teachings of Aleister Crowley nearly a quarter of a century after his death. Violently hostile to Christianity, he saw himself as the Messiah of a new religion.

Poet, novelist, writer of books on magic, eccentric – Crowley was all this and more. He strove hard to assume the mantle of magician, and long before he died he knew that he had succeeded. He is thus in direct line of descent from Sir Edward Kelley,

Cagliostro, the Comte de Saint-Germain, Eliphas Levi and Madame Blavatsky, all of whom were credited with remarkable, if not miraculous powers. While still a Christian and subjected to daily Bible readings in the Crowley household, he had taken a fancy to the 'False Prophet', 'the Beast whose number is 666', and the 'Scarlet Woman', characters or archetypes which were to play a prominent and decisive part in his later life.

He championed the will *(thelema)* or true self in man as opposed to external authority, priests and gods. 'Be strong, o man! lust, enjoy all things of sense and rapture: fear not that any God shall deny thee for this.' Sexual promiscuity and heroin addiction are the chief cause of his infamous reputation.

THE DAVENPORT BROTHERS

Ira Erastus Davenport (1839–1911) and his younger brother, William Henry Harrison Davenport (1841–1877), were two of the most spectacular mediums of the 19th century. Their stage act, with its demonstration of apparently supernatural powers, caused intense excitement and controversy.

The Davenport brothers were able to produce sounds from musical instruments which were hung near them in a darkened room, while they were tied up with heavy ropes. In their later, more elaborate display the brothers were tied hand and foot at opposite ends of a giant box, with doors. When the doors were shut, bells were heard to ring, musical instruments inside the box were played and 'spirit hands' appeared at an opening in one of the doors.

Whether the Davenports had any genuine mediumistic powers, or whether they were nothing more than brilliant showmen and illusionists, was hotly debated. Many people believed in them, and some still do, but stage conjurors of the time, including J. N. Maskelyne and Houdini, the great escape artist who became a violent opponent of Spiritualism, were convinced that they could duplicate the Davenports' effects.

JOHN DEE (1527–1608)

Queen Elizabeth I's astrologer and a noted scientist, John Dee claimed to talk with angels. He was also employed in the Queen's secret service. How far his magical activities were a cover for espionage is a problem which remains unsolved to this day.

In the eyes of many of his contemporaries John Dee was a charlatan, imposter and dabbler in black magic. This portrait of the man was embellished by many writers, especially by Samuel Butler, whose *Hudibras* contains a vicious caricature of Dee, and even the *Biographica Britannica* describes him as 'extremely credulous, extravagantly vain and a most deluded enthusiast'. Although Dee's life story is well documented, little has been done to explain or interpret him. His abundant output of erudite works, his projects and treatises, reveal him as one of the most remarkable of Elizabethan scholars. He was an authority on mathematics, navigation, astronomy and optics, as well as being Astrologer Royal to Elizabeth I.

Below left Top of Aleister Crowley's Janus-headed magical wand Below right The Australian violinist Leila Waddell, 'Laylah' or 'Sister Cybele', one of Crowley's many mistresses and magical assistants, with the mark of the Beast between her breasts.

ARTHUR CONAN DOYLE (1859–1930)

The greatest mystery of all faced the creator of Sherlock Holmes when he tried to find positive proof of life after death.

A keen student of all psychic and paranormal phenomena for nearly half a century, Sir Arthur Conan Doyle spent the last 12 years of his life as an active and leading exponent of the doctrines of Spiritualism.

In his disputations on the Spiritualist controversy Conan Doyle did not at any time attempt to deny the existence of some fraud among mediums and psychic practitioners, but he asserted that it was far less common than was supposed, and that he himself had in fact only encountered it three or four times in his life.

An avowed agnostic, Conan Doyle did not immediately reach the conclusion that there was indeed a life after death, even after he had acknowledged the validity of various supernormal phenomena. For 20 years he was moving towards such a belief, and by 1916 he declared that he was in possession of positive knowledge to this effect. Although opposed to all church dogma he retained a deep respect for the principles of Christianity, as for those of Islam and Buddhism.

MARY BAKER EDDY (1821–1910)

Scandals and law suits marked the spectacular career of the woman known to her many thousands of followers as 'Mother'.

The discoverer and founder of Christian Science, Mary Baker Eddy, was born Mary Baker at Bow, New Hampshire, the youngest of six children. The facts of her early life are, despite her own autobiographical recollections and many official biographies produced

The personality of Mary Baker Eddy, a woman of limited education but strong character, still dominates the Christian Science movement. A legend in her lifetime, she claimed miraculous powers of healing and direct revelation from God

by the Christian Science movement, very much disputed.

Despite the limitations of her education, Mrs Eddy became one of the really remarkable women of the latter part of the 19th century, producing several books, of which one sold many more than a million copies, founding a Church and an international daily newspaper and influencing, through her teachings, the lives of many thousands of people throughout the world.

Mrs Patterson (as she then was) went as a patient to Phineas P. Quimby in Portland, Maine. Until his death in 1866 she was a regular patient of his, once staying for some months under his care. Quimby's system of healing was without doubt the most important influence on Christian Science as Mrs Eddy later developed it. Quimby got his ideas from Charles Poyen, a French mesmerist who had travelled in New England.

Her own reputation as a mental healer is largely based on a number of dramatic, and mainly self-recounted, occasions of healing. The healings are largely unauthenticated by medical testimony – a circumstance which Christian Scientists attribute to the hostility of medical practitioners to mental healing.

DION FORTUNE (1891–1946)

Occultist, psychoanalyst and novelist, Dion Fortune – whose real name was Violet Mary Firth – showed signs at a very early age of extreme sensitivity to people and places and it soon became evident that she possessed strongly developed psychic faculties. Brought up in a Christian Science household, her most characteristic book, *Psychic Defence* (1930), is a study of the abuses of occult power and the ways in which the victim can protect himself.

Her own group – the Fraternity of the Inner Light – was founded in the 1920s and is still in existence.

Under the assumed name Dion Fortune she wrote widely on the occult, her most important book being *The Mystical Qabalah* (1935); much of her material was related to Aleister Crowley's researches in the sphere of magical correspondences and symbolic affinities. Towards the end of her life these two adepts, both of whom were intent upon reviving the ancient mysteries, exchanged a number of letters.

Like many occultists, Dion Fortune also used fiction as a vehicle for her ideas, well aware that in this way she could disseminate truths which would otherwise be incommunicable to uninitiated minds.

EDMUND GURNEY (1847–1889)

Edmund Gurney was a founder of the Society for Psychical Research and one of the most important pioneers in the scientific investigation of ostensibly paranormal phenomena.

Gurney's work in psychical research deals mainly with hypnotism and phantasms of the living. His research into hypnotism falls into two main divisions. The first is a study, theoretical and practical, of the purely psychological features of hypnotism, without regard to any paranormal phenomena which may be associated with it. The second is an experimental study of ostensibly paranormal features in connection with some cases of hypnosis, for example, in the telepathic induction of the hypnotic state, in community of sensation between operator and subject, and in some of the feats performed by subjects under hypnosis.

D. D. HOME (1833–1886)

One of the most celebrated mediums of all time, D. D. Home displayed his gifts before emperors and peers, poets and scientists; despite the closest scrutiny of his demonstrations, he was never discredited. The question of how he did it has remained unanswered to this day. Speculation is endless. The only clue left today is Home's handwriting. If it is possible to control matter magically, that is, to transfer one's psychic force to matter till matter moves, then Home (graphologically considered) was the person to do it. He was certainly inflated enough; and the great men

Below Drawing by Steffi Grant of the Vault of the Adepts of the Golden Dawn. Dion Fortune believed that her initiation into this occult society was responsible for healing her from the damaging effects of a 'psychic attack'

of his age, from the Tsar and the Kaiser and the French Emperor to Lord Adare, who sat before him, provided the terrific stimulus he required. He would not perform for anyone. From time to time he complained that the power had left him, and he was incapable – not the words of a charlatan or a trickster who can always perform until he is found out. He exploited himself ruthlessly; there was nothing to hold him. Like a priest in a fertility cult, he moved his psychic force into the table and made it vibrate and rise. The heaviness of the table had nothing to do with it; and he made himself immune to pain when he picked up red-hot coals. Those who do not believe in the powers of the psyche but only in the power of matter, unable to find a satisfactory explanation, are driven to dispose of the awkward facts by the hypothesis of mass hallucination or deception.

IBN ARABI (1165–1240)

Generally acknowledged as one of the greatest mystics of Islam, Mohammed ibn Ali ibn Arabi, of the Arab tribe of Ta'i, was born at Muriac in south-east Spain. He is known as *Muhyi 'd-Din,* 'the vivifier of the Religion' and *Ash-Shaikh al-Akbar,* 'The Greatest Sheikh'.

He was the most prolific of all Sufi writers. His unique combination of quality with quantity is in a sense a vindication of his claim, repeated again and again throughout

Kenneth Grant

his works, that everything he wrote was forced upon him by the Divine Spirit. His writing was never motivated, he says, by the desire to compose a book. It was simply, as he puts it, 'a way out' from the fire of inspiration which he sometimes felt would burn him up. In addition to his many other gifts, Ibn Arabi is also considered as one of the greatest poets of Islam.

The most exalted and at the same time the most generally known aspect of his writing lies in his formulations of 'Oneness of Being', a doctrine known as 'monism' to Western scholars who have, more often than not, failed to realize that it is in no sense the invention of Ibn Arabi. 'Oneness of Being' is the doctrine that only God *is*, and that the existence of anything else is pure illusion. The created universe is nothing other than the overflowing of God's merciful infinitude, which does not thereby cease to be its one indivisible Self. This has always been the basic doctrine of Islamic mysticism. What characterizes Ibn Arabi is his extreme and sometimes provocative explicitness, where most of his predecessors had preferred to express themselves by aphorism.

ELIPHAS LEVI (1810–1875)

Undoubtedly the most renowned French occultist of his generation, Eliphas Levi (Abbé Louis Constant) was the son of a humble shoe-maker.

Eliphas was born and died in Paris. His best-known books, such as *Transcendental Magic, The History of Magic,* and *The Key of the Mysteries,* which are still available in English translations, have been read by successive generations of students of magic and occultism since the first of them was published in 1856. Levi was, however, an indifferent scholar and though his writings contain much that is illuminating, they should be read as literature rather than as technical manuals.

Although by no means a public figure, his name was now well known in occultist circles in France and Great Britain and to a much lesser extent in Germany.

He never published a complete Tarot manual, but the stray allusions to these cards in his books greatly influenced the generation of French occultists that appeared upon the scene about a decade after his death Papus's theory outlined in his *Tarot of the Bohemians,* that the 22 major trumps are related to the 22 letters of the Hebrew alphabet and hence have a cabalistic significance, derives directly from Levi. The latter once observed that were he to be again condemned to spend a period of time in a prison cell, the only 'book' that he would need would be a Tarot pack since the major trumps, in his opinion, incorporated a complete system of esoteric wisdom.

Although the honesty of Mrs Piper's mediumship was never doubted, many felt that the alleged 'communicators' were aspects of her own personality, 'fed' with information gained telepathically from the living

F. W. H. MYERS (1834–1901)

Frederick William Henry Myers first came into close contact with the two men who became, with him, the chief founders of the Society for Psychical Research, in the 1870s. Both Fellows of Trinity College, Cambridge, they were his senior, and sometime teacher, Henry Sidgwick (1838–1900), and his junior, and sometime pupil, Edmund Gurney (1847–1888). Myers became point Honorary Secretary to the S.P.R. in 1888, after Gurney's untimely death, and President in 1900. He had helped Gurney in the immense labour of preparing *Phantasms of the Living* (1886). During this period almost all important work on such topics as hypnosis, hysteria, multiple personality, and what may be called in general 'abnormal psychology', had been done on the Continent, particularly in France. English psychologists and philosophers had contributed almost nothing, and had largely ignored the work which was being done by others. Myers, who made a thorough study of the material published abroad, was almost the only Englishman at the time who had attempted to do so. His numerous reviews in the S.P.R. *Proceedings* of works by Continental authors on abnormal psychology are masterprices of exposition, and were at the time almost the only source of information on subjects of this nature that were available in English at the time.

Myers's characteristic views on the nature of human personality, and his grounds for holding that it survives the death of the body, are most fully stated in his posthumously published two-volume work *Human Personality and its Survival of Bodily Death* (1903).

MRS PIPER (1875–1950)

Mrs Leonora E. Piper of Boston, Massachusetts, was one of the most remarkable mental mediums of all time.

Mrs Piper's reputation reached William James, Professor of Psychology at Harvard University. James went to sit with her, and received a good deal of information about, and allegedly from, members of his own family.

Richard Hodgson, a leading member of the British Society for Psychical Research, assumed charge of the investigation in 1887. Hodgson arranged for the careful recording of all sittings, and took the most extreme precautions against trickery.

It was agreed by almost everyone who had any extensive first-hand dealings with Mrs Piper and her phenomena that she was completely honest. Richard Hodgson and F. W. H. Myers became in the end convinced that the 'communicators' really were the spirits of deceased persons. But others felt it more likely that the alleged 'communicators' were simply aspects of Mrs Piper's own personality, 'fed' with

Psychic News

information gained telepathically from living people. Her personality showed through the 'communicators' in many ways – for instance in their ignorance of science and literature, their interest in clothes and hats, and the kinds of common associations which they all seemed to possess. Yet the information given by communicators was not infrequently quite unknown to any of the sitters, so that the hypothesis of telepathy with the living has its difficulties.

EUSAPIA PALLADINO (1854–1918)

Born in 1854 at Minervo-Murge, near Bari in Italy, Eusapia Palladino was the daughter of Italian peasants. Her mother died at her birth and when she was 12 years old her father was murdered by brigands. Taken into the household of a Neapolitan family, who were interested in Spiritualism, as a nursery-maid, she soon showed signs of abnormal gifts. From then on her career led from one scientific investigation to another, almost up to her death.

Her phenomena consisted of the occurrences common to physical mediums. While she was said to be securely held or fastened, there would occur raps and bangs on the furniture and walls of the room; touches on the bodies of the investigators and telekinetic movements.

The most notorious feature of Eusapia's strange personality was her incessant resort to trickery. Nevertheless, one of her most outstanding investigators, the French physiologist Professor Richet, stated that, in spite of her many frauds 'all the men of science, without exception, who experimented with her were in the end convinced that she produced genuine phenomena'. No other medium so well illustrates the difficulties and complexities of physical mediumship.

The vast literature on Eusapia is full of interesting comments on her strange psychology. Certainly no more intriguing and illuminating example can be found for studying the problems of physical mediumship.

D. G. ROSSETTI (1828–1882)

Born in London. A poet and painter in the Victorian age, Rossetti mentally dwelt in other worlds. He projected himself, in the imagination, into the Italy of the 13th and 14th centuries, the Florence of his great namesake, Dante Alighieri. The doctrine of 'truth to Nature' that inspired his co-founders of the Pre-Raphaelite Brotherhood, Holman Hunt and John Millais, was to him quite alien. Rossetti might be said to stand rather for 'truth to dreamland'.

In his complex mind the fascination of the weird and the occult was interwoven with ideas of strangely fated romantic loves and psychological encounters. It is dramatically seen in the drawings, of which he made several versions, inspired by the legend of the Doppelgänger or Double.

The drug chloral and unlimited whisky made for a phase of hallucination, another imagined world, this time of universal

Rossetti and his model Jane Morris 'created the mysterious agony of Pre-Raphaelite love with its droop and heavy-lidded frustration'. Detail from The Day-Dream by Rossetti

enmity towards him after he had retrieved from his wife's coffin in Highgate cemetery the manuscript book of his poems which in his grief he had buried with her.

G. W. RUSSELL (1867–1935)

In his first book, Homeward Songs by the Way, lies a clue to the man whom the world knew as 'A.E.' He had signed the book 'Aeon', a word that had come to him unbidden. When he later discovered its occult meaning – Aeon, a rebellious angel, or the divergence of the soul from God and its journey through successive incarnations back to its source – he found in it a confirmation of his own meaning. But since the printer had deciphered it as A.E., he accepted the letters as a name.

A.E. was born in 1867, in Northern Ireland, of evangelical parents who moved to Dublin when he was 11.

He was a pillar of the Irish Renaissance and an assistant with Yeats, Synge and Lady Gregory, at the birth of the Abbey Theatre. His editing of The Irish Statesman

effected a second literary revival in which A.E. was as much the central figure as Yeats had been of the first. He set himself to whip up the Irish conscience.

It is not easy to assess just how much A.E. owned to Theosophy. A.E. himself, in a late letter, said 'I had a natural mysticism of my own before I knew the Indian seers'. He never failed, however, to acknowledge his debt to those who had turned his attention to the classical Sanskrit writer Patanjali and the Upanishads and his copy of the Bhagavad Gita was always with him.

He left the Theosophical Society in 1898 to found the Hermetic Society, where, it has been said, he was careful to discourage students from dabbling in the occult but insisted on the paramount need for the practice of meditation. Throughout his life he constantly reverted to the ancient teaching that every ascent of the soul implies the necessity of a corresponding descent.

RUDOLF STEINER (1861–1925)

The extraordinary originality of Rudolf Steiner's mind led him to a philosophy which linked up the world of natural science with the world of Spirit; his revolutionary ideas took form in a number of enterprises, which spanned a range from art and architecture to education and farming.

The son of a minor official on the Southern Austrian Railway, Rudolf Steiner was born on 27 February 1861 at Kraljevic, then on the borders of Austria and Hungary, but now located in Yugoslavia.

An unusual combination of scientific and artistic interests led him to Goethe, and at the early age of 23 he was responsible for editing Goethe's scientific works which were to be published in an edition of *Deutsche National-literatur*.

His work in the Goethe Archives at Weimar, begun when he was 29 years old, was Steiner's first settled job. In 1897 he accepted an invitation to go to Berlin to edit the *Magazine for Literature* which was associated with a stage society which produced 'modern' plays that were not likely to reach the ordinary theatre. In Berlin he also joined the staff of a working men's college, which gave him a deep insight into prevailing social conditions.

Meditation, however, had become a necessity to him – that 'experience of the whole man through which he reaches the actual spiritual world far more than through ideas'. His first opportunity to speak to an audience esoterically was when a certain Count Brock-dorff, having read an article of Steiner's on Goethe's esoteric fairy tale, *The Green Snake and the Beautiful Lily*, invited him to come as a lecturer and present his views to the members of a theosophical circle.

This led to a ten-year connection with the Theosophical Society, to visits to London where he met Annie Besant, Colonel Olcott and other leaders of the movement, and to his accepting the position of General Secretary to the German branch of the Society. In 1909, being totally opposed to the declaration of a further incarnation of Christ and other theosophical trends, he broke with that society and founded the Anthroposophical Society (from the Greek words *anthropos* and *sophia*, 'man' and 'wisdom'). Characteristic of the man is the recognition of the dangers as well as the difficulties of initiation, and the need to take three steps in morality for everyone which is taken in higher knowledge.

The Waldorf School in Stuttgart was originally founded in 1919 for the employees of a local factory. As its educational director, Steiner gathered teachers from all walks of life, and lectured to them on the three great psychological and physiological periods of childhood, on the temperaments, on the curriculum, and so on, as well as discussing with them the problems of individual children. This educational work roused particular interest in England and the English speaking world.

In his last years he developed with special intensity the subject of karma and reincarnation (the latter in a new and Christian form), which he considered vital for the modern age. And in 1923 he founded the Anthroposophical Society anew, placing at its centre the 'School of Spiritual Science' which was intended for those students who wished to follow a path of self-development.

SWEDENBORG (1688–1772)

Emanuel Swedenborg was born in Stockholm on 29 January 1688, the second son of the Lutheran Bishop of Skara. But it was not until 1745, with the publication of *Worship and the Love of God*, that religion became his one and only concern. His mysticism was not the mysticism of the trance or of the seance – it was a full-blooded avowal of his regular direct communication with beings from heaven. His religious writings are the record of these communications and he makes no concessions.

He was aware of the scepticism that such extraordinary claims would arouse, and in his first theological work he admitted: 'I am well aware that many persons will insist that it is impossible for anyone to converse with spirits and with angels during his life-time in the body; many will say that such intercourse must be mere fancy; some, that I have invented such relations in order to gain credit; whilst others will make other objections. For all these, however, I care not, since I have seen, heard and felt.'

For statements of this kind to have any credence, it is important to remember that Swedenborg was neither a dreamer, nor an ascetic with little experience of the world, but a practical applied scientist who had preferred the real business of mining to becoming the Professor of Astronomy in the University of Uppsala.

Although his work was all based upon his own direct mystical experience of God, he did not neglect scholarship, and the large volumes, written in Latin, were intended for the serious student and were in no sense considered as the means of popularizing a new religion.

Despite the enormous claims made in his writings, Swedenborg remained throughout his life a modest and simple person, working enormously hard, never marrying, and without any intention of founding a new sect, believing that his followers could be of any denomination.

Swedenborg spoke as if heaven and its inhabitants were his 'second home'. He knows them as he knows human beings and his knowledge enables him to maintain that man's real self is in form exactly as is his physical body, and if it had not been for the Fall, the body would have been sloughed off like a snake-skin. Instead, it is quite essential for men to die before they move on to a higher place.

So important is this concept of humanness that Swedenborg continually emphasizes that it is only through man's own eyes that he can see God, that God exists only in the terms that man can see him, and that those terms are human terms. The founding of the Swedenborgian Church – or the New Church, as its adherents prefer – does not imply that other Churches are wrong; it is merely to help to point the way and to complete the revelation which may already be seen by people in other Churches. Much of William Blake's work, for instance, is imbued with the Swedenborgianism he embraced and then left behind.

TEILHARD DE CHARDIN (1881–1955)

Born on 1 May 1881 at Sarcenat near Clermont-Ferrand in the Auvergne, France, Pierre Teilhard de Chardin took his first vows as a Jesuit and remained within the order until his death. But Teilhard was not only a priest but also a scientist – a paleontologist – of some distinction. Before his death he enjoyed a considerable reputation in his chosen field and in 1948 was offered a chair in Prehistory at the Collège de France. This offer he had to decline because his Jesuit superiors in Rome would not allow him to publish his most famous book, *The Phenomenon of Man*. For Teilhard de Chardin had ideas of his own, and these did not correspond to the official Roman Catholic orthodoxy prevalent at the time.

Not long after his death *The Phenomenon of Man* was published in the original French, the English translation appearing with a warmly sympathetic introduction by Sir Julian Huxley, in 1959.

Basically he saw the salvation of the world in terms of a real reconciliation between science and religion, a situation in which religion would be able to re-interpret itself in terms of evolution, and in which science itself would be 'tinged with mysticism and charged with faith', in terms of a 'synthesis of the (Christian) God "above", with the (Marxist) God "ahead"'. In scientific terms he saw the world as evolving to ever-higher stages of 'complexity-consciousness', for, quite rightly, he saw that there was no reason to suppose that evolution had suddenly come to a halt with the emergence of self-conscious man. The very troubles of our times were a sign that the human race was undergoing a new 'mutation', a new qualitative change which would result in a new and higher form of consciousness in which he believed that it would be possible for the individual consciousness to be transcended in some form of collective consciousness.

Teilhard was a pantheist and he knew it, but according to him there were two types of pantheism. These were what he describes as Hindu pantheism – the pantheism of diffusion and dissolution of all individual personality into an indeterminate whole – and a pantheism of 'centration' in which personality, so far from being obliterated, is heightened and clarified through love and centred on to the cosmic Christ who is the point to which all creation (or at least all of it that can be saved) is destined by evolution itself to converge. The 'oriental' pantheism of diffusion, which he had himself experienced time and again, is a blissful experience all right, but it is nonetheless essentially retrograde, a step back into a state of 'co-consciousness' before *self*-consciousness was born. The new mysticism neither abolishes personality nor sinks back into the beatific peace of undifferentiated oneness, but throws itself in a paroxysm of love into him who is both the source and goal of all personality and at the same time constitutes the collective fulfilment of all personalities.

TERESA OF AVILA (1515–1582)

A practical and down-to-earth mystic, Teresa of Avila at the same time attained lofty heights of spiritual experience; on the one hand, an able administrator and on the other, a saint who showed the way to the ultimate fusion of the soul's being with God.

Recognized as one of the greatest Christian mystics, Teresa de Cepeda y Ahumada, in religion Teresa of Jesus, will always be known as Teresa of Avila, from the Castilian town in which she was born on 28 March 1515 and where she spent most of her 67 years until her death on 4 October 1582. She was one of ten children – mostly boys – and when her father's second wife died in 1528, Teresa became something of an anxiety to her father, who finally put her in a boarding school, which she had to leave after 18 months owing to ill-health. He opposed her wish to become a nun, but at the age of 20 she eventually entered the Carmelite convent of the Incarnation in Avila.

In 1567 she was ordered by the general of the Carmelite Order, then on a visit to Spain, to make other foundations. The remaining 15 years of her life were largely spent in travelling, negotiating, working with her own hands – she was, a contemporary declares, the best cook in the order. For, whilst she enjoyed the most remarkable and lofty mystical experiences, she always kept her feet on the ground. 'The Lord walks amongst the saucepans', was a famous saying of hers. In all, she was personally responsible for setting up 19 establishments, including two for men. She was helped in her work by a Carmelite friar, Fr Jerome Gracian. But her chief support in the closing years of her life came from an even greater exponent of mystical theology, John of the Cross.

The seal was set on her life's work when, in 1581, the distinction between the 'calced' or shod, and 'discalced' or shoeless Carmelites, as the relaxed parent body and the stricter reformed order were respectively known, was officially recognized by their separation into two orders, with separate governing bodies. She died in the following year, at Alba, one of her many foundations.

The Interior Castle, written in 1577 and revised three years later, is universally recognized as her greatest achievement. It treats of the progress of the soul from the earliest imperfect stage to the final achievement of the mystic marriage. The 'castle' is pictured as a fabulously rich building, consisting of seven 'mansions' or apartments, the seventh and central one being the dwelling place of the Blessed Trinity, residing in the depths of the soul. Thus the mystic way is a turning away from outward reality to enter 'into oneself', there to find oneself in the embrace of God.

MRS WILLETT (1874–1956)

Until after her death on 31 August 1956, Mrs Charles Coombe Tennant was known in the literature of psychical research as 'Mrs Willett'. She was a most remarkable non-professional medium.

Born on 1 November 1874, and christened Winifred Margaret, she was the only child of George Edward Pearce-Serocold (1828–1912) by his second wife, Mary Richardson of Derwent Fawr, near Swansea.

On 12 December 1895, in her 22nd year, she married Charles Coombe Tennant (1852–1928) of Cadoxton Lodge, Glamorganshire. She was in many aspects a typical Victorian society lady, but she combined this with strong, and rather unusually radical, social and political interests. She was an early and enthusiastic supporter of women's suffrage. In politics she was a strong Liberal, and for a time a great admirer of Lloyd George. She took an active part in local administration in Glamorganshire, and was one of the first women JPs on the bench there. After the end of the First World War the British Government appointed her a delegate to the Assembly of the newly founded League of Nations. Of Welsh descent on her mother's side, she became a keen Welsh nationalist; played an active part and held high office in the National Eisteddfod; and was a discriminating patron of Welsh painting. Beside this, she made for herself a fine collection of modern French pictures.

It was probably through her brother-in-law, F. W. H. Myers, that she first became aware of the Society for Psychical Research and met some of its prominent members.

It was not until after the death of her daughter Daphne that her interest in psychical research became strong and her own very distinctive type of mediumship developed. Its nature, and the course of its development, are thoroughly described in Gerald Balfour's 'Study of the Psychological Aspects of Mrs. Willett's Mediumship', which he contributed to the S.P.R. *Proceedings* in 1935.

Mrs Coombe Tennant died in 1956 in her 82nd year, but on the face of it this was by no means the end of her psychic activities. For from 7 August 1957 to 6 March 1960, Miss Geraldine Cummins, who had been unknown to her personally, obtained a series of 40 automatic scripts purporting to come from her surviving spirit. They were published in 1965 under the title *Swan on a Black Sea*, and they have been the subject of much discussion since.

W. B. YEATS (1865–1939)

The son of Anglo-Irish parents of Protestant stock, William Butler Yeats did not inherit the Catholic faith of the nation for whose cause he worked as a member of the Young Ireland movement, and in whose parliament he afterwards became a Senator.

As an art student in Dublin Yeats formed a friendship with a class-mate, George Russell (A.E.) a natural mystic and visionary. Under the influence of A. P. Sinnett's *Esoteric Buddhism* the Dublin Hermetic Society was founded. On the invitation of this society the theosophist Mohini Chatterjee (named in a poem written many years later) came to Dublin, and from him Yeats learned the rudiments of Hindu philosophy, which remained a lifelong study.

Blake was, during the 1880s, much in vogue in Pre-Raphaelite circles and Yeats set to work on the Blake manuscripts in the possession of the Linnell family to produce the first edition of his longer poems, the three-volume Quaritch edition. Yeats may have come to Swedenborg through Blake.

Yeats was initiated in May or June 1887 into the Society of the Golden Dawn under the motto *Diabolus est Deus Inversus* (Frater D.E.D.I.) and helped Mathers to write the rituals, drawing upon the Chaldean Oracles, the Egyptian Book of the Dead, and Blake.

The original object of the Society was, beyond the study of magical techniques of various kinds, the alchemical 'great work' of self perfection. Subsequent quarrels arose from Mathers's dictatorial attitude and increasing interest in black magic. Yeats was at no time anti-Christian, nor was sexual magic practised by the Golden Dawn.

He was also interested in Spiritualism: he maintained a critical attitude, not from scepticism but because he understood that many explanations of the undoubted phenomena were possible. His play *The Words upon the Window Pane* is drawn from his knowledge of mediums.

A no less important tributary of Yeats's knowledge of occult matters was his interest (continuous from boyhood) in the fairy lore of Ireland, still a living tradition at the end of the 19th century.

Yeats's interest since boyhood in the fairy lore of Ireland, still a living tradition at the end of the 19th century, was an important element in his widespread knowledge of occult matters: Mr W. B. Yeats presenting Mr George Moore to the Queen of the Fairies, a caricature by Max Beerbohm

Index

First published 1975 by
Octopus Books Limited
59 Grosvenor Street London W1

ISBN 0 7064 0431 9

© 1970–1971 BPC Publishing Ltd
© 1975 BPC Publishing Ltd. This book has been produced by Phoebus Publishing Company in cooperation with Octopus Books Limited.

Distributed in the USA by
Crescent Books
a division of Crown Publishers Inc.
419 Park Avenue South
New York NY 10016.

Produced by Mandarin Publishers
Ltd 22a Westlands Road, Quarry
Bay Hong Kong

Printed in Hong Kong

ACKNOWLEDGMENTS

Front jacket: wooden face mask, Ashira-Bapuna tribes (Werner Forman, Kreeger Collection, Washington, D.C.);
Endpapers: Rollright Stones, Oxfordshire (Robert Estall);
Page 5: faith healer Harry Edwards (Peter Goodliffe);
Page 6–7: Wicca wedding ceremony (John Moss);
Page 8–9: Lewes, Sussex bonfire night (Robert Estall).